FINANCIAL ACCOUNTING

MJP PUBLISHERS

FINANCIAL ACCOUNTING

Dr. B. Sivakumar

Associate Professor in Commerce
PSG College of Arts & Science, Coimbatore

ISBN 9789355288882   **MJP Publishers**

All rights reserved   No. 44, Nallathambi Street,
Printed and bound in India   Triplicane, Chennai 600 005

MJP 1686   © Publishers, 2025

Publisher :   C. Janarthanan

ACKNOWLEDGEMENT

I Am very much thankful to the ALMIGHTY for his blessing to complete successfully.

I Feel very happy to express our sincere thanks to the Management and Principal for their continuous encouragement and support to complete this book successfully.

I would like to thank all the people who have helped us to become what am today. Finally, i am indebted to our family members who have rendered their support in all our endeavours.

PREFACE

Financial accounting is a fundamental branch of accounting that focuses on the preparation, presentation, and interpretation of financial statements for external users, such as investors, creditors, regulators, and other stakeholders. This course, *Financial Accounting - I*, serves as the introductory module for students seeking to understand the principles and practices of accounting in a business context.

In this course, we will explore key concepts such as the accounting cycle, the preparation of financial statements, and the application of generally accepted accounting principles (GAAP). We will also delve into the importance of accurate record-keeping and reporting in ensuring transparency and accountability in financial reporting.

The knowledge acquired through *Financial Accounting - I* forms the foundation for more advanced accounting studies and provides essential skills for analyzing financial information, which is crucial for making informed decisions in both personal and business contexts. This subject not only equips students with the technical knowledge of accounting but also emphasizes ethical practices and professional responsibility in financial reporting.

By the end of this course, students will have a solid understanding of the basics of financial accounting, enabling them to prepare financial statements, interpret business transactions, and understand the financial health of an organization.

Unit I

Accountancy principles – double entry system – rules – journal – ledger – trial balance

Unit II

Subsidiary books – Purchase books – Sales book – Purchase return book – Sales statement – Cash Balance.

Unit III

Errors and their rectification – Errors disclosed and not disclosed by Trail Balance.

Unit IV

Bank Reconciliation statement – Reason for preparing bank reconciliation – Over draft model.

Unit V

Final Accounts of sole Trading concern – Adjustment regarding closing stock – depreciation – outstanding and prepaid expenses.

Reference

1. Advanced Accountancy   M.C.Shukla and T.S. Grewal, S.chand NewDelhi.

2. Advanced Accountancy   M.A.Arulananthan & K.S.Raman

3. Advanced Accountancy   Jain and Narang

Contents

Chapter 1

FINANCIAL ACCOUNTING

1.1 INTRODUCTION

Accounting is the language of business. Accounting communicates the result of the business transactions in the form of final accounts, normally two systems for maintaining the accounting records. It is called double entry system and single entry system.

Accounting is a service activity provided in a business organization. In the present business environment, it is impossible to any business man to memories and recollects all the business transaction. Moreover, he is much interested in knowing the business results at the end of the specific period. A businessman wants to know

- What he owes
- How much profit earned
- What are the operating expenses
- How much operating expenses are incurred
- What is the financial position
- What his solvency position is

Much information is required to answer these questions for which a new system has been developed i.e. accounting.

Accounting is concerned with collecting, recording, evaluating and communicating the business results to the interested parties. A system of accounting has been developed according to the changes made in the business world and social needs. Accounting was developed as money across the world. In the period of Stone Age, there is no development of civilization. Even though, the number of business transactions is limited. Moreover, every individual has honesty. Hence, there is no need of maintaining books of accounts. But, the business was changed into a complex and increased a number of business transactions in a day. The system of accounting was developed as a growing child.

In India, the accounting practice was followed when twenty four centuries ago. Kautilya who was a minister in Chandragupta kingdom wrote a book titled, "Arthashastra". This book gave clear picture about how accounting records are to be maintained in olden days. Today, there are many improvements made in the system of accounting. Hence, it is called as modern system of accounting which is based on the principles of double entry.

"Luco Pacioli" who firstly published the Principles of Double Entry System in 1494 at Venice in Italy. Though the system of recording business transactions in a systematic manner has originated in Italy, it was perfected in England and other European countries during the 18th century only i.e., after the Industrial Revolution. Many countries have adopted this system today.

The very success of any modern business is fully based on the accounting system. According to We lsch and Antony, "The growth of business organizations in size, particularly and publicly held corporations, has brought pressured from stock holders, potential investors, creditors, governmental agencies and the public at large, for increased financial disclosure. The public's right to know more about organizations that directly and indirectly affect them is being increasingly recognized as essential. An open society is one that has a degree of freedom the individual level and typically evidences an effective commitment of measuring the quality of life attained.

These characteristics make it essential that the members of that society be provided adequate, understandable and dependable financial information from the major institutions that comprise it". Thus, accounting has gone many phases such as double entry book keeping, financial accounting, cost accounting, management accounting and social accounting.

1.2 MEANING OF ACCOUNTING

In olden days the accounting was used to find the result of business activities for a specific period. But, in due course, the need and importance of accounting were increased. Today, the accounting has to meet the requirements of taxation authorities, investors, creditors, financial institutions, banks, government regulations, management, owners and society. Hence, the scope of accounting is enlarged.

Accounting means an art of recording financial transactions in a set of books, classifying in desired categories and summarizing the information for presentation in a suitable manner to the concerned persons for their benefits.

Accounting is considered as a system which collects and processes financial information of a business. This information is reported to the users to enable them to make appropriate decisions.

1.3 DEFINITION

American Institute of Certified Public Accountants, "Accounting is the art of recording, classifying and summarizing in a significant manner and in terms of money, transactions and events which, in part at least, of a financial character and interpreting the results there of".

American Accounting Associations defines accounting as "the process of identifying, measuring and communicating economic information to permit informed judgments and decisions by users of the information".

Rajeshwara Rao, D.A R. Subrahmanyam, S.Manjula and B.Uma Devi, "Accounting is an art of identifying, recording, summarizing and interpreting business transactions of financial nature".

Smith and Ashburne, "Accounting is the science of recording and classifying business transactions and events, primarily of financial character and the art of making significant summaries, analysis and interpretations of those transactions and events and communicating the results to persons who must make decisions or form judgments".

1.4 OBJECTIVES OF ACCOUNTING

The objective of an accounting is differing from one business to another. The reason is that the requirement of one business unit is differing from another. Moreover, the nature and size of business unit are entirely different. Even though, every business unit requirements are very common in nature. The following are chief objectives of accounting:

- Ascertaining the results of operations during a period
- Ascertaining the financial position
- Maintaining control over assets
- Planning in respect of cash and
- Providing information to tax authorities and Government agencies.

1.5 ADVANTAGES OF ACCOUNTING

The following are the main advantages of accounting.

i) Systematic records

All the business transactions are recorded in the books of accounts. All financial effect is included in the accounting records.

ii) Preparation of financial statements

Results of business operations and the financial position of the concern are provided by accounting periodically.

iii) Decision making

Management of a firm has to make in numerable routine and policy decisions while discharging its functions. Accounting provides the relevant data to make the decisions appropriate and effective.

iv) Taxation

Accounting records are the basic source for computation and settlement of sales tax, income tax and other local tax.

1.6 LIMITATIONS OF ACCOUNTING

We have already discussed the objectives of Accounting. Now we will discuss the limitation or shortcomings of Accounting.

Records only Financial Transactions: Accounting records only financial transaction and events. It ignores qualitative information.

Contradictory Principles: Accounting based on certain principles which appear to be contradictory. For example, according to the principle of conservatism, inventory is valued at the cost or market price whichever is lower. Accordingly the inventory may be valued on cost basis in one year and at market price in another year but it violets the principle of consistency.

Changes in price level ignores: Accounting information is expressed in terms of money and it is assumed that the monetary unit is stable overtime. It ignores the price levels changes in case of financial statements prepared on historical basis.

Historical in nature: The information provided by accounting is historical in nature.

Financial statements are prepared at the end of the accounting periods.

Subjective choice: The accountant faced with a number of alternative choices like choice in the methods of depreciation, valuation of inventory, etc. It is based on the subjective choice which lacks objectivity.

1.7 STEPS INVOLVED IN ACCOUNTING

The following steps are involved in the preparation and maintenance of accounting records in a business organization.

Recording: Each and every business transaction which has financial character recorded in the books of accounts systematically and in chronological order. Each transaction should be supported by reliable documentary evidence. Journal is passed for each transaction. Moreover, transactions are recorded in the subsidiary books also.

Classification: The books of accounts are classified on a pre - determined basis. Classification of accounts helps to merging numerous business transactions which are having common significances. Separate accounts are opened for each income, expenses, asset, liability, group of customers and suppliers and the like.

Summarizing: The classified accounts are presented periodically in the summarized manner which is easily understandable by an ordinarily individual. Moreover, these accounts are highly useful to the owners of the business unit and other interested parties of accounting information. Summarizing takes place as in form of trial balance, trading account, profit and loss account and balance sheet. The trial balance ensures the arithmetical accuracy of the recording and classification of accounts. The financial position of the business is shown in the balance sheet.

Specified Manner: The nature, size and type of business is differing from one business to another. Hence, each business has its own significances, special problems and different requirements. Even though, the accounts are recorded, classified and summarized in a significant manner. The chief executive of a business unit requires specific information for controlling and decision making purpose.

In terms of Money: All the business transactions are measured in terms of money. It is the medium through which all the business transactions are expressed. Stock can be expressed in terms of Kg or units, land and building may be expressed in terms of Sq.ft., furniture and fittings may be expressed in terms of number and the like.

Financial Characteristics events and transactions: All the financial character business transactions alone are recorded in the books of accounts. At the same time, if the business transaction has no financial character such type of business transactions are not recorded in the books of accounts and ignored in the accounting process.

Interpretation of Results: The accounting results are interpreted for various purposes. The purchase, sales and expenses of different periods are prepared to find out trend percentage. It is used for future planning of business operations. The detail of payment made to suppliers is used to decide purchase policy. The collection of amount from debtors is used to frame sales policy. Ratio, fund flow statement and cash flow statement are used for the interpretation of business results. Such interpretation provides guidance for future plans and operations.

1.8 FUNCTIONS OF ACCOUNTS

The functions of accounting help the organization to keep the business transactions in a ready manner.

1. **Recording**

    The basic function of accounting is recording the monetary aspect of all the business transaction in an orderly manner for the purpose of memory and reference in a future period. Recording is done in a book called Journal.

2. **Classifying**

    The transactions recorded in journal are classified and posted to the main book of accounts known as Ledger.

3. **Summarizing**

    The transactions recorded in the ledger will be summarized and the balance in each account will be ascertained and list of such balance is called Trial Balance will be prepared at the end of accounting period.

4. **Interpreting**

    The final stage in the accounting process is analyzing and interpreting the financial data contained in the final account. It will help in planning for the future in a better way.

5. **Communicating**

    It communicates the results of the business to the various categories of persons as owners, investors, creditors, employees, management, Government etc.

1.9 LEGAL STATUTARATION

Provident fund for employees, employees state insurance contributions, deduction of tax at source (DTS), filling of tax returns are properly fulfilled with the help of accounting.

Branches of Accounting

Accounting has five main branches

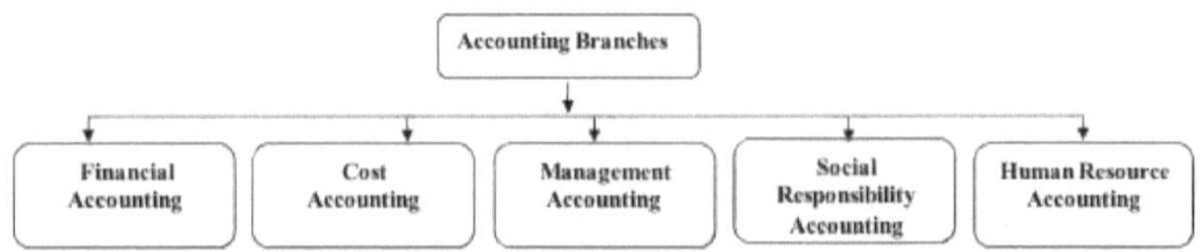

1. **Financial Accounting**

    Financial accounting is concerned with recording and processing all transactions with outsiders and events affecting the financial position of the firm.

2. **Cost Accounting**

    Cost accounting seeks to ascertain the cost of each product or each job by the firm. Cost accounting data is useful to the management.

3. Management Accounting

Management accounting has the objective of collecting systematically and regularly all such information as will help management in discharging its functions of planning, control decision making.

4. Social Responsibility Accounting

Social responsibility accounting describes the impact of corporate decisions on environmental pollutions, the consumption of non-renewable resources and ecological and groups on the maintenance of public services, on public safety, on health, and education and many other such social concerns.

5. Human Resource Accounting

Human resource accounting is a process to identify, qualify and report investments made in human resources as employees are the assets of company, they must be duly recognized.

1.10 FINANCIAL ACCOUNTING VS COST ACCOUNTING

The followings are the differences between financial accounting and cost accounting.

S.No	Financial Accounting	Cost Accounting
1	It is prepared on the basis of historical records	It is prepared on the current records
2	It is recording, classifying and analyzing the business expenses in total	It is recording, classifying and analyzing the costs in stage wise production on the current records.
3	It does not control the future cost	It controls the future costs
4	It is prepared at the end of the accounting period	It is prepared at the end of the production of goods and services.

S.No	Financial Accounting	Cost Accounting
5	It prepared according to the requirements of Companies Act, Income Tax Act, Sales Tax Act.	It is not like so
6	It facilitates the preparation of Profit and Loss Account and Balance Sheet	It does not facilitate the preparation of Profit and Loss Account and Balance Sheet.
7	Management is not in a position to plan.	The business transaction are preplanned
8	It emphasis the ascertainment of profit or loss of the concern.	It emphasis the ascertainment of profit or loss of the product.
9	It is prepared at the end of the accounting period	It is prepared at the end of the production of goods and services.

1.11 ACCOUNTING PRINCIPLES

Accounting principles may be defined as "procedure which are adopted by the accountants universally, while recording the accounting transactions". The accounting principles can be classified into two categories.

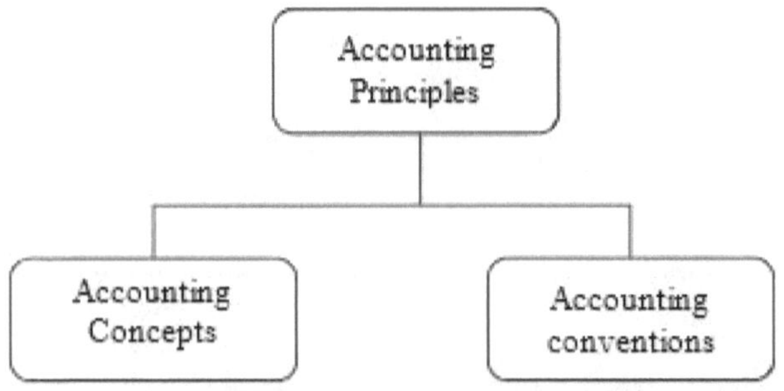

1.12 ACCOUNTING CONCEPTS AND CONVENTIONS

Under financial accounting, all the financial character transactions are recorded, classified and summarized. It discloses the operating results of the business concern for a specific period at regular intervals. The operating results are presented as in the form of financial statements, which are highly useful to internal and external users. The financial reports have to be prepared by the accountant and understood by the users in the same sense.

It is possible through following uniform accounting principles and practices in the maintenance of books of accounts and preparing financial statements. If different principles, concepts and conventions are adopted for maintaining books of accounts, there is no uniformity. Moreover, it is very difficult to make comparative analysis of financial statement of two firms. If compared, nothing can be understood and there is wastage of time and energy. Besides, a lot of confusion is raised in the business world. Hence, some of the accounting principles, postulates, concepts and conventions were developed and used as basis for maintaining books of accounts and preparing financial statements in a business concern.

1.13 ACCOUNTING CONCEPTS

These concepts guide how business transactions are reported. On the basis of the above four assumptions the following concepts (principles) of accounting have been developed.

Business Entity concept

A business entity is an organization of person established or created to accomplish an economic goal. Such an entity in distinct from its owners, managers and employees of the enterprise. The accounting entity maybe the business unit as a whole or part of business unit or an amalgamation of related business.

All the business transactions are recorded from the point of view of the business unit and not from the point of view of owner, managers, customers, creditors etc. Sometimes, a dividend maybe paid by a company. It is treated as dividend is paid by the company and not received by the share holders.

A joint stock company is an artificial person in the eye of law. Hence, it has separate legal entity form its shareholder. Even though, partnership firms and sole trader concerns are registered as per the law, they have no legal entity. But, they have business entity for accounting purpose.

According to the business entity concept, owner is treated as financier to the business concern. But, he or she is eligible for profit and responsible for losses.

Going Concern Concept

A business unit has infinite life as per going concern concept. Hence, it can continue its operation for an indefinite period of time. The life of an individual is limited. But, the business unit has the life even after death of owner of business concern.

According to International Accounting Standard, "The enterprise is normally viewed as a going concern, that its, as continuing in operation for the foreseeable future. It is assumed that the enterprise has neither the intention nor the necessity of liquidation".

Anybody can enter into a contract with the business unit. Anybody can give loan to the business unit. Any customer can buy goods on credit basis from the company. Any supplier can supply goods on credit basis. These things are happening only on the assumption of going concern concept. Similarly, prepaid expenses and accrued incomes are treated as assets on the presumption of continuation of business.

This concept is very important for the valuation of assets and liabilities of business concern. The assets and liabilities of the business are valued only on the basis of their productivity and not on the basis of their realizable value. If the business unit is going to be closed down, the assets and liabilities are valued at their realizable value.

Money Measurement Concept

The money measurement concept excludes the transactions which are not expressed in terms of money. Moreover, some transactions cannot be expressed in terms of money. If so, the transactions are not recorded in the books of accounts. For example efficiency of employees utilized quality of the product, production of sales and personal policies, loyalty of employees, working conditions, working environment and organization culture. These cannot be recorded in the books of accounts. Even though they are highly required for effective functioning of business. In addition, this information is useful for preparation of Balance Sheet and financial statements. Managerial planning and control are possible if the transactions are expressed in terms of money.

The business transactions which are having financial character alone enter in the books of accounts. The financial character of the business transaction is expressed only in terms of money.

Dual Aspect Concept

Dual aspect principle is the basis for Double Entry System of book-keeping. All business transactions recorded in accounts have two aspects-receiving benefit and giving benefit. For example, when a business acquires an asset (receiving of benefit) it must pay cash (giving of benefit).

Salaries paid are one of the business transactions. In this transaction, service of employees received is benefit received aspect, hence, salaries account is debited and cash is paid to employees considered as benefit giving aspect, hence, cash account is credited. Rent outstanding, in this transaction using the building is the benefit received aspect, hence, rent accounts is debited and create an obligation for payment of rent in future which is considered as benefit to be given aspect, hence, personal account of the landlord is credited.

Accounting Period Concept

Accounting period concept is used as basis for segregation of capital expenditure from revenue expenditure. All expenses whose benefit is derived within the accounting period are revenue expenses. If the benefit of expenses is available in more than one accounting period that expenses is capital expenditure. All incomes pertaining to the period are revenue incomes.

The accounting period should not be too short which results in the preparation of financial statements frequently as a burden. Likewise, the accounting period should not be too lengthy which results in the presentation financial statements as useless. Normally, the accounting periods is fixed as one year. If so, the seasonal fluctuations in business are easily absorbed and assess the income tax for payment and undertake any remedial measures to rectify poor performance.

Accounting period helps to measure the income generated during the specific accounting period. Moreover, the business unit can distribute its income to the owners without any ambiguity. Besides, it helps to compare to results of one accounting period with another accounting period, leading to comparative performance evaluation.

Cost Concept

The cost concept is criticized is three ways. Firstly, the cost does not reveal the true value of the asset. Secondly, if the assets are shown on cost basis, the accounting records do not show the true and fair view of financial position of business unit. Thirdly, inflation is not considered under cost concept. Therefore, the true value of money is not known and difficult to find true worth of assets.

Accounting creates history to a business unit through recording of business transactions. The assets are recorded the price at which they are acquired under cost concept. This cost is the basis for all the subsequent accounting for the assets. The depreciation is provided on basis of cost and effective life of such assets. The market values of assets are not considered either for valuation and depreciation. The reason is that the market values of assets cannot be accurately ascertained. There are a lot of changes in traditional accounting system. At present some measurement bases are also used for recording assets along with cost concept. They are net present value, present value of future cash flows of assets, current cost, replacement cost, opportunity cost and the like.

Revenue Realization Concept

It is otherwise called realization concept. According to this concept, revenue is considered as the income earned on the date when it is realized. Unearned or unrealized revenue should not be taken into account. The realization concept is vital for determining income pertaining to an accounting period. It avoids the Possibility of inflating incomes and profits.

In the case of hire purchase system, the down payment, installments received and installments due are treated as income. The reason is that the title to the goods is passed only when last installment is paid. Till such time, all the amounts paid under hire purchase system are treated income as hire charges.

Historical Cost Concept

Under this concept, assets are recorded at the price paid to acquire them and this cost is the basis for all subsequent accounting for the asset. For example, if a piece of land is purchased for ₹5,00,000 and its market value is ₹8,00,000 at the time of preparing final accounts the land value is recorded only for ₹5,00,000. Thus, the balance sheet does not indicate the price at which the asset could be sold for.

Matching Concept

Matching the revenues earned during an accounting period with the cost associated with the period to ascertain the result of the business concern is called the matching concept. It is the basis for finding accurate profit for a period which can be safely distributed to the owners.

There are two stages involved in matching concept. In the first stage, the direct costs are matched with sales revenue to find out gross profit. In the second stage, indirect costs are matched with gross profit and other incomes are also taken into consideration to find out net profit. Besides, both non operation losses and capital expenses to be written off are also matched with operating profit.

The term non operating losses include loss on sale if fixed assets, abnormal losses due to that, fire accident and the like. Preliminary expenses, underwriting commission, discount on issue of shares and debentures, goodwill and the like are the examples for capital expenses. Periodical matching of costs with revenue leads to finding of periodical operating results.

The main objective of any business unit is profit making. The profit making is ascertained through matching the revenues earned in anyone of the accounting period with the cost incurred in the corresponding accounting period. Accurate and reliable profit can be ascertained by adopting matching concept. All the expenses and revenues for a specific period are properly identified and recorded. Outstanding and prepaid expenses and incomes are properly entered in the books of accounts, adequate depreciation and necessary provisions are also properly made.

Accrual Concept

Under this concept, all outstanding expenses and prepaid expenses must be recorded. Similarly, all incomes associated with the period should be included whether they are received or not.

The accrual concept is focusing both revenues and expenses. This concept makes a difference between receipt of cash and the right to receive cash and payment of cash and the legal obligation to pay cash in relation to revenues and expenses respectively. On the basis of this distinction, on outflow of cash is treated as expenses if there is any legal obligation to pay even though cash might not have been paid for them.

Full Disclosure Concept

Accounting statements should disclose fully and completely all the significant information. Based on this, decisions can be taken by various interested parties. It involves proper classification and explanations of accounting information which are published in the financial statements.

Verifiable and Objective Evidence Concept

This principle requires that each recorded business transactions in the books of accounts should have an adequate evidence to support it. For example, cash receipt for payments made. The documentary evidence of transactions should be free from any bias. As accounting records are based on documentary evidence which is capable of verification, it is universally acceptable.

1.15 ACCOUNTING CONVENTIONS

Accounting conventions are also very important to record business transactions in the books of accounts. There are four accounting conventions. They are briefly explained below.

Convention of Conservatism

According to this convention, the assets are valued under two methods but one method if asset value i.e. least value is recorded in the books of accounts instead of high value. It is applied in the valuation of stock for balance sheet purpose. The closing stock is valued at cost price or market price whichever is low. At the same time, it is also necessary to provide all possible losses such as doubtful debts, discount on debtors, provisions for contingencies. Thus, conservatism may result in underestimate of assets and income and over statement of provisions and liabilities.

This convention is based on the maximum of anticipate no profit and provide for all possible losses. Conservatism is a policy of playing safe. According to Kohler, "conservatism is a guideline which chooses between acceptable accounting alternatives for recording events and transactions so that the least favourable immediate effect on assets, income and owner's equity is reported".

Convention of full Disclosure

The Companies Act 1956 has many provisions for preparing and presenting accounting information with full disclosure. The basis for valuation of closing stock and investments are given in the Companies Act Contingent liabilities should be listed out. Convention of full disclosure should be a transparency in the preparation and presentation of financial statements. The reason is that the financial statements are essentially meant for external users. Modern business world is dominated by joint stock companies. May joint stock companies are functioning in more than one country as multinational companies. Companies share holders of many companies are scattered all over the world. The ownership is completely separated from management. Hence, the convention of full disclosure gets much importance statements which are necessary to owners, investors and creditors.

Convention of Consistency

The basic aim of the convention of consistency is to preserve the comparability and reliability of financial statements. The reason is that the decision makes are highly used the financial statements. Here, the decision makers refer to top management executives. The financial statements should be comparable year after year and one business unit with another. If so, the management can take quality decision for the success of business unit. Accounting to this convention, the rules, practices and concepts used in accounting in a year should be continuously observed and applied year after year.

Convention of Materiality

The term material may be interpreted by the accountant in many ways. It means that one information is material to one business unit but the same information is immaterial to another business unit. Besides, what is material in one accounting year may be immaterial in the subsequent year. But, anyway, all the material facts should be included in the book of accounts.

Materiality means relative importance. As per this convention, all the material facts of business operation should be disclosed in the books of accounts. It means that irrelevant and immaterial facts need not be included or disclosed in the books of accounts. If all the facts are expected to include in the books of account, the work of accountant is increased. At the same time, the value of benefits derived from such books of accounts is less than the cost incurred for maintaining books of accounts.

According to the American Accounting Association, "An item should be regarded as material if there is reason to believe that knowledge, it would influence the decision of informed investor".

1.16 BOOK KEEPING

The dictionary meaning of Book-keeping is the "art of keeping accounts in a regular and systematic manner". This means that a business concern has to record the events affecting it in such a way that a correct picture can emerge whenever needed.

Book keeping is the recording of financial character business transactions correctly and systematically in a set of books that result in the transfer of money or money's worth. An emphasis is given to the recording of transactions very clearly systematically. The reason is that raw materials may be purchased on credit basis from several persons.

Moreover, goods may be sold to many persons on credit basis. How, the businessman would like to know how much amount is owed to suppliers and due from the customers from time to time. One cannot memory all these business transactions at all times. Besides, the businessman likes to know how much profit he or she has earned during the course of the year. For this purpose, proper maintenance of books of accounts is indispensable a business man. Hence, initially book keeping system of accounts was developed.

1.17 DEFINITION OF BOOK KEEPING

R.N. Carter, "Book keeping is the science and art of correctly recording in books of accounting all those business transactions that result in the transfer money or money's worth".

C.Mohan Juneja. R.C Chawla and K.K. Sexena, "Book keeping is the science and art of recording transactions in money or money's worth so accurately and systematically that the true state of a businessman's affairs can be correctly ascertained".

K.L. Nagarajan, N.Vinayakam and P.L Mani, "Book keeping is the systematic recording of business transactions in a manner which enables the financial relationship of a business with other persons to be clearly disclosed and the combined effect of the transactions on the financial position of the business itself to be ascertained".

L.C.Cropper, "Book keeping is the science of recording transactions in money or money's worth in such a manner that at any subsequent date, their nature and effect may be clearly understood and that when required a combined statement of their result may be prepared".

Rajeshwara Rao, S.Majla, D.A.R Subrahmanyam and B.Uma Devi, "Book keeping is recording of the financial transactions of a business in a methodical manner so that information on any point in relation to them may be quickly obtained".

A.R.Rosenrampff, "Book keeping is the art of recording business transactions in a systematic manner".

1.18 OBJECTIVES OF BOOK KEEPING

The objectives of book keeping are listed below

1. To maintain proper records for each business transactions permanently
2. To know the financial effect of each business transaction

3. To know the combined effect of all business transactions for a specific period

4. To know the financial position of the company as a whole on a specified date

5. To know how much the business man or the company owes to others and or how much others owes to him or her or the company

6. To know the details of various incomes, expenses, gains, losses, assets and liabilities and utilized for rational decision making.

1.19 DIFFERENCES BETWEEN BOOK KEEPING AND ACCOUNTING

The following are the differences between the Book Keeping and Accounting.

S. No	Book Keeping	Accounting
1	The nature of book keeping work is mechanical and repetitive in nature	The nature of accounting work is not mechanical and no repetitive in nature.
2	Book keeping is the recording of business transactions in a set of books systematically	Accounting is the preparation of financial statements, cost statements through designing suitable accounting system.
3	Book keeping is the basic for accounting	Accounting is not the basic for book keeping.
4	Book keeping work is done by the lower level executives of the accounting department	The accounting statements are prepared by the experienced top level executives of the accounting department.

S. No	Book Keeping	Accounting
5	There is no need of specialized skill and knowledge to do book keeping work.	Special knowledge of accounts is required to maintain accounting records.
6	Book keeping work is done by a book keeper	Accounting work is done by the accountant.
7	More knowledge of accounts is enough to maintain book keeping records	Special knowledge of accounts is required to maintain accounting records.
8	Book keeping is the fore runner of accounting	Accounting is started after book keeping
9	Book keeping is a part of accounting	Accounting is started after book keeping
10	The recorded financial transactions are not analyzed	The financial statements are to be analyzed and interpreted.

1.20 METHODS OF ACCOUNTING

The methods of accounting are classified into two. They are:

1. Single Entry System
2. Double Entry System

Single Entry System

Under single entry system of accounting, no principles are adopted to record the business transactions. Moreover, all transactions are not also recorded. A transaction has two aspects. These two aspects are recorded. But, there is no entry. Incomplete accounts are maintained and the accounts are maintained on systematically. Hence, the accounts maintained under single entry are not reliable. Trial balance is not able to prepare the accurate profit and loss account to know the correct amount of profit or loss. Generally single entry system is followed by small business concerns.

Only personal accounts of the debtors and creditors and cash book of the business are maintained under this system. Purchase and sales accounts are not maintained. Hence, it is very difficult to find errors, frauds and misappropriations. There is no hard and fast rule for maintaining records even for personal accounts. The circumstances and the needs of the business concern are deciding the maintenance of accounts under this system.

Double Entry System

It is the most common system of keeping records whereby the two aspects of every transaction – the giving aspect and the receiving aspect – are recorded in the books of accounts. Each aspect will be recorded in one account and this method of writing every transaction in two accounts is known as Double entry system of book keeping. This is the most scientific, complete and accurate system of accounting.

Definition

This system was invented by an Italian named Luco Pacioli in 1494 A.D. Double entry system is a scientific way of presenting accounts. The preparation of accounts is very easy if double entry system of accounting is followed. The taxation authorities are also compel the business man to prepare the accounts under double entry system. The two aspects of a business transaction are considered for prepare the accounts. Receiving aspect and giving aspect are such two aspects. Receiving aspect is known as debit aspect and giving aspect is known as credit aspect. The preparation of trial balance and final accounts are very easy since the two aspects of a business transaction are considered in double entry system of accounting.

According to **J.R.Batliboi** "Every business transaction has a two-fold effect and that it affects two accounts in opposite directions and if a complete record were to be made of each such transaction, it would be necessary to debit one account and credit another account. It is this recording of the two fold effect of every transaction that has given rise to the term Double Entry System".

1.21 ADVANTAGES OF DOUBLE ENTRY SYSTEM

- It provides a complete record of every transaction
- It provides an arithmetical check on the records as the total of debit entries must be equal to the total credit of all entries.
- The amount owing to outsiders and the amount due to the business can be ascertained with the help of personal accounts
- The profit and loss account can be prepared with the help of nominal accounts which is helpful to the business to ascertain the operating results of the business
- It helps to prepare the balance sheet of the business which is helpful to ascertain the financial position of the business
- It helps to reduce the occurrence of the errors/frauds and when occurred can be deducted easily.

Disadvantages of double entry system

- This system requires the maintenance of a number of books of accents which is not practical in small concerns.
- The system is costly because a number of records are to be maintained
- There is no guarantee of absolute accuracy of the books of account inspite of agreement of the trial balance.

1.22 PRINCIPLES OF DOUBLE ENTRY

Every business transaction has linked with at least two accounts. Out of two accounts, one account should be debited with one amount and another account should be credited with equal amount. It means that one account receives benefit and another account is giving benefit or some other thing. The benefit receiving account is debited and the benefit given up or giving account is credited.

The principle of double entry is based on the fact that there can be no giving without receiving nor can there be receiving without something being given. Hence, both debit and credit aspects of business transactions are properly recorded in the books of accounts. According to this principle, every debit must necessarily have a corresponding credit and vice versa.

1.23 DISTINCTIONS BETWEEN DOUBLE ENTRY AND SINGLE ENTRY SYSTEMS

Double Entry	Single Entry
For every debit there is a corresponding credit and vice versa	Debits and credits do not agree
Maintaining a complete record of personal accounts, real accounts and nominal accounts	Only personal account and cash accounts are maintained
A balance sheet and profit & loss account can be prepared	A balance sheet and profit & loss account cannot be prepared
Double entry is the only scientific system of keeping books of accounts	Single entry is not a system. It is an incomplete and unscientific.
Trial balance can be prepared	Trial balance cannot be prepared
Internal check is possible	Internal check is not possible
Suitable for all business	Suitable for small business
Most acceptable method for income tax and other tax purpose	This method is not acceptable for taxation.

1.24 STAGES OF DOUBLE ENTRY SYSTEM

The following are the stages of a complete system of double entry.

Books of original entry: All the business transactions are recorded in the books of accounts which are having financial character as and when they take place. Transactions are recorded as in the form of journal or subsidiary book. The process is called as "Entering". The books of accounts are called as, "Books of original entry".

Posting: All the journal entries or entries made in the subsidiary books are posted to the appropriate ledger accounts. If so, the total effect of such all business transactions in a particular account can be find out. This process is known as posting.

Trial balance: All the accounts are closed at the end of the specified period to find out their balances. A list of such balances is prepared i.e. Trial Balance.

Profit & Loss Account and Balance Sheet: With the help of trial balance, the trading result of the business concern is find out through preparing profit & loss account. Balance sheet is prepared to know the financial position of the business concern.

1.25 CLASSIFICATION OF ACCOUNTS

Every transaction has two aspects and each aspect has an account. It is stated that 'an account is a summary of relevant transactions at one place relating to a particular head'.

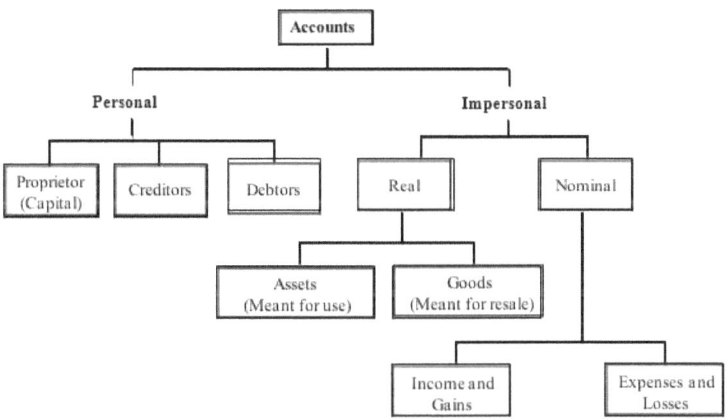

Personal Accounts

The personal accounts are classified into three categories. They are proprietor, creditor and debtor. When a person starts a business, he is called proprietor. He or she brings cash to run the business initially. The initial amount is called capital. For which, capital account is prepared. Thereafter, he or she may withdraw amount from the business at regular or irregular intervals. Hence, one more account is prepared i.e Drawings Account. Both capital account and drawings account are treated as personal accounts.

These accounts record a business dealing with person or firms. The person receiving something is given debit and the person giving something is given credit. Generally, the personal accounts take the following forms.

Natural Persons: It denotes natural human beings and includes both male and female.

Artificial Persons or Legal Bodies: A person is artificially created by law or an institution is treated as a person in the eye of law. It covers partnership Firm's Account, Private Limited and Public Limited Company Accounts, Club Accounts, Co-operative Society Account etc.

Representative Personal Account: All accounts representing the outstanding expenses and accrued or prepaid expenses.

Real accounts

Accounts relating to properties or assets are known as Real Accounts. Every business needs some assets which are used only for the business purposes. Hence, separate account is opened for each asset. Real accounts are of two types.

A tangible real account, intangible real accounts is another. Furniture, computer and machinery are some of the examples for tangible real accounts. Goodwill, Patents and Copy right are some of the examples for intangible real accounts. Goods is one of the best examples for real account. Goods are treated as in the following ways for accounting purpose.

These are the accounts of assets. An asset entering the business is given debit and asset leaving from the business is given credit.

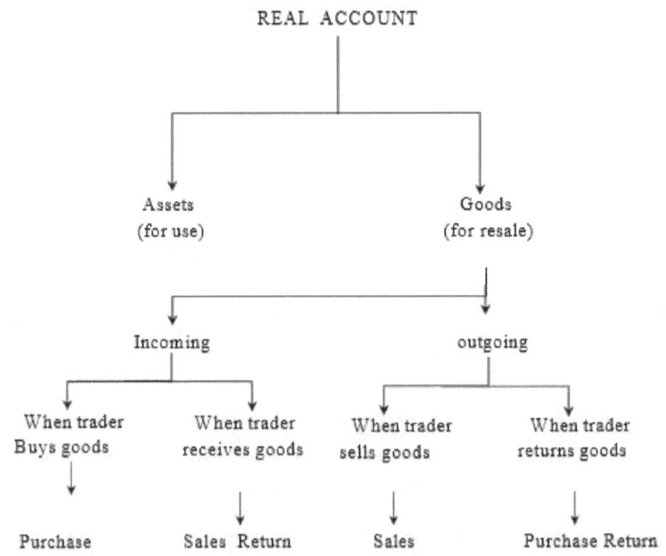

If a thing is purchased for use, that is treated as assets. If a same thing is purchase for resale, that is treated as goods. The goods may be entering the business concern in two ways. One way is that goods are bought by the trader i.e. treated as purchase. Another way is that goods may be received from the customer i.e. treated as sales returns. The goods may leave the business concern under two circumstances. One time is that when the trader sells goods treated as sales. Another time is that when trader returns the goods treated as purchase returns.

Nominal Accounts

Accounting related to expenses, losses, incomes and gains are known as Nominal Account. A separate account is maintained for each item of expense, loss, income and gain. Examples for nominal accounts are Wages, Salaries, rent paid, commission paid, commission received, interest paid and interest received etc.

These accounts deal with expenses, incomes, profits & losses. Accounts of all expenses and losses are debited and accounts of all incomes and gains are credited.

1.26 OTHER TERMS

Proprietor

A person who has own business is called its proprietor.

Capital

Capital is the amount invested by the proprietor in the business. This amount is increased by the amount of profits earned and the amount of additional capital introduced. It is decreased by the amount of losses incurred and the amounts withdrawn.

Drawings

A drawing is the amount of cash or value of goods withdrawn from the business by the proprietor for his personal use. It is deducted from the capital.

Sales

Sales refer to the amount of goods sold that are already bought or manufactured by the business. When goods are sold for cash, they are cash sales but if goods are sold and payment is not received at the time of sale, it is credit sales. Total sales include both cash and credit sales.

1.27 NATURE OF DEBIT AND CREDIT

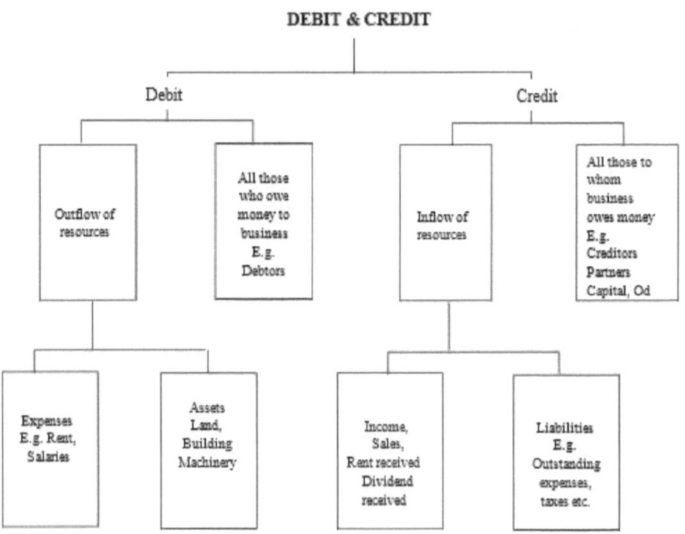

If there is an increase or decrease in one account, there will be equal decrease or increase in another account. Accordingly, the following rules of debit and credit in respect of the various categories of accounts can be obtained. The rules may be summarized as below:

Elements of Accounting equation	Debit	Credit	Normal Balance
Assets	Increase	Decrease	Debit
Liabilities	Decrease	Increase	Credit

Elements of Accounting equation	Debit	Credit	Normal Balance
Capital	Decrease	Increase	Debit
Revenues	Decrease	Increase	Credit
Expenses	Increase	Decrease	Debit

QUESTIONS

CHOOSE CORRECT ANSWERS

1. As per the business entity assumption, the business is different from the
   a) Owners
   b) Banker
   c) Government
   d) Debtors
2. As per dual aspect concept, every business transaction has
   a) Three aspects
   b) One aspect
   c) Two aspects
   d) Four
3. Going concern assumption tell us the life of the business is
   a) Very short
   b) Very long
   c) None
   d) Both a and b
4. The receiving aspect in a transaction is called as
   a) Debit aspect
   b) Credit aspect
   c) Neither of the two
   d) None
5. The giving aspect in a transaction is called as
   a) Debit aspect
   b) Credit aspect
   c) Neither of the two
   d) Capital aspect
6. Murali account is an example for
   a) Personal A/c
   b) Real A/c
   c) Nominal A/c
   d) None

7. Nominal Account is classified under

    a) Personal A/c

    b) Impersonal A/c

    c) Neither of the two

    d) Asset a/c

8. Outstanding rent A/c is an example for

    a) Nominal account

    b) Personal account

    c) Representative
        personal account

    d) Real account

9. Drawings account is classified under

    a) Real A/c.

    b) Personal A/c.

    c) Nominal A/c.

    d) None

10. Assets are usually shown in the balance sheet at

    a) Revalued cost

    b) Replacement
        cost

    c) Unexpired cost

    d) Real cost

11. Which one of the following is an example of current assets?

    a) Capital

    b) Stock

    c) Investment

    d) Building

12. The object of financial accounting is not

    a) To prepare future financial plans

    b) To prepare and communicate final accounts

    c) To record all transactions and interpret the financial data

    d) To take into consideration the historical data

13. What do you mean by concept?

    a) Reasonable assumption

    b) Universal characteristics

    c) A regulated condition

    d) A willful prediction

14. What is the purpose of preparing a voucher?

    a) A mere formality

    b) Helpful for finalizing final accounts

    c) Some supportive document

    d) To safeguard all cash disbursement

15. Credit sales create

    a) Creditors   b) Debtors   c) Suppliers   d) Agent

16. Another meaning of capital expenditure is

    a)   Payment of expenses

    b)   Payment of Interest

    c)   Purchase of fixed assets

    d)   The cost of train fare

17. Which of the following are the fixed assets?

    a) Cash   b) Debtors   c) Bank balance d) Computers

18. Payment of stationary, rent, salary, merchandise, etc, can be termed as

    a) Transaction   b) Events   c) Results d) Activities

19. Accounting is an information system

    a) True   b) False   c) None of these

20. Which is the function of accounting?

    a)   Decision making   b)   Measurement

    c)   Forecasting   d)   All of these

21. Contingent liability is shown in the balance sheet. This arises out of

    a) Convention of disclosure

    b) Convention of materiality

    c) Convention of consistency

22. Revenue is generally recognized as being earned at the point of time

    a) Sale is effected   b) Cash is received

    c) Production   d) All of these

23. Balance Sheet is not a valuation statement. This concept is

    a)   Period concept

    b)   Cost and going concern concept

    c)   Realisation concept

[**Answers:** 1 (a), 2 (c), 3 (b), 4 (a), 5 (b), 6 (a), 7(b), 8 (c), 9 (b), 10 (a), 11 (b),12 (a), 13 (a), 14 (d), 15 (b), 16 (c), 17 (d), 18 (a), 19 (a), 20 (d), 21 (a), 22 (a), 23 (b)]

FILL IN THE BLANKS

---

1. Business concern must prepare financial statements at least once in a year is based on _______ assumption.
2. ____________ principle requires that the same accounting methods should be followed from one accounting period to the next.
3. Transactions between owner and business are recorded separately due to _____assumption.
4. Every business transaction reveals ___ aspects.
5. The incoming aspect of a transaction is called ________
6. Impersonal accounts are classified into _______ types.
7. The outgoing aspect of a transaction is called .
8. Plant and machinery is an example of _______ account.
9. Commission received will be classified under . account.
10. On July 15, Amir paid to his clerk ₹ 6,000 as salary. This can be classified as _
11. A credit to equity account __ balance
12. When an asset balance is to be reduced the account is to be _

[**Answers:** 1. Accounting period, 2. Consistency, 3. Business entity, 4. two, 5. Debit, 6. Two, 7.Credit, 8. Real, 9.Nominal, 10. Atransactions, 11. Increases, 12. Credited]

OTHER QUESTIONS

1. What is accounting?
2. Mention the objectives of accounting
3. State the functions of accounting.
4. What do you mean by business entity assumption?
5. What do you mean by going concern assumption?
6. What are the basic concepts of accounting?
7. Explain in detail the principles of accounting.
8. Briefly explain the various accounting concepts.
9. Explain the meaning of Double Entry System.
10. What are branches of accounting?
11. Write a short note on personal accounts.
12. Differentiate double entry from single entry system.
13. Define book keeping?
14. Who is a proprietor? What is capital?
15. What is meant by drawings?
16. What is a sale?
17. Outline the objectives of book keeping.
18. Give a note on social responsibility accounting
19. What do you mean by Human Resource Accounting?
20. What is dual aspect concept
21. Explain briefly the concepts of accounting.
22. What do you mean by business entity concept?
23. What is going concern concept?

Chapter 2

JOURNAL

Accounting process starts with identifying the transactions to be recorded in the books of accounts. Accounting identifies only those transactions and events which involve money. They should be of financial character. Accountant does so by sorting out various cash memos, invoices, bills, receipts and vouchers. In the accounting process, the first step is the recording of transactions in the books of accounts. The origin of a transaction is derived from the sourcedocument.

2.1 SOURCE DOCUMENTS

Source documents are the evidences of business transactions which provide information about the nature of the transaction, the date, the amount and the parties involved in it. Transactions are recorded in the books of accounts when they actually take place and are duly supported by source documents. According to the verifiable objective principle of Accounting, each transaction recorded in the books of accounts should have adequate proof to support it. These supporting documents are the written and authentic proof of the correctnessof the recorded transactions. These documents are required for audit and tax assessment. Theyalso serve as the legal evidence in case of a dispute. The following are the most common source documents.

2.2 CASH MEMO

When a trader sells goods for cash, he gives a cash memo and when he purchases goods for cash, he receives a cash memo. Details regarding the items, quantity, rate and the price are mentioned in the cash memo.

<table>
<tr><td colspan="4" align="center">Cash Memo</td></tr>
<tr><td colspan="4" align="center">Vinoth Watch Co.</td></tr>
<tr><td colspan="4" align="center">62, North RK Nagar, Chennai 72.</td></tr>
<tr><td colspan="2">No: 152</td><td colspan="2">Date: 05.12.2015</td></tr>
<tr><td colspan="4">To ……………………………………………………………</td></tr>
<tr><td>Qty</td><td>Description</td><td>Rate ₹</td><td>Amount ₹</td></tr>
<tr><td>2</td><td>Titan Sonata</td><td>2,500</td><td>5,000</td></tr>
<tr><td>1</td><td>Titan Swash</td><td>1,750</td><td>1,750</td></tr>
<tr><td></td><td colspan="2"></td><td>6,750</td></tr>
<tr><td></td><td colspan="2" align="right">Less: 10% Discount</td><td>675</td></tr>
<tr><td>3</td><td>Total</td><td></td><td>6,075</td></tr>
<tr><td colspan="3" align="center">(Six thousand and seventy five only)</td><td></td></tr>
<tr><td colspan="2" align="center">Goods once sold are not taken back</td><td colspan="2" align="center">Manager
for Vinoth Watch Co</td></tr>
</table>

2.3 INVOICE OR BILL

When a trader sells goods on credit, he prepares a sale invoice. It contains full detailsrelating to the amount, the terms of payment and the name and address of the seller and buyer. The original copy of the sale invoice is sent to the purchaser and its duplicate copy is kept formaking records in the books of accounts. Similarly, when a trader purchases goods on credit,he receives a credit bill from the supplier of goods.

<table>
<tr><td colspan="4" align="center">Invoice</td></tr>
<tr><td colspan="4" align="center">Viji Electronics</td></tr>
<tr><td colspan="4" align="center">72, Gandhiji Salai, Chennai- 27.</td></tr>
<tr><td colspan="2">No: 504</td><td colspan="2">Date: 04.12.2015</td></tr>
<tr><td colspan="4">Name & Address of the Customer: Bhavan Enterprises,
105, Balaji Nagar,
Chennai – 92</td></tr>
<tr><td colspan="4">Terms: 5% cash discount if payment is made within 15 days.</td></tr>
<tr><td>Qty</td><td>Description</td><td>Rate ₹</td><td>Amount ₹</td></tr>
<tr><td>6</td><td>Washing Machines</td><td>10,000</td><td>60,000</td></tr>
<tr><td>10</td><td>Refrigerators</td><td>14,500</td><td>1,45,000</td></tr>
<tr><td></td><td></td><td></td><td>2,05,000</td></tr>
<tr><td></td><td>Sales Tax 12%</td><td></td><td>24,600</td></tr>
<tr><td></td><td></td><td></td><td>1,80,400</td></tr>
<tr><td></td><td>Handling and Delivery charges</td><td></td><td>1,500</td></tr>
<tr><td>16</td><td>Total</td><td></td><td>1,81,900</td></tr>
<tr><td colspan="4">(Rupees One lakh eighty one thousand and nine hundred only)</td></tr>
<tr><td colspan="2"></td><td colspan="2">Partner</td></tr>
<tr><td colspan="2">E & O.E</td><td colspan="2">for Viji Electronics</td></tr>
</table>

Note: E.&O.E., means errors and omissions excepted. In other words, if there is any error in theinvoice, the same has to be adjusted accordingly.

2.4 RECEIPT

When a trader receives cash from a customer, he issues a receipt containing the date,the amount and the name of the customer. The original copy is handed over to the customer and the duplicate copy is kept for record. In the same way, whenever we make payment, we obtain a receipt from the party to whom we make payment.

RECEIPT

Saravanan Book House,

34, First Street, Thanjavur

Receipt No: 505   Date: 02.11.2015

Received with thanks a sum of ₹ 15,000 (Rupees fifteen thousand only) from M/s.Sulthan & Sons being the supply of books as per the list enclosed

Cheque/DD/ No. 2458 Dt: 25.10.2015

Canara Bank, Thanjavur

Signature

Seal

Note: If the amount is more than ₹ 5,000, affix a revenue stamp.

2.5 DEBIT NOTE

A debit note is prepared by the buyer and it contains the date of the goods returned, name of the supplier, details of the goods returned and reasons for returning the goods. Eachdebit note is serially numbered. A duplicate copy or counter foil of the debit note is retainedby the buyer. On the basis of debit note, the suppliers account is debited in the books.

<table>
<tr><td colspan="5" align="center">DEBIT NOTE</td></tr>
<tr><td colspan="3">Murugan Traders</td><td colspan="2">No. 555</td></tr>
<tr><td colspan="3">22, RR Nagar,</td><td colspan="2">Date: 15.11.2015</td></tr>
<tr><td colspan="5">Madurai – 613001</td></tr>
<tr><td colspan="5">Name & Address of Supplier: Guru Nagar,</td></tr>
<tr><td colspan="5">777, Second Street,</td></tr>
<tr><td colspan="5">Coimbatore- 600 075</td></tr>
<tr><td colspan="5">Terms: 5% cash discount if payment is made within 30 days</td></tr>
<tr><td>Date</td><td colspan="2">Particulars</td><td>₹</td><td>₹</td></tr>
<tr><td>2015
October</td><td colspan="2">50 FM Radio sets purchased
under your invoice No.394, dated,
2nd October, 2015,now returned,
as the sets are not in working</td><td></td><td></td></tr>
<tr><td>15</td><td colspan="2">conditions @ ₹ 50 per set.</td><td>2,500</td><td></td></tr>
<tr><td></td><td colspan="2">Add : Packing expenses 100</td><td>100</td><td>2,600</td></tr>
<tr><td></td><td>Total</td><td></td><td></td><td>2,600</td></tr>
<tr><td colspan="5">E &O.E</td></tr>
<tr><td colspan="5" align="right">Manager</td></tr>
</table>

2.6 CREDIT NOTE

A credit note is prepared by the seller and it contains the date on which goods are returned, name of the customer, details of the goods received back, amount of such goods and reasons for returning the goods. Each credit note is serially numbered. A duplicate copy of the credit note is retained for the record purpose. On the basis of credit note, the customer's account is credited in the books.

<table>
<tr><td colspan="5" align="center">CREDIT NOTE</td></tr>
<tr><td colspan="5">No. 555   Date: 15.11.2015</td></tr>
<tr><td colspan="5" align="center">KUMAR SHIRTS</td></tr>
<tr><td colspan="5" align="center">Anna Salai, Thanjavur – 613001</td></tr>
<tr><td colspan="5">Name & Address: Muthusamy & Sons,</td></tr>
<tr><td colspan="5">555, Mela Masi Veethi,</td></tr>
<tr><td colspan="5">Madurai – 10</td></tr>
<tr><td colspan="5">Term: 5% cash discount if payment is made within 30 days</td></tr>
<tr><td>Date</td><td>Particulars</td><td>₹</td><td>₹</td></tr>
<tr><td>2015
October
25</td><td>T-Shirts - 32" - 100 Nos @ ₹ 100 each</td><td>10,000</td><td></td></tr>
<tr><td></td><td>Less : Discount @10%</td><td>1,000</td><td>9,000</td></tr>
<tr><td></td><td align="right">Total</td><td></td><td>9,000</td></tr>
<tr><td colspan="4">E &O.E</td></tr>
<tr><td colspan="4" align="right">Manager</td></tr>
</table>

Pay-in-slip

Pay-in-slip is a form available in banks and is used to deposit money into a bank account. Each pay-in-slip has a counterfoil which is returned to the depositor duly sealed and signed by the bank official. This source document relates to bank transactions. It gives details regarding date, account number, amount deposited (in cash or cheque) and name of the account holder.

Cheque

A cheque is a document in writing drawn upon a specified banker to pay a specified sum to the bearer or the person named in it and payable on demand. Each cheque book has acounterfoil in which the same details in the cheque are filled. The counterfoil remains with theaccount holder for his future reference. The counterfoil forms the source document for entries to be made in the books of accounts.

Vouchers

A voucher is a written document in support of a business transaction. Vouchers are prepared by an accountant and each voucher is counter signed by an authorised person of the organisation. The vouchers are properly filed according to their serial numbers so that the auditors may easily vouch them and these may also serve as documentary evidence in future. Bills receivable, bills payable, wages, salaries pay acquaintance, correspondence etc., also serve as the source documents. Thus, there must be a source document for each transaction recorded in the books of accounts.

2.7 ACCOUNTING EQUATION

The source document is the origin of a transaction and it initiates the accounting process, whose starting point is the accounting equation. Accounting equation is based on dual aspect concept (Debit and Credit). It emphasizes on the fact that every transaction has a two sided effect i.e., on the assets and claims on assets. Always the total claims (those of outsidersand of the proprietors) will be equal to the total assets of the business concern. The claims arealso known as equities, are of two types:

- i.) Owners equity (Capital);
- ii.) Outsiders' equity (Liabilities).

Assets = Equities

Assets = Capital + Liabilities (A = C+L)

Capital = Assets – Liabilities (C = A–L)

Liabilities = Assets – Capital (L = A–C)

Books of accounts

Business concerns, which follow the double entry system of book keeping, maintain aset of accounts books in small concerns.

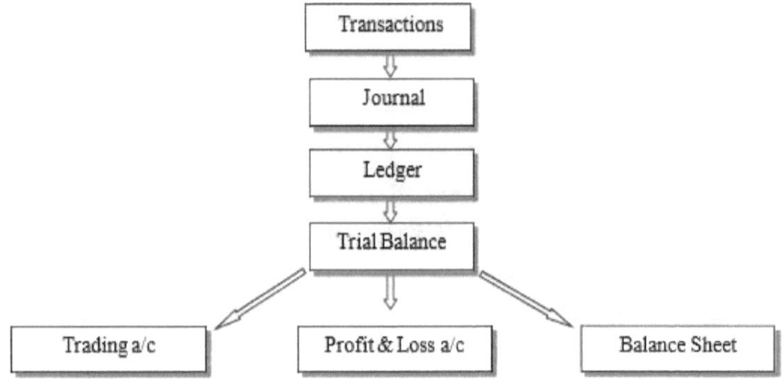

2.8 RULES FOR DEBITING AND CREDITING

In actual practice, the individual transactions of similar nature are recorded, added andsubtracted at one place. Such place is customarily the meaning of debit and credit, it is essential to understand the meaning and form of an account.

An account is a record of all business transactions relating to a particular person or asset or liability or expense or income. In accounting, we keep a separate record of each individual, asset, liability, expense or income. The place where such a record is maintained istermed as an 'Account'.

All accounts are divided into two sides. The left hand side of an account is called Debit side and the right hand side of an account is called Credit side. In the abbreviated formDebit is written as Dr. and Credit is written as Cr. For example, the transactions relating to cash are recorded in an account, entitled 'Cash Account' and its format will be as given below:

Debit (Dr)	Cash a/c	Credit (Cr)

In order to decide when to write on the debit side of an account and when to write onthe credit side of an account, there are two approaches They are: 1) Accounting Equation Approach, 2) Traditional Approach.

2.9 NATURE OF ACCOUNT

The accounting equation is a statement of equality between the debits and the credits. The rules of debit and credit depend on the nature of an account. For this purpose, all the accounts are classified into the following five categories in the accounting equation approach:-

1. Assets Accounts
2. Capital Account
3. Liabilities Accounts
4. Revenues or Incomes Accounts
5. Expenses or Losses Accounts

If there is an increase or decrease in one account, there will be equal decrease or increase in another account. Accordingly, the following rules of debit and credit in respect ofthe various categories of accounts can be obtained.

The rules may be summarized as below:-

1. Increases in assets are **debits;**
    Decreases in assets are **credits.**
2. Increases in capital are **credits;**
    Decreases in capital are **debits.**
3. Increases in liabilities are **credits;**
    Decreases in liabilities are **debits.**
4. Increases in incomes and gains are **credits;**
    Decreases in incomes and gains are **debits.**
5. Increases in expenses and losses are **debits;**
    Decreases in expenses and losses are **credits.**

Elements of Accounting equation	Debit	Credit
Assets	Increase	Decrease
Liabilities	Decrease	Increase
Capital	Decrease	Increase
Revenues	Decrease	Increase
Expenses	Increase	Decrease

In the traditional approach, all the accounts are classified into the following three types.

1. Personal Accounts
2. Real Accounts
3. Nominal Accounts

GOLDEN RULES OF DEBIT AND CREDIT

Personal Accounts   *Debit the Receiver*

credit the Giver

Real Accounts   *Debit what comes in*

Credit what goes out

Nominal Accounts   *Debit Expenses and Losses*

Credit Incomes and Gains

2.10 BOOKS OF ORIGINAL ENTRY

The books in which a transaction is recorded for the first time from a source documentare called *Books of Original Entry* or *Prime Entry.* Journal is one of the books of original entry in which transactions are originally recorded in a chronological (day-to-day) order according to the principles of Double Entry System.

2.11 JOURNAL

Journal is derived from the French word 'Jour" which means a day. Journal is a date-wise record of all the transactions *with* details of the accounts *debited* and credited and the amount of each transaction. Journal is a book of original entry.

Journal format

Date	Particulars	L.F.	Dr ₹	Cr ₹

1. ***Date:*** In the first column, the date of the transaction is entered. The year and the monthis written only once, till they change. The sequence of the dates and months should bestrictly maintained.

2. ***Particulars:*** Each transaction affects two accounts, out of which one account is debited and the other account is credited. The name of the account to be debited is written first,very near to the line of particulars column and the word **Dr.** is also written at the end ofthe particulars column. In the second line, the name of the account to be credited is written, starts with the word '**To**', a few space away from the margin in the particulars column to the make it distinct from the debit account.

3. ***Narration:*** After each entry, a brief explanation of the transaction together with necessary details is given in the particulars column with in brackets called ***narration***. The words 'For' or 'Being' are used before starting to write down narration. Now, it isnot necessary to use the word 'For' or 'Being'.

4. **Ledger Folio (L.F)**: All **entries** from the journal are later posted into the ledger accounts. The page number or folio number of the Ledger, where the posting has beenmade from the Journal is recorded in the L.F column of the Journal. Till such time, this column remains blank.

5.   ***Debit Amount:*** In this column, the amount of the account being debited is written.

6.   ***Credit Amount:*** In this column, the amount of the account being credited is written.

2.12 PRONS OF JOURNAL

The main advantages are:

1.   It reduces the possibility of errors.
2.   It provides an explanation of the transaction.
3.   It provides a chronological record of all transactions.

2.13 CONS OF JOURNAL

The limitations are:

1.   It will be too long if all transactions are recorded here.
2.   It is difficult to ascertain the balance of each account.

2.14 BASIC ACCOUNTING PROCEDURE

S.No	*Account*	*Accounting approach*
1	Building	Real account
2	Purchase a/c	Real account
3	Sales a/c	Nominal account
4	Rent a/c	Nominal account
5	Rent outstanding	Personal account
6	Bank deposit	Personal account
7	Cash a/c	Real account
8	Closing stock	Real account
9	Investment a/c	Real account

S.No	Account	Accounting approach
10	Debtors a/c	Personal account
11	Capital a/c	Personal account
12	Drawings a/c	Personal account
13	Provision for depreciation	Real account
14	Interest receivable	Personal account
15	Rent received in advance	Personal account
16	Bad debts	Nominal account
17	Depreciation	Nominal account
18	Income tax	Personal account
19	Stock reserve	Real account
20	Provision for discount on debt.	Personal account

2.15 STEPS IN JOURNALISING

The process of analysing the business transactions under the heads of debit and credit and recording them in the Journal is called ***Journalising***. An entry made in the journal is called a '***Journal Entry***'.

Step 1 Determine the two accounts which are involved in the transaction.

Step 2 Classify the above two accounts under Personal, Real or Nominal.

Step 3 Find out the rules of debit and credit for the above two accounts.

Step 4 Identify which account is to be debited and which account is to be credited.

Step 5 Record the date of transaction in the date column. The year and monthis written once, till they change. The sequence of the dates and monthsshould be strictly maintained.

Step 6 Enter the name of the account to be debited in the particulars column very close to the left hand side of the particulars column followed bythe abbreviation Dr. in the same line. Against this, the amount to be debited is written in the debit amount column in the same line.

Step 7 Write the name of the account to be credited in the second line starts with the word '**To**' a few space away from the margin in the particulars column. Against this, the amount to be credited is written in the credit amount column in the same line.

Step 8 Write the narration within brackets in the next line in the particulars column.

Step 9 Draw a line across the entire particulars column to separate onejournal entry from the other.

For Example:

1. Kannan Commenced business with capital

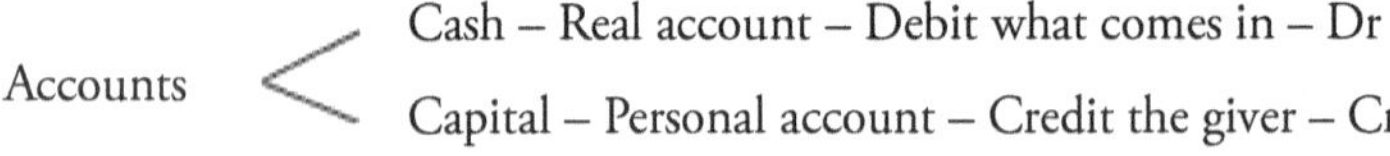

2. Paid into bank

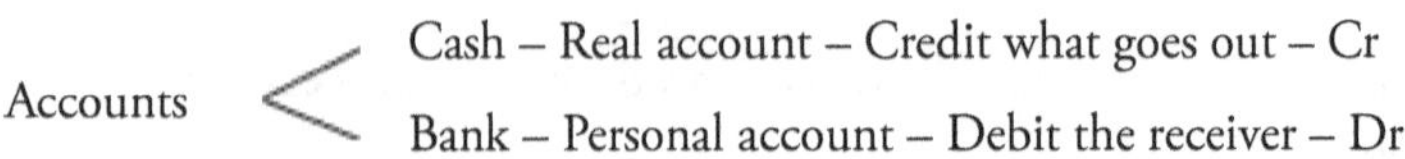

3. Goods for cash

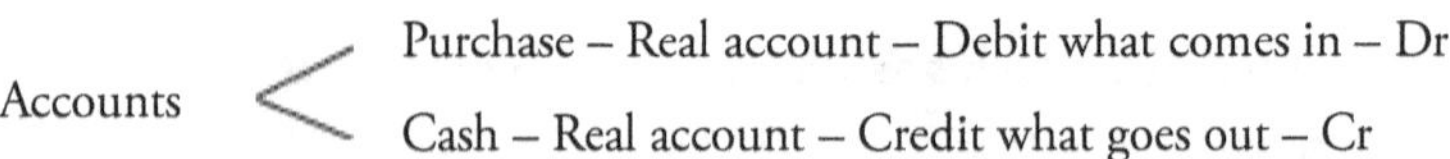

4. Cash sales

Accounts ⟨
Cash – Real account – Debit what comes in– Dr
Sale – Real account – Credit what goes out – Cr

5. Sold goods to Selvi on credit

Accounts ⟨
Sales – Real account – Credit what goes out – Cr
Selvi – Personal account – Debit the receiver – Dr

6. Received cash from Mukesh

Accounts ⟨
Cash - Real account – What comes in- Dr
Mukesh – Personal account – Credit the giver - Cr

7. Paid cash to Hari

Accounts ⟨
Cash – Real account – Credit What goe–s out   - Cr
Hari – Personal account – Debit the receiver – Dr

8. Paid rent by Cheque

Accounts ⟨
Cash – Real account – Credit Whatgoes out – Cr
Hari – Personal account – Debit the receiver – Dr

9. Paid salaries in cash

Accounts ⟨
Cash – Real account –Credit What goes out – Cr
Hari – Personal account – Debit the receiver – Dr

10. Received commission

Accounts ⟨
Commission–Nominal account – Credit all income & gains – Cr

Cash – Real account – Debit what comes in – Dr

Illustration: 1 Pass journal entries for the following transactions.

   i)   Capital introduced ₹ 1,50,000

   ii)   Cash purchases ₹ 40,000

   iii)   Purchases from A ltd ₹ 50,000

   iv)   Goods sold to Z Ltd ₹ 1,25,000

Solution:

Journals

Date	Particulars		L.F.	Debit ₹	Credit ₹
(i)	Cash a/c	Dr		1,50,000	
	To Capital a/c				1,50,000
	(Being cash introduced in business)				
(ii)	Purchase a/c	Dr		40,000	
	To Cash a/c				40,000
	(Being cash purchases)				
(iii)	Purchase a/c	Dr		50,000	
	To A ltd a/c				50,000
	(Being credit purchases from A ltd)				
(iv)	Z Ltd a/c	**Dr**		1,25,000	
	To Sales a/c				1,25,000
	(Being credit sales to Z Ltd)				

Illustration: 2 Journalise the following transactions in the books of Mr. Santhanam

2013	₹
April business with a capital	1 Commenced 10,000
5 cash from Ragavan	Bought goods for 5,000
7 account and deposited	Opened bank 2,000
10	Purchased stationeries 200

Solution:

Journals in the books of Mr. Santhanam

Date	Particulars		L.F.	Debit ₹	Credit ₹
2013	Cash a/c	Dr		10,000	
Apr	To Capital a/c				10,000
1	(Being commenced business)				
5	Purchase a/c To Cash a/c	Dr		5,000	
	(Being bought goods for cash)				5,000
7	Bank a/c	Dr		2,000	
	To Cash a/c				2,000
	(Being cash deposited into bank)				
10	Printing & Stationery s a/c			200	
	To Cash a/c	**Dr**			200
	(Being stationeries purchased)				

Illustration: 3 Journalise the following transactions in the book of Densing in Chennai

March	1	Sold goods to Ramesh for cash	₹ 900
	2	Sold goods to Mukesh	₹ 700
	3	Cash sales	₹ 1,200
	4	Ganesh bought goods	₹ 450
	5	Sold machinery	₹ 1,500

Solution

In the books of Densing Journals

Date	Particulars		L.F.	Debit ₹	Credit ₹
March 1	Cash a/c	Dr		900	
	To Sales a/c				900
	(Being cash sales)				
2	Mukesh a/c	Dr		700	
	To Sales a/c				700
	(Being credit sales to Mukesh)				
3	Cash a/c	Dr		1,200	
	To Sales a/c				1,200
	(Being cash sales)				
4	Ganesh a/c	Dr		450	
	To sales a/c				450
	(Being credit sales to Ganesh)				
5	Cash a/c	Dr		1,500	
	To Machinery a/c				1,500
	(Being machinery sold for cash)				

Illustration:4 Journalise the following transactions in the books of Sri Tamil in Chennai

2015	1. Commenced business with	₹ 50,000
April	2. Purchased goods for cash @ 5% trade discount	₹ 10,000
	3. Paid carriage	₹ 50
	4. Purchase Machinery	₹ 20,000
	5. Sold goods to Mohan on account	₹ 1,500

Solution:

In the Books of TamilJournal entries

Date	Particulars		L.F.	Debit ₹	Credit ₹
2015	Cash a/c	Dr		50,000	
April	To Tamil's Capital a/c				50,000
1	(Being business commenced with capital)				
2	Purchase a/c	Dr		10,000	
	To Discount a/c				
	To Cash a/c				500
	(Being cash purchase & discount @5%)				9,500
3	Carriage a/c	Dr		50	
	To Cash a/c				50
	(Being carriage paid)				
4	Machinery a/c	Dr		20,000	
	To Cash a/c				20,000
	(Being machinery purchased)				
5	Mohan a/c	Dr		1,500	
	To Sales a/c				1,500
	(Being credit sales to mohan)				

Illustration: 5 Journalise the following transactions in the books of Mr.Rabik in Bangalore

April	1 Bought goods from Subash for cash	₹ 7,300
2015	2 Bought Machinery	₹ 67,000

3 Paid for stationery   ₹ 1,200

4 Bought goods from Aravinth   ₹ 8,750

5 Received four tables from Mullai & Co   ₹ 2,250

8 Bought packing material from Sakthi & Co   ₹ 1,750

Solution:

Journal entries in the books of Mr. Rabik

Date	Particulars		L.F.	Debit ₹	Credit ₹
April 1	Purchase a/c	Dr		7,300	
	To Cash a/c				7,300
	(Being cash purchase)				
2	Machinery a/c	Dr		67,000	
	To Cash a/c				67,000
	(Being purchase of machinery)				
3	Printint & Stationary a/c	Dr		1,200	
	To Cash a/c				1,200
	(Being purchase of stationery)				
4	Purchase a/c	Dr		8,750	
	To Aravinth a/c				8,750
	(Being purchase goods from aravinth)				
5	Furniture a/c	Dr		2,250	
	To Mullai a/c				2,250
	(Being 4 tables purchase from mullai & co)				

Date	Particulars		L.F.	Debit ₹	Credit ₹
6	Packing Expenses a/c	Dr		1,750	
	To Sakthi & co a/c				1,750
	(Being purchase of packing material)				

Illustration: 6 Journalise the following transaction in the books of Mr. Raja.

- i) Sold goods for cash   ₹ 15,000
- ii) Purchased goods for cash   ₹ 10,000
- iii) Sold goods to Mr. Z   ₹ 25,000
- iv) Purchased goods from Mr.A   ₹ 30,000
- v) Paid salary   ₹ 5,000
- vi) Paid rent to Raman the land lord   ₹ 4,000

Solution:

Books of Mr. RajaJournal entries

Date	Particulars		L.F.	Debit ₹	Credit ₹
(i)	Cash a/c	Dr		15,000	
	To Sales a/c				15,000
	(Being sales made in cash)				
(ii)	Purchase a/c	Dr		10,000	
	To Cash a/c				10,000
	(Being goods purchased for cash)				
(iii)	Mr.Z a/c	Dr		25,000	
	To Sales a/c				25,000
	(Being goods sold to Mr. Z on credit)				

Date	Particulars		L.F.	Debit ₹	Credit ₹
(iv)	Purchase a/c	Dr		30,000	
	To Mr.A a/c				30,000
	(Being goods purchased from Mr.A on credit)				
(v)	Salary a/c	Dr		5,000	
	To Cash a/c				5,000
	(Being salary paid in cash)				
(vi)	Rent a/c	Dr		4,000	
	To Cash a/c				4,000
	(Being rent paid to Raman, the land lord)				

Illustration: 7 Journalise the following transactions in the books of Stella in Coimbatore

2015		
Jan 1	Started business with a capital of	₹ 5,000
3	Purchased goods from Ganesan	₹ 2,500
5	Sold goods to Kumaran	₹ 1,000
10	Cash sales	₹ 2,000
13	Purchased furniture	₹ 1,000
18	Received interest	₹ 500
20	Withdrew cash from bank for personal use	₹ 2,500
22	Deposited cash into bank	₹ 2,000

Solution:

Journal entries in the books of Stella

Date	Particulars		L.F.	Debit ₹	Credit ₹
2015	Cash a/c	Dr		5,000	
Jan 1	To capital a/c				5,000
	(Being business started with capital)				
3	Purchase a/c	Dr		2,500	
	To Ganesh a/c				2,500
	(Being credit purchase from ganesh)				
5	Kumaran a/c	Dr		1,000	
	To Sales a/c				1,000
	(Being credit sales to kumaran)				
10	Cash a/c	Dr		2,000	
	To Sales a/c				2,000
	(Being cash sales)				
13	Furniture a/c	Dr		500	
	To Interest a/c				500
	(Being interest received)				
20	Bank a/c	Dr		2,500	
	To Drawings a/c				2,500
	(Being cash withdrew from bank for personal use)				
22	Bank a/c	Dr		2,000	
	To Cash a/c				2,000
	(Being cash deposited in to bank)				

Illustration: 8 Enter the following transactions in the book of Mr. Joseph.

2015		
Jan 1	Started business with cash	₹ 1,00,000
2	Deposited into bank	₹ 70,000
3	Goods purchased for cash	₹ 5,000
5	Withdraw from bank for office use	₹ 1,000
7	Credit sales to Johnson	₹ 1,500
9	Credit purchase from Moses	₹ 5,000

Solution:

Books of Mr. JosephJournal entries

Date	Particulars		L.F.	Debit ₹	Credit ₹
2015	Cash a/c	Dr		1,00,000	
Jan 1	To Joseph's capital a/c				1,00,000
	(Being business started with capital)				
2	Bank a/c	Dr		70,000	
	To Cash a/c				70,000
	(Being cash deposited to bank)				
3	Purchase a/c	Dr		5,000	
	To Cash a/c				5,000
	(Being cash purchase)				
5	Cash a/c	Dr		1,000	
	To Bank a/c				1,000
	(Being cash sales)				

Date	Particulars		L.F.	Debit ₹	Credit ₹
7	Johnson a/c	Dr		1,500	
	To Sales a/c				1,500
	(Being credit sales to Johnson)				
9	Purchase a/c	Dr		5,000	
	To Moses a/c				5,000
	(Being credit purchase from Moses)				
22	Bank a/c	Dr		2,000	
	To Cash a/c				2,000
	(Being cash deposited in to bank)				

Illustration: 9 Journalise the following transactions in the books Mr.Mohamed Sidhik

2014			₹
Jan 1	Received cash from Raman		15,000
3	Purchased goods		2,500
11	Sold goods to Lakshmanan		3,500
15	Paid Mahadevan		1,500
17	Received from Raju		1,100
19	Bought furniture on credit		5,000
27	Paid rent		500
31	Paid salary		2,000

Solution:

Journal entries in the books of Mr.MohamedSidhik

Date	Particulars		L.F.	Debit ₹	Credit ₹
2014	Cash a/c	Dr		15,000	
Jan 1	To Raman a/c				15,000
	(Being cash received from Raman)				
3	Purchase a/c	Dr		2,500	
	To Cash a/c				2,500
	(Being goods purchased)				
11	Lakshmanan a/c	Dr		3,500	
	To Salas a/c				3,500
	(Being sales made to Lakshmanan)				
15	Madhavan a/c	Dr		1,500	
	To Cash a/c				1,500
	(Being cash paid to Madhavan)				
17	Cash a/c	Dr		1,100	
	To Raju a/c				1,100
	(Being cash received from Raju)				
19	Furniture a/c	Dr		5,000	
	To Kannan a/c				5,000
	(Being furniture purchased)				
27	Rent a/c	Dr		500	
	To Cash a/c				500
	(Being rent paid)				

Date	Particulars		L.F.	Debit ₹	Credit ₹
31	Salary a/c	Dr		2,000	
	To Cash a/c				2,000
	(Being salary paid)				

Illustration: 10 Journalise the following transactions in the books of Mr. Kumar

2014			₹
April 1	Kumar started with capital of		1,00,000
3	Purchase of machinery		20,000
11	Cash purchases		15,000
15	Cash sales		22,000
17	Paid salaries		1,500
19	Rent paid		2,400
27	Wages paid		1,500
31	Credit purchase from Balaji		1,000

Solution:

Books of Mr. Kumar Journal entries

Date	Particulars		L.F.	Debit ₹	Credit ₹
2014	Cash a/c	Dr		1,00,000	
Apr 1	To Kumar's capital a/c				1,00,000
	(Being business started with capital)				

Date	Particulars		L.F.	Debit ₹	Credit ₹
3	Machinery a/c	Dr		20,000	
	To Cash a/c				20,000
	(Being machinery purchased)				
11	Purchase a/c	Dr		15,000	
	To Cash a/c				15,000
	(Being cash purchase)				
15	Cash a/c	Dr		22,000	
	To Sales a/c				22,000
	(Being cash sales)				
17	Salary a/c	Dr		1,500	
	To Cash a/c				1,500
	(Being salary paid)				
19	Rent a/c	Dr		2,400	
	To Cash a/c				2,400
	(Being rent paid)				
27	Wages a/c	Dr		1,500	
	To Cash a/c				1,500
	(Being wages paid)				
31	Purchase a/c	Dr		1,000	
	To Balaji a/c				1,000
	(Being credit purchase from Balaji)				

Illustration:11 Journalise the following transactions in the books of Mr. Miller

Started business with	₹ 10,000
Bought furniture for	₹ 900
Purchased goods from Mohan for	₹ 4,000
for cashSold goods for cash	₹ 1,700
Paid in to bank	₹ 2,000
Sold goods to James	₹ 2,000
Purchased stationary	₹ 500
Rent paid	₹ 800
Wages paid	₹ 500
Paid salary	₹ 8,000

Solution:

Journal entry in the books of Miller

Date	Particulars		L.F.	Debit ₹	Credit ₹
	Cash a/c	Dr		10,000	
	To capital a/c				10,000
	(Being cash brought in as capital)				
	Furniture a/c	Dr		900	
	To Cash a/c				900
	(Being furniture purchased)				
	Purchase a/c	Dr		4,000	
	To Cash a/c				4,000
	(Being cash purchase)				

Date	Particulars		L.F.	Debit ₹	Credit ₹
	Cash a/c	Dr		1,700	
	To sales a/c				1,700
	(Cash sales)				
	Bank a/c	Dr		2,000	
	To cash a/c				2,000
	(Being cash deposited in to bank)				
	James a/c	Dr		2,000	
	To Sales a/c				2,000
	(Being credit sales)				
	Stationary a/c	Dr		500	
	To Cash a/c				500
	(Being stationary purchased)				
	Rent a/c	Dr		800	
	To Cash a/c				800
	(Being rent paid)				
	Wages a/c	Dr		500	
	To cash a/c				500
	(Being wages paid)				
	Salary a/c	Dr		8,000	
	To cash a/c				8,000
	(Being salary paid)				

Illustration: 12 Write the journal entries for the following transaction in the books of Mr.Raju

			₹
2014	1	Started business with	10,000
January	1	Paid into bank	5,000
	3	Bought furniture	500
	5	Bought goods	500
	10	Bought one bicycle from A & Co, on credit	2,500
	13	Sold goods to Sona on Credit	1,000
	14	Bought goods from Amutha on Credit	2,000
	15	Paid advertisement charges	1,000
	21	Sold goods to Raja on cash	2,000
	26	Paid salaries	1,200
	29	Withdrew from bank for Private use	3,000
	30	Paid rent by cheque	4,500
	31	Withdrew from bank	7,000

Solution:

Journal entries in the books of Mr. Raju

Date	Particulars		L.F.	Debit ₹	Credit ₹
2014	Cash a/c	Dr		10,000	
January	To capital a/c				10,000
1	(Being cash brought in as capital)				

Date	Particulars		L.F.	Debit ₹	Credit ₹
1	Bank a/c	Dr		5,000	
	To Cash a/c				5,000
	(Being cash paid into bank)				
3	Furniture a/c	Dr		500	
	To Cash a/c				500
	(Being furniture bought)				
5	Purchase a/c	Dr		500	
	To Cash a/c				500
	(Being goods purchase)				
10	Bicycle a/c	Dr		2,500	
	To A & Co a/c				2,500
	(Being bicycle bought from A & Co)				
13	Sona a/c	Dr		1,000	
	To Sales a/c				1,000
	(Being goods sold)				
14	Purchase a/c	Dr		2,000	
	To Amutha a/c				2,000
	(Being goods purchased on credit)				
15	Advertisement a/c	Dr		1,000	
	To Cash a/c				1,000
	(Being advertisement amount paid)				

Date	Particulars		L.F.	Debit ₹	Credit ₹
21	Cash a/c	Dr		2,000	
	To Sales a/c				2,000
	(Being cash sales)				
26	Salaries a/c	Dr		1,200	
	To cash a/c				1,200
	(Being salary paid)				
29	Drawings a/c	Dr		3,000	
	To Bank a/c				3,000
	(Being cash withdrew for private use)				
30	Rent a/c	Dr		4,500	
	To Bank a/c				4,500
	(Being rent paid)				
31	Cash a/c	Dr		7,000	
	To Bank a/c				7,000
	(Being cash withdrew from bank)				

Illustration: 13 Journalise the following transactions of Amirtharaj for the month ofSeptember as given below:

2014 1		Amirtharaj commenced business with cash	₹ 50,000
Sept	1	Paid into bank	30,000
	3	Bought goods for cash	10,000
	5	Drew cash from Bank	1,000
	13	Sold goods to Krishnan on credit	11,000

20	Bought from Shyam goods on credit		10,000
24	Received from Krishnan		10,900
	Allowed him discount		100
28	Paid to Shyam cash		9,800
	Discount allowed		200
30	Cash sales for the month		8,000
	Paid rent		500
	Paid salary		1,000

Solution:

In the book of Mr.Amirtharaj Journals

Date	Particulars		L.F.	Debit ₹	Credit ₹
2014	Cash a/c	Dr		50,000	
Sep 1	To Capital a/c				50,000
	(Being amount invested in the business)				
1	Bank a/c	Dr		30,000	
	To Cash a/c				30,000
	(Being cash paid in to bank)				
3	Purchase a/c	Dr		10,000	
	To Cash a/c				10,000
	(Being goods purchased for cash)				
5	Cash a/c	Dr		1,000	
	To Bank a/c				1,000
	(Being cash withdraw from bank)				

Date	Particulars		L.F.	Debit ₹	Credit ₹
13	Krishnan a/c	Dr		11,000	
	To Sales a/c				11,000
	(Being goods sold on credit)				
20	Purchase a/c	Dr		10,000	
	To Shyam a/c				10,000
	(Being goods purchases on credit from shyam)				
24	Cash a/c Discount a/c	Dr		10,900	
	To Krishnan a/c	Dr		100	11,000
	(Being cash received Krishnan & discount allowed)				
28	Shyam a/c	Dr		10,000	
	To Cash a/c				9,800
	To Discount a/c				200
	(Being cash paid to shyam and discount allowed)				
30	Cash a/c	Dr		8,000	
	To Sales a/c				8,000
	(Being cash sales)				
30	Rent a/c	Dr		500	
	Salary a/c	Dr		1,000	
	To cash a/c				1,500
	(Being salary and rent paid on cash)				

2.16 COMPOUND JOURNAL ENTRY

When two or more transactions of similar nature take place on the same date, such transactions can be entered in the journal by means of a combined journal entry is called **Compound Journal Entry**. The only precaution is that the total debits should be equal to total credits.

Opening Entry

Opening Entry is an entry which is passed in the beginning of each current year to record the closing balance of assets and liabilities of the previous year. In this entry asset accounts are debited and liabilities and capital account are credited. If capital is not given in the question, it will be found out by deducting total of liabilities from total of assets.

Example: The following balances appeared in the books of Poonkodi as on 1ˢᵗ January 2014 – Cash ₹ 700, Bank ₹ 7,000, Stock ₹ 8,000, Furniture ₹ 1,000, Computer ₹ 5,000, Debtors ₹ 3,300 and Creditors ₹ 9,000.

The opening entry is

Solution:

In the book of Poonkodi Journals

Date	Particulars		L.F.	Debit ₹	Credit ₹
2014	Cash a/c	Dr		700	
Jan 1	Bank a/c	Dr		7,000	
	Stock a/c	Dr		8,000	
	Debtors a/c	Dr		3,300	
	Furniture a/c	Dr		1,000	
	Computer a/c	Dr		5,000	
	To Creditors a/c				9,000
	To Capital a/c				16,000
	(Being assets and liabilities are brought forward)				

2.17 ADVANTAGES OF JOURNAL

The main advantages of the Journal are:

1. It reduces the possibility of errors.
2. It provides an explanation of the transaction.
3. It provides a chronological record of all transactions.

2.18 LIMITATIONS OF JOURNAL

The limitations of the Journal are:

1. It will be too long if all transactions are recorded here.
2. It is difficult to ascertain the balance of each account.

2.19 LEDGER

The ledger is the main book of account. The journal is a subsidiary book. The wordsubsidiary means 'giving additional helps to'. The journal helps a businessman to take the various transactions to the right place. The journal is the base, the ledger the middle of the pyramid. The balance Sheet and Profit & Loss statements can be prepared from the main book of account. Recording the business transactions under the heads of debit and credit is known as journalizing. Processing these transactions further and taking them to the appropriate accounts is known as Posting. The work of the journal is similar to the constablein that it merely tells the account to be debited and the account to be credited. Then the entries are posted under appropriate accounts. All similar transactions must be brought to gather. Transactions with customers and suppliers are grouped under appropriate personal accounts.Transactions connected with various assets are recorded under each asset account separately.The expenses and incomes of the business are recorded under appropriate nominal accounts. Ledger is the main book of the business containing Personal, Real and Nominal accounts of the business. But transactions are not normally recorded in the ledger directly. They are firstentered in the Journal and then posted to the concerned accounts in the ledger.

The Journal, each transaction is dealt with separately. Therefore, it is not possible to know at a glance, the net result of many transactions. So, in order to ascertain the net effect ofall the transactions relating to a particular account are collected at one place in the Ledger. ALedger is a book which contains all the accounts whether personal, real or nominal, which are first entered in journal or special purpose subsidiary books.

According to **L.C. Cropper**, 'the book which contains a classified and permanent record of all the transactions of a business is called the Ledger'.

The ledger that is normally used in a majority of business concern is a bound note book. This can be preserved for a long time. Its pages are consequently numbered. Each account in the ledger is opened preferably on a separate page. If one page is completed, the account will be continued in the next or some other page.

The Ledger is the main book of account. The Journal is a subsidiary book. An accountis divided in the middle and the two sides are called the debit side and the credit side.

Sub divisional Ledger

In a small business it will be possible to keep all the ledger accounts in one ledger, especially if the ledger be a loose leaf one. But as the business grows, it will be convenient tosub divide the ledger to facilitate easy reference as under.

General or Simple Ledger

This section contains all accounts other than Debtors and Creditors. It includes proprietorship accounts asset accounts, goods accounts, liabilities other than creditors and allnominal accounts.

Debtors Ledger

This will contain the accounts of those people to whom the business sells goods on credit, showing goods sold, cash received etc. This section of the ledger will enable the businessman to calculate the amount owing by his customers rapidly.

Creditors ledger

This section will contain the accounts of those people from whom the business purchases goods on credit, showing goods purchased, cash paid etc. This part of the ledger will enable the trader to calculate rapidly the balance due to each creditor.

2.20 RELATIONSHIP BETWEEN JOURNAL AND LEDGER

1. The journal is a subsidiary book, the ledger is the main book of account.

2. Transactions are first entered in Journal subsequently these entries are posted to the appropriate accounts in the ledger.

3. The Journal is a daily record. Business transactions are entered in this book in the order of dates. Posting from the journal is done periodically, may be weekly or fortnightly as per the convenience of the business.

4. Entering the transactions in the journal is called journalizing the act of recording in theledger is called posting.

2.21 DISTINCTION BETWEEN JOURNAL AND LEDGER

Basis of Distinction	Journal	Ledger
1. Book	It is the book of prime entry	It is the main book of account
2. Stage	Recording of entries in thesebooks is the first stage	Recording of entries in theledger is the second stage
3. Process	The process of recording entries in these books is called "Journalizing".	The process of recording entries in the ledger is called "Posting".
4. Transactions	Transactions relating to a person or property or expense are spread over	Transactions relating to a particular account are found together on a particular page.
5. Net effect	The final position of a particular account cannot be found.	The final position of a particular account can be ascertained just at a glance.
6. Next stage	Entries are transferred to theledger	From the ledger, first the Trialbalance is drawn and then final accounts are prepared.

Basis of Distinction	Journal	Ledger
7. Tax authorities	Do not rely upon these books	Rely on the ledger for assessment purpose.

2.22 ADVANTAGES OF LEDGER

Ledger is a principal or main book which contains all the accounts in which the transactions recorded in the books of original entry are transferred. Ledger is also called the **'Book of Final Entry'** or **'Book of Secondary Entry'**, because the transactions are finally incorporated in the Ledger. The following are the advantages of ledger.

Complete information at a glance: All the transactions pertaining to an account are collected at one place in the ledger. By looking at the balance of that account, one can understand the collective effect of all such transactions at a glance.

Arithmetical Accuracy: With the help of ledger balances, Trial balance can be prepared to know the arithmetical accuracy of accounts.

Result of Business Operations: It facilitates the preparation of final accounts for ascertaining the operating result and the financial position of the business concern.

Accounting information

The data supplied by various ledger accounts are summarised, analysed and interpreted for obtaining various accounting information.

Ledger format

Date	Particulars	L.F.	Amount ₹	Date	Particulars	L.F.	Amount ₹
Year Month Date	To (Name of Credit Accountin Journal)			Year Month Date	By (Name of Debit account in Journal)		

1. Each ledger account is divided into two parts. The left hand side is known as the debitside and the right hand side is known as the credit side. The words 'Dr.' and 'Cr.' areused to denote Debit and Credit.

2. The name of the account is mentioned in the top (middle) of the account.

3. The date of the transaction is recorded in the date column.

4. The word 'To' is used before the accounts which appear on the debit side of an account in the particulars column. Similarly, the word 'By' is used before the accountswhich appear on the credit side of an account in the particulars column.

5. The name of the other account which is affected by the transaction is written either inthe debit side or credit side in the particulars column.

6. The page number of the Journal or Subsidiary Book from where that particular entry istransferred is entered in the Journal Folio (J.F) column.

7. The amount pertaining to this account is entered in the amount column.

Personal Accounts

Debit (Dr)	Rajesh a/c	Credit (Cr)
Debit Rajesh when he receives goods. Money or value from the business		Credit Rajesh when he gives goods, money or value to the business

Real Accounts

Debit (Dr)	Furniture a/c	Credit (Cr)
Debit purchase of assets	Credit sale of asset	

Nominal Accounts

Debit (Dr)	Salaries a/c	Credit (Cr)
Debit expenses or losses		

Debit (Dr)	**Rent Received a/c**	Credit (Cr)
	Credit incomes or gains	

Book of Accounts

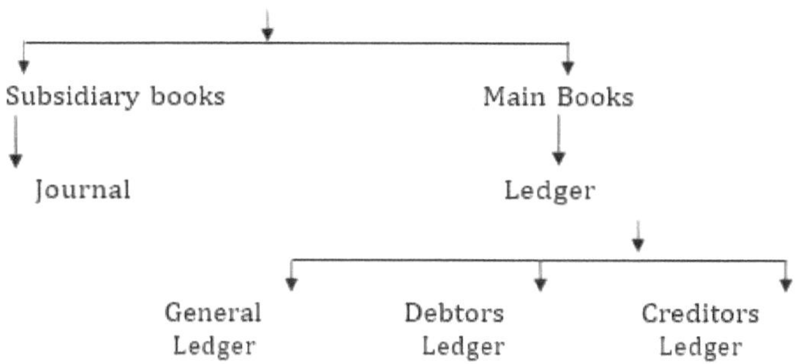

2.23 POSTING

The process of transferring the entries recorded in the journal or subsidiary books to the respective accounts opened in the ledger is called **Posting**. In other words, posting meansgrouping of all the transactions relating to a particular account at one place. It is necessary topost all the journal entries into various accounts in the ledger because posting helps us to know the net effect of various transactions during a given period on a particular account. In simply says the technique of recording the journal entries into the ledger is known as"Posting".

Example

Date	Particulars		L.F.	Debit ₹	Credit ₹
2014	Cash a/c	Dr		50,000	
Jan 1	To Capital a/c				50,000
	(Being amount invested in business)				

This journal entry indicates to the ledger keeper that the cash account is to be debited and the capital account is to be credited. Debiting an account means entering the transaction on the debit side of that account. Crediting an account signifies recording the transaction on the credit side of that account. To post the above journal entry we have to record on the debit side of the cash account and on the credit side of the capital account in the ledger.

Dr Cash   **Cr**

Date	Parti culars	J.F	₹	Date	Parti culars	J.F	₹
1.1.2014	To Capital a/c		50,000				

Dr   **Capital**   **Cr**

Date	Parti culars	J.F	₹	Date	Parti culars	J.F	₹
				1.1.2014	By Cash a/c		50,000

Note: it is customary to write "To" on the debit side and "By" on the credit side.

A ledger entry gives us three details

1. Whether it is a debit or a credit
2. The amount
3. The direction

Illustration: 14 Journalising the following transaction and post to proper accounts

2014				₹
Jan	1	Vijay started business with a capital of		20,000
"	4	Bought goods from Suriya		13,500
"	7	Cash Purchase		6,000
"	10	Cash Sales		8,000
"	13	Bought goods from Suriya		4,000
"	16	Sold goods to Ajith		10,000
"	18	Paid cash to Suriya		5,700
"	19	Sold goods to Ajith		1,000
"	24	Paid Suriya on account		4,800
"	26	Received cash from Ajith		3,300
"	27	Paid salaries		2,500
"	30	Received cash from Ajith		400

Solution:

Journal of Mr. Vijay

Date	Particulars		L.F.	Debit ₹	Credit ₹
2014	Cash a/c	Dr		20,000	
Jan 1	To Capital a/c				20,000
	(Being the cash invested in business)				
4	Purchase a/c	Dr		13,500	
	To Suriya a/c				30,000
	(Being credit purchase of goods)				
7	Purchase a/c	Dr		6,000	
	To Cash a/c				6,000
	(Being cash purchase)				
10	Cash a/c	Dr		8,000	
	To Sales a/c				8,000
	(Being cash sales)				
13	Purchase a/c	Dr		4,000	
	To Suriya a/c				4,000
	(Being credit purchase of goods)				
16	Ajith a/c	Dr		10,000	
	To Sales a/c				10,000
	(Being credit sales of goods)				
18	Suriya a/c	Dr		5,700	
	To Cash a/c				5,700
	(Being cash paid to Suriya)				

19	Ajith a/c	Dr	1,000	
	To Sales a/c			1,000
	(Being credit sales of goods)			

24	Suriya a/c	Dr	4,800	
	To Cash a/c			4,800
	(Being cash paid to suriya account)			

26	Cash a/c	Dr	3,300	
	To Ajith a/c			
	(Being cash received from ajith)			3,300

27	Salaries a/c	Dr	2,500	
	To cash a/c			2,500
	(Being salaries paid)			

30	Cash a/c	Dr	400	
	To Ajith a/c			400
	(Being cash received)			

Ledger of Mr. Vijay

Dr Capital Account   **Cr**

Date	Particulars	J.F	₹	Date	Particulars	J.F	₹
Jan 31	To Balance c/d		20,000	2014	By Cash a/c		20,000
			20,000				20,000
				Feb 1	By Balance b/d		20,000

Dr				Cash account			Cr
Date	Parti culars	J.F	₹	Date	Parti culars	J.F	₹
2014				2014			
Jan 1	To Capital a/c		20,000	Jan 7	By Purchase		6,000
10	To Sales		8,000	18	By Suriya		5,700
26	To Ajith		3,300	24	By Suriya		4,800
30	To Ajith		400	30	By Salaries		2,500
				31	By Balance c/d		12,700
			31,700				31,700
Feb 1	To Balance b/d		12,700				

Dr Purchase account			Cr				
Date	Parti culars	J.F	₹	Date	Parti culars	J.F	₹
2014							
Jan 4	To Suriy a/c		13,500	2014			
7	To Cash a/c		6,000	Jan 31	By Balance c/d		23,500
13	To Suriya a/c		4,000				
			23,500				23,500
Feb 1	To Balance b/d		23,500				

Dr				Sales account			Cr
Date	Particulars	J.F	₹	Date	Particulars	J.F	₹
				2014			
2014				Jan 10	By Cash a/c		8,000
Jan 31	To Balance c/d		19,000	16	By Ajith		10,000
				19	By Ajith		1,000
			19,000				19,000
				Feb 1	By Balance b/d		19,000

Dr				Ajith account	Cr		
Date	Particulars	J.F	₹	Date	Particulars	J.F	₹
2014				2014			
Jan 16	To Sales		10,000	Jan 26	By Cash		3,300
19	To Sales		1,000	30	By Cash		400
				Jan 31	By Balance c/d		7,300
			11,000				11,000
Feb 1	To Balance b/d		7,300				

Dr			₹	Suriya account			Cr ₹
Date	Parti culars	J.F	₹	Date	Parti culars	J.F	₹
2014				2014			
Jan 19	To Cash		5,700	Jan 4	By Purchase		13,500
24	To Cash		4,800	13	By Purchase		4,000
31	To Balance c/d		7,000				
			17,500				17,500
				Feb 1	By Balance b/d		7,000

Note:

1. If you carefully analyse the postings into the ledger you will find that there are 12 debit entries and 12 credit entries in the ledger.
2. The journal contained 12 transactions i.e 12 accounts to be debited and 12 accounts tobe credited.
3. A debit entry in the journal is taken to the debit of the appropriate account in the ledger.
4. A credit entry in the journal is taken to the credit of the appropriate account in the ledger.
5. The total value of debits corresponds to the total value of credits reminding us the veryfoundation of the Double Entry System – for every debit there is a corresponding credit.

2.24 BALANCING AN ACCOUNT

1. After all transactions have been posted to the various accounts the balances of variousaccounts are ascertained as under.
2. Total the two sides of an account in a work sheet.
3. Enter the higher amount on the side obtained, e.g. if the debits total ₹ 31,700. The figure ₹ 19,000 is first inserted in the total on the debit side

4. Extend the same total on the other side of the amount i.e the total of ₹ 19,000 is written against the total on the credits side also

5. Ascertain the difference between the two sides of the accounts and place it on the lighter side of the account writing in the particulars column "….. Balance c/d", are meaning that the amount is again shown under.

6. Bring down the balance on the heavier side writing in the particulars column "…..Balance b/d", meaning that the balance in the account has been brought down.

Illustration: 15 The following are transactions of Mr. Mathialagan.

2015

April	1	Started business with ₹10,000 cash
	2	received a loan of ₹ 50,000 from Mr.Narmatha by cheque

2 bank account opened and above cheque paid

3 bought machinery for cash ₹ 600

8   took ₹ 3,000 out of the bank and put it into the cash till

15   repaid part of Mr. Narmatha loan by cheque

24   repaid part of Mr.Narmatha's loan by cash ₹ 1,000

31   bought additional machinery ₹ 5000

You are required to write up the journal and ledger to record the above.

Solution:

In the Books of MathialaganJournal entries

Date	Particulars	L.F.	Debit ₹	Credit ₹
2015	Cash a/c Dr		10,000	
April	To Capital a/c			10,000
1	(Being business started with capital)			

Date	Particulars		L.F.	Debit ₹	Credit ₹
2	Bank a/c	Dr		50,000	
	To Narmatha a/c				50,000
	(Being loan amount received fromnarmatha)				
3	Machinery a/c	Dr		600	
	To Cash a/c				600
	(Being machinery bought from cash)				
8	Cash a/c	Dr		3,000	
	To Bank a/c				3,000
	(Being took from bank)				
15	Narmatha a/c	Dr		8,000	
	To Bank a/c				8,000
	(Being loan paid to narmatha thro Cheq)				
24	Narmatha a/c	Dr		1,000	
	To Cash a/c				1,000
	(Being part loan amount paid tonarmatha)				
31	Machinery a/c	Dr		5,000	
	To Cash a/c				5,000
	(Being additional machinery bought)				

Ledger of Mr. Mathialagan

Dr	Capital account				Cr			
Date	Parti culars	J.F	₹	Date	Parti culars	J.F	₹
2015				2015			
Jan 31	To Bal c/d		10,000	Jan 1	By Cash a/c		10,000
			10,000				10,000
				Feb 1	By Bal b/d		10,000

Dr			Cash account					Cr
Date	Parti culars	J.F	₹	Date	Parti culars	J.F	₹
2015				2015			
Jan 1	To Capital a/c		10,000	Jan 3	By Machinery		600
8	To Bank a/c		3,000	24	By Narmatha		1,000
				31	By Machinery a/c		5,000
				31	By Balance c/d		6,400
			13,000				13,000
Feb 1	To Bal b/d		6,400				

Dr Bank account		Cr					
Date	**Particulars**	**J.F**	**₹**	**Date**	**Particulars**	**J.F**	**₹**
2015				2015			
Jan 2	To Narmatha a/c		50,000	Jan 8	By Cash a/c		3,000
				15	By Narmatha a/c		8,000
				31	By Balance c/d		39,000
			50,000				50,000
Feb 1	To Bal b/d		39,000				

Dr		Narmatha account				Cr	
Date	**Particulars**	**J.F**	**₹**	**Date**	**Particulars**	**J.F**	**₹**
2015				2015			
Jan 15	To Bank a./c		8,000	Jan 2	By Bank a/c		50,000
24	To Cash a/c		1,000				
31	To Balance c/d		41,000				
			50,000				50,000
				Feb 1	By Bal b/d		41,000

Dr	Machinery Account			Cr			
Date	Particulars	J.F	₹	Date	Particulars	J.F	₹
2015				2015			
Jan 3	To Cash a/c		600	Jan 31	By Balance c/d		5,600
31	To Cash a/c		5,000				
			5,600				5,600
Feb 1	To Bal b/d		5,600				

Illustration: 16 Journalise the following transactions in the journal of Mr. Joseph Sundaram, post them in ledger and balance them.

2015

Aug. 1	Statred business with		₹ 4,50,000
3	Goods purchased		₹ 70,000
5	Goods sold		₹ 51,000
9	Deposited into Bank		Rs. 40,000
10	goods purchased from Samy		₹ 2,00,000
16	Goods returned to Samy		₹ 5,000
23	Drew from bank		₹ 30,000
26	Furniture purchased		₹ 10,000
27	Settled samy account		
31	Salary paid		₹ 12,000

Solution:

In the Books of Joseph Sundaram Journal entries

Date	Particulars		L.F.	Debit ₹	Credit ₹
2015	Cash a/c	Dr		4,50,000	
Aug	To Capital a/c				4,50,000
1	(Being business started with capital)				
3	Purchase a/c	Dr		70,000	
	To Cash a/c				70,000
	(Being goods purchased for cash)				
5	Cash a/c	Dr		51,000	
	To Sales				51,000
	(Being goods sold for cash)				
10	Purchase a/c	Dr		2,00,000	
	To Samy a/c				2,00,000
	(Being goods purchased from samy oncredit)				
16	Samy a/c	Dr		5,000	
	To Purchase return a/c (Being goods returned to samy)				5,000
23	Cash a/c	Dr		30,000	
	To Bank a/c				30,000
	(Being cash with draw from bank)				

Date	Particulars		L.F.	Debit ₹	Credit ₹
26	Furniture a/c	Dr		10,000	
	To Cash a/c				10,000
	(Being furniture bought for cash)				
27	Samy a/c	Dr		1,95,000	
	To Cash a/c				1,95,000
	(Being samy account is settled)				
31	Salary a/c	Dr		12,000	
	To Cash a/c				12,000
	(Being salary paid)				

Ledger of Mr. Joseph Sundaram

Dr			Cash Account		Cr		
Date	Particulars	J.F	₹	Date	Particulars	J.F	₹
2015				2015			
Aug 1	To Capital a/c		4,50,000	Aug 3	By Purchse a/c		70,000
5	To Sales a/c		51,000	9	By Bank a/c		40,000
				26	By Furniture a/c		10,000
23	To Bank a/c		30,000	27	By Samy a/c		1,95,000
				31	By Salary a/c		12,000
				31	By Balance c/d		2,44,000
			5,31,000				5,31,000
Sep 1	To Bal b/d		2,44,000				

Dr				Capital Account			Cr
Date	**Particulars**	**J.F**	**₹**	**Date**	**Particulars**	**J.F**	**₹**
2015				2015			
Aug 31	To Bal c/d		4,50,000	Aug 1	By Cash a/c		4,50,000
			4,50,000				4,50,000
				Sep 1	By Bal b/d		4,50,000

Dr	Purchase Account				Cr		
Date	**Particulars**	**J.F**	**₹**	**Date**	**Particulars**	**J.F**	**₹**
2015				2015			
Aug 3	To Cash a/c		70,000	Aug 31	By Balance c/d		2,70,000
10	To Samy a/c		2,00,000				
			2,70,000				2,70,000
Sep 1	To Bal b/d		2,70,000				

Dr				Sales Account			Cr
Date	**Particulars**	**J.F**	**₹**	**Date**	**Particulars**	**J.F**	**₹**
2015				2015			
Aug 31	To Balance c/d		51,000	Aug 5	By Cash a/c		51,000
			51,000				51,000
				Sep 1	By Bal b/d		51,000

Dr Samy Account   Cr

Date	Particulars	J.F	₹	Date	Particulars	J.F	₹
2015				2015			
Aug 16	To Purchase return		5,000	Aug 10	By Purchase a/c		2,00,000
27	To Cash a/c		1,95,000				
			2,00,000				2,00,000

Dr   Purchase Returns Account   Cr

Date	Particulars	J.F	₹	Date	Particulars	J.F	₹
2015				2015			
Aug 31				Aug 16			
	To Balance c/d		5,000		By Samy a/c		5,000
			5,000				5,000
				Sep 1	By balance b/d		5,000

Dr Bank Account Cr

Date	Particulars	J.F	₹	Date	Particulars	J.F	₹
2015				2015			
Aug 9	To Cash a/c		40,000	Aug 23	By Cash a/c		30,000
Aug 31			30,000	Aug 23	By Balance c/d		10,000
			30,000				40,000
Sep 1	To Balance b/d		10,000				

Dr				Furniture Account			Cr
Date	**Parti culars**	**J.F**	**₹**	**Date**	**Parti culars**	**J.F**	**₹**
2015				2015			
Aug 26	To Cash a/c		10,000	Aug 31	By Balance c/d		10,000
			10,000				10,000
			10,000				
Sep 1	To Bal b/d						

Dr				Salary Account			Cr
Date	**Parti culars**	**J.F**	**₹**	**Date**	**Parti culars**	**J.F**	**₹**
2015				2015			
Aug 31	To Cash a/c		12,000	Aug 31	By Balance c/d		12,000
			12,000				12,000
			12,000				
Sep 1	To Bal b/d						

Illustration: 17 Journalise the following transactions, post them into ledger and balance the ledgers.

Started business with ₹ 50,000

Paid into bank ₹ 20,000

Bought furniture 5000 and machinery

₹ 10,000 Purchased goods for ₹ 14,000

Sold goods for ₹ 8,000

Purchased goods from Mahindra & Co ₹ 11,000

Paid telephone rent by cheque ₹ 500

Solution:

Journal entries

Date	Particulars		L.F.	Debit ₹	Credit ₹
	Cash a/c	Dr		50,000	
	To Capital a/c				50.000
	(Being business started with capital)				
	Bank a/c	Dr		20,000	
	To Cash a/c				20,000
	(Being cash paid into bank)				
	Furniture a/c	Dr		5,000	
	To Cash a/c				5,000
	(Being furniture bough)				
	Machinery a/c	Dr		10,000	
	To Cash a/c				10.000
	(Being machinery bought)				
	Purchase a/c	Dr		14,000	
	To Cash a/c				14,000
	(Being goods purchased)				
	Cash a/c	Dr		8,000	
	To Sales a/c				8,000
	(Being goods sold for cash)				

Date	Particulars		L.F.	Debit ₹	Credit ₹
	Purchase a/c	Dr		11,000	
	To Mahindra & Co				11,000
	(Being goods purchased from Mahindra &Co)				
	Postage & Telephone a/c	Dr		500	
	To Cash a/c				500
	(Being telephone rent paid)				

Ledger Accounts

Dr			Cash Account		Cr		
Date	Parti culars	J.F	₹	Date	Parti culars	J.F	₹
	To Capital a/c		50,000		By Bank a/c		20,000
	To Sales a/c		8,000		By Furniture a/c		5,000
					By Machinery a/c		10,000
					By Purchase a/c		14,000
					By Balance c/d		9,000
			58,000				58,000
	To Bal b/d		9,000				

Dr **Capital Account** **Cr**

Date	Particulars	J.F	₹	Date	Particulars	J.F	₹
	To Bal c/d		50,000		By Cash a/c		50,000
			50,000				50,000
							50,000
					By Bal b/d		

Dr **Bank Account** **Cr**

Date	Particulars	J.F	₹	Date	Particulars	J.F	₹
	To Cash a/c		20,000		By Telephone rent		500
					By Balance c/d		19,500
			20,000				20,000
	To Balance b/d		19,500				

Dr **Furniture Account** **Cr**

Date	Particulars	J.F	₹	Date	Particulars	J.F	₹
	To Cash a/c		5,000		By Balance c/d		5,000
			5,000				5,000
	To Balance b/d		5,000				

Dr				Machinery Account			Cr
Date	**Particulars**	**J.F**	**₹**	**Date**	**Particulars**	**J.F**	**₹**
	To Cash a/c		10,000		By Balance c/d		10,000
			10,000				10,000
	To Balance b/d		10,000				

Dr				Purchase Account			Cr
Date	**Particulars**	**J.F**	**₹**	**Date**	**Particulars**	**J.F**	**₹**
	To Cash a/c		14,000		By Balance c/d		25,000
	To Mahindra & Co		11,000				
			25,000				25,000
	To Balance b/d		25,000				

Dr				Sales Account			Cr
Date	**Particulars**	**J.F**	**₹**	**Date**	**Particulars**	**J.F**	**₹**
	To Balance c/d		8,000		By Cash a/c		8,000
			8,000				8,000
					By Balance b/d		8,000

Dr				Mahindra & Co Account				Cr
Date	**Parti culars**	**J.F**	**₹**	**Date**	**Parti culars**	**J.F**	**₹**	
	To Balance c/d		11,000		By Purchase a/c		11,000	
			11,000				11,000	
					By Balance b/d		11,000	

Dr				Postage & Telephone Account				Cr
Date	**Parti culars**	**J.F**	**₹**	**Date**	**Parti culars**	**J.F**	**₹**	
	To Bank a/c		500		By Balance c/d		500	
			500				500	
	To Balance b/d		500					

Illustration: 18 Balance of Rajesh's account on 31st March, 2014 from the following transactions.(without using journals)

01.03.2014	Goods sold to Rajesh on credit	₹ 2,00,000
05.03.2014	Sales return by Rajesh	₹ 20,000
20.03.2014	Cash received from Rajesh	₹ 40,000
31.03.2014	Cheque received from Rajesh	₹ 60,000
31.03.2014	Discount allowed to him	₹ 2,000

Dr				Rajesh's Account			Cr
Date	**Parti culars**	**J.F**	**₹**	**Date**	**Parti culars**	**J.F**	**₹**
01.03.15	To Sales a/c		2,00,000	05.03.14	By sales return a/c		20,000
				20.03.14	By Cash a/c		40,000
				31.03.14	By Bank a/c		60,000
				31.03.14	By Discount a/c		2,000
				31.03.14	By Balance c/d		78,000
			2,00,000				2,00,000
31.03.14	To Balance b/d		78,000				

2.25 TRIAL BALANCE

The Double Entry System offers greet advantages in checking the accuracy of books of account. Every debit has a corresponding credit and vice versa. This principle of double entry has never been violated in the sub division of the Journal into Purchases book, Sales book, Purchases returns book, Sales returns book, Cash book, Petty cash book, Bills receivable book, and Bills Payable book. The sub division might have resulted in one debit having a series of credits or a series of debits having a consolidated credit.

It follows therefore the total value of debit in the ledger should be equal to the total value of credit in the ledger. As a result it can be stated that the total of debit balances foundin the various accounts must equal the total of credit balances found in the ledger. If the totalsof the debit and credit balances do not agree, then, obviously some errors must have been made in the records. It is necessary to find out the mistakes and rectify them before we proceed to ascertain the profit or loss. In double entry book keeping, trial balance offers a means of checking arithmetical errors in writing up books of account.

The 'Trial Balance is nothing but a summary of the various transactions entered in thebooks of accounts. **Trial balance** is a statement which shows debit balances and credit balances of all accounts in the ledger. Since, every debit should have a corresponding credit asper the rules of double entry system, the total of the debit balances and credit balances should tally. *Trial of ledger balances like a tailor taking a trial of a suit.*

Trial balance is a statement prepared with the balances or total of debits and credits ofall the accounts in the ledger to test the arithmetical accuracy of the ledger accounts. As the name indicates it is prepared to check the ledger balances. If the total of the debit and credit amount columns of the trail balance are equal, it is assumed that the posting to the ledger in terms of debit and credit amounts is accurate. The agreement of a trail balance ensure arithmetical accuracy only, A concern can prepare trail balance at any time, but its preparationas on the closing date of an accounting year is compulsory.

2.26 DEFINITION

"Trial balance is a statement, prepared with the debit and credit balances of ledger accounts to test the arithmetical accuracy of the books" – **J.R. Batliboi**.

According to M.S. Gosav "Trail balance is a statement containing the balances of allledger accounts, as at any given date, arranged in the form of debit and credit columns placedside by side and prepared with the object of checking the arithmetical accuracy of ledger postings".

2.27 OBJECTIVES OF PREPARING A TRIAL BALANCE

a   It gives the balances of all the accounts of the ledger. The balance of any account can be found from a glance from the trail balance without going through the pagesof the ledger.

b   It is a check on the accuracy of posting. If the trail balance agrees, it proves

c   That both the aspects of each transaction are recorded

d   That the books are arithmetically accurate.

e   It facilitates the preparation of profit and loss account and the balance sheet.

f   Important conclusions can be derived by comparing the balances of two or Morethan two years with the help of trail balances of those years.

2.28 FEATURES OF TRIAL BALANCE

The following are the important features of a trail balances:

i)   A trail balance is prepared as on a specified date.

ii) It contains a list of all ledger account including cash account.

iii) It may be prepared with the balances or totals of Ledger accounts.

iv) Total of the debit and credit amount columns of the trail balance must tally.

v)   If the debit and credit amounts are equal, we assume that ledger accounts arearithmetically accurate.

vi) Difference in the debit and credit columns points out that some mistakes havebeen committed.

viii) Tallying of trail balance is not a conclusive profit of accuracy of accounts.

2.29 ADVANTAGES

The advantages of the trial balance are

i)   It helps to ascertain the arithmetical accuracy of the book-keeping work doneduring the period.

ii) It supplies in one place ready reference of all the balances of the ledger accounts.

iii) If any error is found out by preparing a trial balance, the same can be rectifiedbefore preparing final accounts.

iv) It is the basis on which final accounts are prepared.

2.30 LIMITATIONS OF TRIAL BALANCE

The following are the important limitations of trail balances:

a) The trail balance can be prepared only in those concerns where double entrysystem of book- keeping is adopted.

b) This system is too costly.

c) A trail balance is not a conclusive proof of the arithmetical accuracy of the booksof account.

d) It the trail balance agrees, it does not mean that now there are absolutely no errorsin books. On the other hand, some errors are not disclosed by the trail balance.

e) It the trail balance is wrong, the subsequent preparation of Trading, P&L Account and Balance Sheet will not reflect the true picture of the financial position of the business concern.

2.31 METHODS OF TRIAL BALANCE

A trail balance refers to a list of the ledger balances as on a particular date. It can be prepared in the following manner.

Total Method: The total of debits and credits of all accounts. This method is also known as "gross trial balance".

Balance Method: According to this method, only balance of each account of ledger is recorded in trail balance. Some accounts may have debit balance and the other may have credit balance. All these debit and credit balances are recorded in it. This method is widely used.

Compound Method: It is the combination of balance method and total method in which trial balance is prepared by taking the total of each side as well as balances of all the accounts.

Ruling of a trial balance:

The following is the form of a trail balance

Total Method

Trial Balance as on

S.No	Name of the account	L.F.	Debit Total Balance	Credit Total Balance

Balance Method

Trial Balance as on

S.No	Name of the account	L.F.	Debit Balance	Credit Balance

Note: Accounts of all assets, expenses, losses and drawings are debit balances. Accounts of all liabilities, incomes, gains, and capital are credit balances. Trial balance disclosed some of the errors and does not disclosed some other errors. This is given below.

A) Trial Balance disclosed by the Errors

1. Wrong totaling of subsidiary books
2. Posting of an amount on the wrong side
3. Omission to post an amount into ledger
4. Double posting or omission of posting
5. Posting wrong amount
6. Error in balancing

B) Trial Balance not disclosed by the Errors

1. Error of principle
2. Error of omission

3. Errors of Commission
4. Recording wrong amount in the books of original entry
5. Compensating errors

2.32 DIFFERENCES BETWEEN TRIAL BALANCE AND BALANCE SHEET

Trial Balance	Balance Sheet
1 It is prepared to verify the arithmetical accuracy of books of accounts	1 It is prepared to disclose the true financial position of the business
2 It is prepared with balance of all theledger accounts	2 It is prepared with the balance of assetsand liabilities accounts
3 It is not a part of final accounts	3 It is an important part of final accounts
4 It is prepared before the preparation offinal accounts	4 It is prepared after the preparation of trading and profit and loss account
5 It may be prepared a number of timein an accounting year	5 It is generally prepared once at the endof accounting year
6 Generally it includes opening stockbut not closing stock	6 It is always includes closing stock butnot opening stock
7 There is no rule for arranging the ledger balance in it	7 Assets and liabilities must be shown init according to the rule of marshaling
8 It is not required to be filed to any body	8 It must be filed with the registrar of companies if the business is a company

A trial balance contains in it the balances found in all the ledger accounts which maybe grouped as under

1. Assets and liabilities
2. Expenses or losses and incomes or gains
3. Trading account items
4. Special items like provisions and reserves.

Assets & liabilities: if an account is an asset, it must have a debit balance. If an account is a liability it must have a credit balance. Capital is the liability of the business to theproprietor - it is a credit balance. In the specimen trial balance land, furniture bank and cashare all assets and therefore debit balances.

Expenses or losses and income or gains: These are the times which are grouped in the final accounts to ascertain the profit or loss. Some of them are taken to the Trading account. But, most of them are taken to the Profit and Loss account. If an account representsan expense or loss it must be a debit. On the other hand an income or gain is a credit balance.

Trading account items: The following accounts relating to buying and selling of goods are found in the Trial balance.

Debit items	*Credit items*
Stock at commencement	Sales
Purchases	Purchases return
Sales returns	

Special items: Reserves and provision are generally credit balances. The details given abovemay be summarized as under.

Rules

The following generalized rules, that

Debit Balance(due to that)

Drawings Assets Losses Expenses

Sundry DebtorsOpening Stock

Purchases Sales Returns

Credit Balance(due for that)

Capital LiabilitiesGains Incomes

Sundry CreditorsClosing Stock Purchase Returns Sales

2.33 PREPARATION OF TRIAL BALANCE

A trial balance contains in it the balances found in all the Ledger Accounts which maybe grouped as under

- Assets & Liabilities
- Expenses or losses and incomes or gains
- Trading account items
- Special items (Provisions etc)

Assets & Liabilities

An asset must have a debit balance. If an account is a liability it must have a credit balance. Capital is the Liability of the business to the proprietor it is a credit balance. Land,Furniture, Bank, Sundry Debtors and Cash are all debit balances.

Expenses or Losses and Incomes or gains

If an account represents an expenses or loss it must be a debit. On the other hand anincome or gain is a **credit** balance.

Trading account items

Opening stock, purchases and sales returns are debit balance. Sales, purchase returnsare credit balance.

Special Items

Reserves and Provisions are generally speaking credit balances.

Sundry Debtors and Creditors

A list of debit balances found in the various customers' accounts is prepared and the consolidated total of this list is shown under the title "Sundry Debtors". A list of credit balance in personal accounts consolidated total is called "Sundry Creditors".

2.34 SUSPENSE ACCOUNT

The difference in the trial balance is transferred to newly open imaginary and temporary account called 'Suspense Account'. Suspense account is prepared to avoid the delay in the preparation of final accounts.

If the total debit balance of the trial balance exceeds the total credit balances, the difference is transferred to the credit side of the suspense account. On the other hand, if the total credit balances of the trial balance exceeds the total debit balances the difference is transferred to the debit side of the suspense account.

Specimen form of Trial Balance

The common format of a trial balance is given below:

Trial Balance of as on

S.No	Name of the Account	L.F	Debit ₹	Credit ₹

Illustration: 19 The following balances are extracted from the books of Ramdass on 31st December 2012. Prepare a Trial balance.

Particulars	₹	Particulars	₹
Capital	19,000	Outstanding rent	1,000
Plant & Machinery	12,000	Opening Stock	2,000
Purchases	8,000	Sales Returns	4,000
Sales	24,000	Investments	14,000
Sundry Creditors	8,000	Sundry Debtors	12,000

Solution:

Mr. Ramdass's Statement of Trial Balance as on 31.12.2012

S. No	Name of the Account	Debit ₹	Credit ₹
1	Capital		19,000
2	Purchases	8,000	
3	Stock (Opening)	2,000	
4	Plant & Machinery	12,000	
5	Sundry Creditors		8,000
6	Investments	14,000	
7	Sales		24,000
8	Sales returns	4,000	
9	Sundry Debtors	12,000	
10	Outstanding Rent		1,000
	TOTAL	**52,000**	**52,000**

Illustration: 20 From the following mentioned balances extracted from the books of a trader on 31ˢᵗ March 2014, prepare a trial balance.

	₹		₹
Capital	2,00,000	Bills payable	44,000
Sundry Debtors	3,00,000	Cash in hand	2,400
Purchases	2,40,000	Stock (opening)	70,000
Wages	32,000	Sundry Creditors	48,000
Sales	4,00,400	Plant	1,20,000
Furniture	30,000		
Bills receivable	40,000	Bad debts reserve	2,000
Salaries	40,000	Rent	20,000

Solution:

Trial Balance as on 31ˢᵗ March 2014

Particulars	Debit ₹	Credit ₹
Capital		2,00,000
Bills Payable		44,000
Cash in hand	2,400	
Purchases	2,40,000	
Stock (Opening)	70,000	
Bad debts reserve		2,000
Plant	1,20,000	
Sundry Creditors		48,000
Furniture	30,000	
Bills Receivable	40,000	

Particulars	Debit ₹	Credit ₹
Salaries	40,000	
Sales		4,00,400
Sundry Debtors	3,00,000	
Wages	32,000	
Rent	20,000	
TOTAL	**6,94,400**	**6,94,400**

Illustration: 21 The following balances were extracted from the ledger of Mukesh Engineering work on 31st March 2015. You are required to prepare a trial balance as on that date in proper form.

Particulars	₹	Particulars	₹
Drawings	6,000	Salaries	9,500
Capital	24,000	Sales return	1,000
Sundry creditors	43,000	Purchase returns	1,100
Bills payable	4,000	Travelling expenses	4,600
Loan	10,000	Commission paid	100
Furniture	14,700	Trading expenses	2,500
Opening stock	51,000	Discount earned	4,000
Cash in hand	900	Rent	2,000
Cash at bank	22,500	Bank overdraft	6,000
Tax payable	3,500	Purchases	70,800
Sales	1,20,000	Sundry debtors	30,000

Solution:

Statement of Trial Balance of Mr.Mukesh Engineering work on 31st March 2015

Particulars	Debit ₹	Credit ₹
Drawings	6,000	
Capital		24,000
Sundry creditors		43,000
Bills payable		4,000
Loan		10,000
Furniture	14,700	
Opening stock	51,000	
Cash in hand	900	
Cash at bank	22,500	
Sales		1,20,000
Salaries	9,500	
Sales returns	1,000	
Purchase returns		1,100
Travelling expenses	4,600	
Commission paid	100	
Trading expenses	2,500	
Discount earned		4,000
Rent	2,000	
Bank overdraft		6,000
Purchases	70,800	

Particulars	Debit ₹	Credit ₹
Sundry debtors	30,000	
Tax payable		3,500
TOTAL	**2,15,600**	**2,15,600**

Illustration: 22 From the following balances you are required to prepare a trial balance as on31st December 2014.

Particulars	₹	Particulars	₹
Capital	50,000	Plant and machinery	80,000
Sales	1,77,000	Purchases	60,000
Return outwards	750	Return inwards	1,000
Stock (1.1.2014)	30,000	Discount (Dr)	350
Discount (Cr)	800	Bank charges	75
Debtors	45,000	Creditors	25,000
Salaries	6,800	Carriage inwards	750
Wages	10,000	Carriage outwards	1,200
Bad debts provision (Cr)	525	Rent and taxes	10,000
Advertisement	2,000	Cash in hand	900
		Cash at bank	6,000

Solution:

Trial Balance as on 31st December 2014

Particulars	Debit ₹	Credit ₹
Capital		50,000
Sales		1,77,000
Return outwards		750
Stock	30,000	
Discount (Cr)		800
Debtors	45,000	
Salaries	6,800	
Wages	10,000	
Bad debts provision		525
Advertisement	2,000	
Plant & Machinery	80,000	
Purchases	60,000	
Return inwards	1,000	
Discount (Dr)	350	
Bank charges	75	
Creditors		25,000
Carriage inwards	750	
Carriage outwards	1,200	
Rent and taxes	10,000	

Particulars	Debit ₹	Credit ₹
Cash in hand	900	
Cash at bank	6,000	
TOTAL	**2,54,075**	**2,54,075**

Illustration: 23: The following balances you are required to prepare a trial balance as on 31ˢᵗMarch 2014 in proper form.

Particulars	₹	Particulars	₹
Opening stock	50,000	Debtors	3,000
Wages	2,200	Income tax paid	500
Carriage	200	Drawings	700
Commission (Dr)	300	Return outwards	150
Purchases	12,000	Sales	25,200
Returns inwards	440	Discount received	400
Trade expenses	580	Capital	7,000
Rent	200	Creditors	830
Cash in hand	200	Loan (Cr)	1,400
Cash at bank	1,000		

Solution:

Statement of Trial Balance

Name of account	Debit Balance ₹	Credit Balance ₹
Opening stock	10,600	
Wages	2,200	

Name of account	Debit Balance ₹	Credit Balance ₹
Carriage	200	
Debtors	3,000	
Income tax paid	500	
Drawings	700	
Commission (Dr)	300	
Purchases	12,000	
Returns inwards	440	
Trade expenses	580	
Rent	200	
Plant	2,600	
Repairs to plant	460	
Cash in hand	200	
Cash at bank	1,000	
Return outwards		150
Sales		25,200
Discount received		400
Capital		7,000
Creditors		830
Loan (Cr)		1,400
	34,980	34,980

Illustration: 24 The following balances you are required to prepare a trial balance.

Particulars	₹	Particulars	₹
Opening stock	10,000	Loan (Cr)	15,000
Purchases	49,000	Sundry debtors	42,000
Wages	15,000	Capital	50,000
Rent	1,000	Provision for bad debts	2,800
Salaries	8,000	Sales returns	2,000
General expenses	900	Discount allowed	500
Plant	15,000		
Sundry creditors	20,000		
Furniture	8,000		
Cash at bank	5,000		
Sales	1,28,600		
Building	60,000		

Solution:

Account	Debit ₹	Credit ₹
Opening stock	10,000	
Purchases	49,000	
Wages	15,000	
Rent	1,000	
Salaries	8,000	
General expenses	900	
Plant	15,000	

Account	Debit ₹	Credit ₹
Sundry creditors		20,000
Furniture	8,000	
Cash at bank	5,000	
Sales		1,28,600
Building	60,000	
Loan (Cr)		15,000
Sundry debtors	42,000	
Capital		50,000
Provision for bad debts		2,800
Sales returns	2,000	
Discount allowed	500	
	2,16,400	**2,16,400**

Illustration: 25 From the following ledger accounts data of Mr. Senthil, prepare trial balance under the balance method, total method and compound method for the month of April 2015.

Name of account	Debit ₹	Credit ₹
Cash a/c	6,400	5,950
Stock a/c	1,000	
Capital of Senthil		6,000
Purchases a/c	2,900	
Equipment a/c	3,250	
Dinesh a/c		900
Salary a/c	360	

Name of account	Debit ₹	Credit ₹
Drawings a/c	350	
Sales return a/c	300	
Diwakar a/c	3,000	1,300
Sales a/c		3,400
Dixon a/c	750	750
Discount received a/c		10

Trial balance of Senthil as on April 30, 2015

(Balance Method)

Name of account	L.F.	Credit ₹	Credit ₹
Cash a/c		450	
Stock a/c		1,000	
Capital of Senthil			6,000
Purchases a/c		2,900	
Equipment a/c		3,250	
Dinesh a/c			900
Salary a/c		360	
Drawings a/c		350	
Sales return a/c		300	
Diwakar a/c		1,700	
Sales a/c			3,400
Discount received a/c			10
		10,310	10,310

Trial balance of Senthil as on April 30, 2015

(Total Method)

Name of account	L.F.	Debit ₹	Credit ₹
Cash a/c		6,400	5,950
Stock a/c		1,000	
Capital of Senthil			6,000
Purchases a/c		2,900	
Equipment a/c		3,250	
Dinesh a/c			900
Salary a/c		360	
Drawings a/c		350	
Sales return a/c		300	
Diwakar a/c		3,000	1,300
Sales a/c			3,400
Dixon		750	750
Discount received a/c			10
		18,310	18,310

Trial balance of Senthil as on April 30, 2015

(Compound Method)

Name of account	L.F.	Debit ₹	Credit ₹	Debit ₹	Credit ₹
Cash a/c		6,400	5,950	450	5,950
Stock a/c		1,000	--	1,000	-
Capital of Senthil		--	6,000	--	6,000
Purchases a/c		2,900	--	2,900	-
Equipment a/c		3,250	--	3,250	-
Dinesh a/c		--	900	--	900
Salary a/c		360	--	360	-
Drawings a/c		350	--	350	-
Sales return a/c		300	--	300	-
Diwakar a/c		3,000	1,300	1,700	-
Sales a/c		--	3,400	--	3,400
Dixon a/c		750	750	--	-
Discount received a/c		--	10	---	10
		18,310	**18,310**	**10,310**	**10,310**

Illustration: 26 The following balances were extracted from the ledger of Gopu EngineeringWorks on 31ˢᵗ March 2007. You are required to prepare a trial balance as on that date in proper form.

Name of the Accounts	₹	Name of the Accounts	₹
Drawings	6,000	Salaries	9,500
Capital	24,000	Sales Returns	1,000
Sundry Creditors	43,000	Purchase Returns	1,100
Bills Payable	4,000	Travelling expenses	4,600
Sundry debtors	50,000	Commission paid	100
Bills receivable	5,200	Trading expenses	2,500
Loan from Karthik	10,000	Discount earned	4,000
Furniture	4,500	Rent	2,000
Opening stock	47,000	Bank overdraft	6,000
Cash in hand	900	Purchases	70,800
Cash at bank	12,500	Tax paid	3,500
Sales	1,28,000		

Solution:

Trial Balance of Gopu as on 31ˢᵗ March 2007

Particulars	Debit	Credit
Drawings	6,000	
Capital		24,000
Sundry creditors		43,000
Bills payable		4,000

Particulars	Debit	Credit
Sundry debtors	50,000	
Bills receivable	5,200	
Loan from Karthik		10,000
Furniture	4,500	
Opening stock	47,000	
Cash in hand	900	
Cash at bank	12,500	
Tax paid	3,500	
Sales		1,28,000
Salaries	9,500	
Sales returns	1,000	
Purchase returns		1,100
Travelling expenses	4,600	
Commission paid	100	
Trading expenses	2,500	
Discount earned		4,000
Rent	2,000	
Bank overdraft		6,000
Purchases	70,800	
TOTAL	**2,20,100**	**2,20,100**

Illustration: 27: *Prepare Trial balance of Mr. Tinku as on 31ˢᵗ March 2010*

Capital	1,00,000	Motor Van	30,000
Drawings	25,000	Salaries	25,000
Purchases	4,50,000	Rent	10,000
Sales	6,50,000	Taxes	1,500
Returns inwards	4,500	Insurance	3,000
Carriage inwards	5,550	Sundry Debtors	40,000
Carriage outwards	4,000	Sundry Creditors	30,000
Duty on purchase	10,000	Cash in hand	2,500
Stock(opening)	55,000	Cash at Bank	12,500
		Furniture	5,000
		Land	1,02,000

Solution:

Trial balance of Mr. Tinku as on 31ˢᵗ March 2010

Particulars	Debit	Credit
Capital		1,00,000
Drawings	25,000	
Purchase	4,50,000	
Sales		6,50,000
Returns outwards		4,500
Returns inwards	3,500	
Carriage inwards	5,500	
Carriage outwards	4,000	

Particulars	Debit	Credit
Duty on Purchase	10,000	
Stock(Opening)	55,000	
Motor Van	30,000	
Salaries	25,000	
Rent	10,000	
Taxes	1,500	
Insurance	3,000	
Sundry Debtors	40,000	
Sundry Creditors		30,000
Cash in hand	2,500	
Cash at Bank	12,500	
Furniture	5,000	
Land	1,02,000	
TOTAL	**7,84,500**	**7,84,500**

Illustration 28: The following trial balance has been prepared wrongly. You are asked toprepare the trial balance correctly

Trial Balance as on ....

Particulars	Debit ₹	Credit ₹
Capital a/c	22,000	
Stock		10,000
Debtors	8,000	
Creditors		12,000

Particulars	Debit ₹	Credit ₹
Machinery		20,000
Cash in hand		2,000
Bank overdraft	14,000	
Sales returns		8,000
Purchase returns	4,000	
Misc. expenses	12,000	
Sales		44,000
Purchases	26,000	
Wages	10,000	
Salaries		12,000
Prepaid insurance		200
Bills payable	10,800	
Outstanding salaries	1,400	
Total	**1,08,200**	**1,08,200**

Solution:

Corrected Trial balance

Trial Balance as on …

Particulars	Debit ₹	Credit ₹
Capital a/c		22,000
Stock	10,000	
Debtors	8,000	
Creditors		12,000

Particulars	Debit ₹	Credit ₹
Machinery	20,000	
Cash in hand	2,000	
Bank overdraft		14,000
Sales returns	8,000	
Purchase returns		4,000
Misc. expenses	12,000	
Sales		44,000
Purchases	26,000	
Wages	10,000	
Salaries	12,000	
Prepaid insurance	200	
Bills payable		10,800
Outstanding salaries		1,400
Total	**1,08,200**	**1,08,200**

Illustration 29: A book-keeper submitted to you the following Trail Balance, which he hasnot been able to agree. Rewrite the Trial Balance.

Trial Balance as on ....

Particulars	Debit ₹	Credit ₹
Capital		15,000
Drawings	3,250	
Stock (1.1.2014)	17,445	
Return inwards		554

Particulars	Debit ₹	Credit ₹
Carriage inwards	1,240	
Deposits		1,375
Return outwards	840	
Carriage outwards		725
Loan to Ananth		1,000
Interest on the Ananth loan		25
Rent	820	
Rent outstanding	130	
Stock (31.12.2014)		18,792
Purchases	12,970	
Debtors	4,000	
Goodwill	1,730	
Creditors		3,000
Advertisement	954	
Provision for doubtful debts		1,200
Bad debts	400	
Patents and patterns	500	
Cash	62	
Sales		27,914
Discount allowed		330
Wages	754	
Total	**45,095**	**45,095**

Solution

Corrected Trail Balance as at 31st December 2014

Particulars	Debit ₹	Credit ₹
Capital		15,000
Drawings	3,250	
Stock (1.1.2014)	17,445	
Return inwards	554	
Carriage inwards	1,240	
Deposits	1,375	
Return outwards		840
Carriage outwards	725	
Loan to Ananth	1,000	
Interest on the Ananth loan		25
Rent	820	
Rent outstanding		130
Purchases	12,970	
Debtors	4,000	
Goodwill	1,730	
Creditors		3,000
Advertisement	954	
Provision for doubtful debts		1,200
Bad debts	400	
Patents and patterns	500	
Cash	62	
Sales		27,914
Discount allowed	330	
Wages	754	
Total	**48,109**	**48,109**

Note: *Closing stock is an adjustment, so it has not been taken in the Trial balance.*

Illustration: 30 Journalise the following transactions in the books of SomaSundaram and postthem in the Ledger and prepare Trial balance:-

2014 March	1	Bought goods for cash	₹ 25,000
	2	Sold goods for cash	₹ 50,000
	3	Bought goods for credit from Gopi	₹ 19,000
	5	Sold goods on credit to Robert	₹ 8,000
	7	Received from Robert	₹ 6,000
	9	Paid to Gopi	₹ 5,000
	10	Bought furniture for cash	₹ 7,000

Solution:

In the Books of SomaSundaram

Journal entries

Date	Particulars		L.F.	Debit ₹	Credit ₹
2014	Purchase a/c	Dr		25,000	
March	To Cash a/c				25,000
1	(Being cash purchase)				
2	Cash a/c	Dr		50,000	
	To Sales a/c				50,000
	(Being cash sales)				
3	Purchase a/c	Dr		19,000	
	To Gopi a/c				19,000
	(Being credit purchase)				

Date	Particulars		L.F.	Debit ₹	Credit ₹
5	Robert a/c	Dr		8,000	
	To Sales a/c				8,000
	(Being credit sales)				
7	Cash a/c			6,000	
	To Robert a/c				6,000
	(Being cash received)				
9	Gopi a/c	Dr		5,000	
	To Cash a/c				5,000
	(Being cash paid to Gopi)				
20	Furniture a/c	Dr		7,000	
	To Cash a/c				7,000
	(Being furniture purchased)				

Ledger Account of SomaSundaram

Dr	Cash Account				Cr			
Date	Particulars	J.F	₹	Date	Particulars	J.F	₹
2004				2004			
Mar 5	To Sales a/c		50,000	Mar 1	By Purchase a/c		25,000
7	To Robert a/c		6,000	9	By Gopi a/c		5,000
				20	By Furniture a/c		7,000
				31	By Balance c/d		19,000
			56,000				56,000
Apr 1	To Balance b/d		19,000				

Dr	Purchase Account						Cr
Date	**Particulars**	**J.F**	**₹**	**Date**	**Particulars**	**J.F**	**₹**
2004				2004			
Mar 1	To Cash a/c		25,000	Mar 31	By Balance c/d		44,000
3	To Gopi a/c		19,000				
			44,000				44,000
Apr 1	To Balance b/d		44,000				

Dr	Sales Account						Cr
Date	**Particulars**	**J.F**	**₹**	**Date**	**Particulars**	**J.F**	**₹**
2004				2004			
Mar 31	By Balance c/d		58,000	Mar 2	By Cash a/c		50,000
				5	By Robert a/c		8,000
			58,000				58,000
				Apr 1	By Balance b/d		58,000

Dr	Furniture Account						Cr
Date	**Particulars**	**J.F**	**₹**	**Date**	**Particulars**	**J.F**	**₹**
2004				2004			
Mar 20	To Cash a/c		7,000	Mar 31	By Balance c/d		7,000
			7,000				7,000
Apr 1	To Balance b/d		7,000				

Dr					Gopi Account			Cr
Date	Parti culars	J.F	₹	Date	Parti culars	J.F	₹
2004				2004			
Mar 19	To Cash a/c		5,000	Mar 3	By Purchase a/c		19,000
31	To Balance c/d		14,000				
			19,000				19,000
				Apr1	By Balance b/d		14,000

Dr					Robert Account			Cr
Date	Parti culars	J.F	₹	Date	Parti culars	J.F	₹
2004				2004			
Mar 5	To Sales a/c		8,000	Mar 7	By Cash a/c		6,000
				31	By Balance c/d		2,000
			8,000				8,000
Apr1	To Balance b/d		2,000				

Trial Balance of Mr. Soma Sundaram

Particulars	Debit ₹	Credit ₹
Cash a/c	19,000	
Purchase a/c	44,000	
Sales a/c		58,000
Furniture	7,000	
Gobi a/c		14,000
Robert a/c	2,000	
	72,000	72,000

Illustration: 31 Journalise the following transactions in the journal of Mr. James, post them inledger.

			₹
2014	1	James commenced business with	21,000
April	2	Bought goods for cash	9,200
	4	Sold goods to Peter on credit	5,600
	5	Purchased goods from Stephen	3,300
	9	Received cash from Antony	3,600
	10	Withdrew for personal use	2,000
	11	Paid Stephen on account	2,100
	16	Sold goods to Martin	3,500
	21	Cash sales	7,500
	26	Paid Stephen	1,200
	29	Received cash from Martin	3,500
	30	Paid rent	450
	31	Paid salaries to office Staff	700

Solution:

Journal entries in the books of Mr. James

Date	Particulars		L.F.	Debit ₹	Credit ₹
2014	Cash a/c	Dr		21,000	
April	To Capital a/c				21,000
1	(Being cash brought in as capital)				

Date	Particulars		L.F.	Debit ₹	Credit ₹
2	Purchase a/c	Dr		9,200	
	To Cash a/c				9,200
	(Being cash purchased)				
4	Peter a/c	Dr		5,600	
	To Sales a/c				5,600
	(Being credit sales to peter)				
5	Purchase a/c	Dr		3,300	
	To Stephen a/c				3,300
	(Being credit purchase)				
9	Cash a/c	Dr		3,600	
	To Antony a/c				3,600
	(Being cash received from Antony)				
10	Drawings a/c	Dr		2,000	
	To Cash a/c				2,000
	(Being amount with draw for personaluse)				
11	Stephen a/c	Dr		2,100	
	To Cash a/c				2,100
	(Being cash paid to Stephen)				
16	Martin a/c	Dr		3,500	
	To Sales a/c				3,500
	(Being credit sales)				

Date	Particulars		L.F.	Debit ₹	Credit ₹
21	Cash a/c	Dr		7,500	
	To Sales a/c				7,500
	(Being cash sales)				
26	Stephen a/c	Dr		1,200	
	To Cash a/c				1,200
	(Being cash paid to Stephen)				
29	Cash a/c	Dr		3,500	
	To Martin a/c				3,500
	(Being cash received from martin)				
30	Rent a/c	Dr		450	
	To Cash a/c				450
	(Being rent paid)				
31	Salaries a/c	Dr		700	
	To Cash a/c				700
	(Being salaries paid for the month)				

Ledger Account

	Dr	Cash Account			Cr		
Date	Particulars	J.F	₹	Date	Particulars	J.F	₹
2014				2014			
Apri 1	To Capital a/c		21,000	Apr 2	By purchase		9,200
9	To Antony		3,600	10	By Drawings		2,000

21	To Sales	7,500	11	By Stephen	2,100
29	To Martin	3,500	26	By Stephen	1,200
			30	By Rent	450
			31	By Salaries	700
			31	By Balance c/d	19,950
		35,600			35,600
May 1	To Balance b/d	19,950			

Dr		Capital Account					Cr

Date	Parti culars	J.F	₹	Date	Parti culars	J.F	₹
Apr 30	To Balance c/d		21,000	2014 Apr 1	By Cash a/c		21,000
			21,000				21,000
				May 1	By Balance b/d		21,000

	Dr	Purchase Account		Cr			

Date	Parti culars	J.F	₹	Date	Parti culars	J.F	₹
2014				2014			
Apr 2	To Cash		9,200	Apr 30	By Balance c/d		12,500
5	To Stephen		3,300				
			12,500				12,500
May 1	To Balance b/d		12,500				

Dr				Peter Account			Cr
Date	**Parti culars**	**J.F**	**₹**	**Date**	**Parti culars**	**J.F**	**₹**
2014				2014			
Apr 4	To Sales		5,600	Apr 30	By Balance c/d		5,600
			5,600				5,600
May 1	To Balance b/d		5,600				

Dr	Sales Account			Cr			
Date	**Parti culars**	**J.F**	**₹**	**Date**	**Parti culars**	**J.F**	**₹**
2014				2014			
Apr 30	To Balance c/d		16,600	4	By Peter		5,600
				16	By Martin		3,500
				21	By Cash		7,500
			16,600				16,600
				May 1	By Balance b/d		16,600

Dr				Stephen Account			Cr
Date	**Parti culars**	**J.F**	**₹**	**Date**	**Parti culars**	**J.F**	**₹**
2014				2014			
11	To Cash		2,100	5	By Purchase		3,300
26	To Cash		1,200				
			3,300				3,300

Dr	Antony Account			Cr			
Date	Particulars	J.F	₹	Date	Particulars	J.F	₹
2014				2014			
Apr 30	To Balance c/d		3,600	9	By Cash		3,600
			3,600				3,600
				May 1	By Balance b/d		3,600

Dr	Drawings Account						Cr
Date	Particulars	J.F	₹	Date	Particulars	J.F	₹
2014				2014			
Apr 10	To Cash		2,000	Apr 30	By Balance c/d		2,000
			2,000				2,000
May 1	To Balance b/d		2,000				

Dr	Martin Account			Cr			
Date	Particulars	J.F	₹	Date	Particulars	J.F	₹
2014				2014			
Apr 16	To Sales		3,500	Apr 29	By Cash		3,500
			3,500				3,500

Dr					Rent Account				Cr
Date	**Parti culars**	**J.F**	**₹**		**Date**	**Parti culars**	**J.F**	**₹**	
2014					2014				
Apr 30	To Cash		450		Apr 30	By Balance c/d		450	
			450					450	
May 1	To Balance b/d		450						

	Dr	Salary Account				Cr			
Date	**Parti culars**	**J.F**	**₹**		**Date**	**Parti culars**	**J.F**	**₹**	
2014					2014				
Apr 30	To Cash		700		Apr 30	By Balance c/d		700	
			700					700	
May 1	To Balance b/d		700						

Trial Balance

Particulars	Debit ₹	Credit ₹
Cash a/c	19,950	
Capital a/c		21,000
Purchase a/c	12,500	
Peter a/c	5,600	
Sales a/c		16,600
Antony a/c		3,600
Drawings	2,000	
Rent	450	
Salary	700	
	41,200	**41,200**

Illustration: 32: From the following transactions, Prepare Journal, Ledger and Trial balanceof Mr.Nazer.

			₹
2012	1	Started business with Cash	45,000
January	1	Paid into bank	25,000
	2	Goods purchased for cash	15,000
	3	Furniture purchase and payment by Cheque	5,000
	5	Sold goods for cash	8,500
	8	Sold goods to Subash	4,000
	10	Goods purchased from Amirtha	7,000
	12	Goods returned to Amirtha	1,000
	15	Goods returned by Subash	200
	18	Cash received from Subash in full settlement	3,760
	21	Withdrew from bank for private use	1,000
	25	Telephone rent paid	5,000
	28	Cash paid to Amirtha in full settlement	5,940
	30	Rent paid	1,000
	30	Stationary paid	200
	30	Salaries paid	2,500

Solution:

Journals

Date	Particulars		L.F.	Debit	Credit
2012	Cash a/c	Dr		45,000	
January 1	To Nazer's Capital a/c				45,000
	(Being capital contributed)				
1	Bank a/c	Dr		25,000	
	To Cash a/c				25,000
	(Being cash deposited)				
2	Purchase a/c	Dr		15,000	
	To Cash a/c				15,000
	(Being cash purchase)				
3	Furniture a/c	Dr		5,000	
	To Bank a/c				5,000
	(Being furniture Purchased)				
5	Cash a/c	Dr		8,500	
	To Sales a/c				8,500
	(Being sales made)				
8	Subash a/c	Dr		4,000	
	To Sales a/c				4,000
	(Being cash sales)				
10	Purchase a/c	Dr		7,000	
	To Amirtha a/c				7,000
	(Being purchase made)				

12	Amirtha a/c	Dr	1,000	
	To Purchase returns a/c			1,000
	(Being goods returned)			
15	Sales returned a/c	Dr	200	
	To Subash a/c			200
	(Being goods returned by subash)			
18	Cash a/c Discount a/c	Dr	3,760	
	To Subash a/c	Dr	40	
	(Being cash received from Subash)			4,000
21	Drawings a/c	Dr	1,000	
	Cash a/c	Dr	5,000	6,000
	To Bank a/c			
	(Being cash drawn for personal and office use)			
25	Telephone rent a/c	Dr	400	
	To Cash a/c			400
	(Being telephone rent paid)			
28	Amirtha a/c	Dr	6,000	
	To Cash a/c			5,940
	To Discount a/c			60
	(Being cash paid to Amirtha)			
30	Printing & Stationary a/c	Dr	200	
	Rent a/c	Dr	1,000	
	Salary a/c	Dr	2,500	
	To Cash a/c			3,700

Hint: (4,000 – 3,760) = 40 is assumed as Discount

Dr	Capital Account			Cr			
Date	Parti culars	J.F	₹	Date	Parti culars	J.F	₹
2012				2012			
Jan 31	To Balance c/d		45,000	Jan 1	By Cash a/c		45,000
			45,000				45,000
				Feb 1	By Balance b/d		45,000

Dr	Cash Account						Cr
Date	Parti culars	J.F	₹	Date	Parti culars	J.F	₹
2012				2012			
Jan 1	To Capital a/c		45,000	Jan 1	By Bank a/c		25,000
5	To Sales a/c		8,500	2	By Purchase a/c		15,000
18	To Subash a/c		3,760	25	By Telephone rent		400
21	To Bank a/c		5,000	28	By Amirtha a/c		5,940
				30	By Stationary a/c		200
				30	By Rent a/c		1,000
				30	By Salary a/c		2,500
				30	By Balance c/d		12,220
			62,260				62,260
Feb 1	To Balance b/d		12,220				

Dr	Bank Account				Cr			
Date	**Particulars**	**J.F**	**₹**		**Date**	**Particulars**	**J.F**	**₹**
2012					2012			
Jan 1	To Cash a/c		25,000		Jan 3	By Furniture a/c		5,000
					21	By Drawings a/c		1,000
					21	By Cash a/c		5,000
					30	By Balance c/d		14,000
			25,000					25,000
Feb 1	To Balance b/d		14,000					

Dr	Purchase Account							Cr
Date	**Particulars**	**J.F**	**₹**		**Date**	**Particulars**	**J.F**	**₹**
2012					2012			
Jan 2	To Cash a/c		15,000		Jan 31	By Balance c/d		22,000
	To Amirtha a/c		7,000					
			22,000					22,000
Feb 1	To Balance b/d		22,000					

Dr	Furniture Account				Cr			
Date	**Particulars**	**J.F**	**₹**		**Date**	**Particulars**	**J.F**	**₹**
2012					2012			
Jan 3	To Bank a/c		5,000		Jan 31	By Balance c/d		5,000
			5,000					5,000
Feb 1	To Balance b/d		5,000					5,000

Dr				Sales Account			Cr
Date	**Parti culars**	**J.F**	**₹**	**Date**	**Parti culars**	**J.F**	**₹**
2012				2012			
Jan 31	To Balance c/d		12,500	Jan 5	By Cash a/c		8,500
				8	By Subash a/c		4,000
			12,500				12,500
				Feb 1	By Balance b/d		12,500

Dr	Subash Account			Cr			
Date	**Parti culars**	**J.F**	**₹**	**Date**	**Parti culars**	**J.F**	**₹**
2012				2012			
Jan 8	To Sales a/c		4,000	Jan 15	By Return inwards		200
				18	By Cash a/c		3,760
				18	By Discount a/c		40
			4,000				4,000

Dr				Amirtha Account			Cr
Date	**Parti culars**	**J.F**	**₹**	**Date**	**Parti culars**	**J.F**	**₹**
2012				2012			
Jan 12	To Return outwards		1,000	Jan 10	By Purchase a/c		7,000
28	To Cash a/c		5,940				
28	To Discount a/c		60				
			7,000				7,000

Dr	Return inwards / Sales return Account						Cr
Date	**Particulars**	**J.F**	**₹**	**Date**	**Particulars**	**J.F**	**₹**
2012				2012			
Jan 15	To Subash a/c		200	Jan 31	By Balance c/d		200
			200				200
Feb 1	To Balance b/d		200				

Dr	Return outwards / Purchase return Account						Cr
Date	**Particulars**	**J.F**	**₹**	**Date**	**Particulars**	**J.F**	**₹**
2012				2012			
Jan 31	To Balance c/d		1,000	Jan 12	By Amirtha a/c		1,000
			1,000				1,000
				Feb 1	By Balance b/d		1,000

Dr	Discount Account			Cr			
Date	**Particulars**	**J.F**	**₹**	**Date**	**Particulars**	**J.F**	**₹**
2012				2012			
Jan18	To Subash a/c		40	Jan 28	By Amirtha a/c		60
28	To Balance c/d		20				
			60	Feb 1	By Balance b/d		20

Dr **Drawings Account** **Cr**

Date	Particulars	J.F	₹	Date	Particulars	J.F	₹
2012				2012			
Jan 21	To Bank a/c		1,000	Jan 30	By Balance c/d		1,000
			1,000				1,000
Feb 1	To Balance b/d		1,000				

Dr **Postage & Telephone a/c** **Cr**

Date	Particulars	J.F	₹	Date	Particulars	J.F	₹
2012				2012			
Jan 25	To Cash a/c		400	Jan 30	By Balance c/d		400
			400				400
Feb 1	To Balance b/d		400				

Dr **Stationary a/c** **Cr**

Date	Particulars	J.F	₹	Date	Particulars	J.F	₹
2012				2012			
Jan 25	To Cash a/c		200	Jan 30	By Balance c/d		200
			200				200
Feb 1	To Balance b/d		200				

Dr				Rent a/c				Cr
Date	Particulars	J.F	₹	Date	Particulars	J.F		₹
2012				2012				
Jan 25	To Cash a/c		1,000	Jan 30	By Balance c/d			1,000
			1,000					1,000
Feb 1	To Balance b/d		1,000					

Dr	Salary a/c		Cr					
Date	Particulars	J.F	₹	Date	Particulars	J.F		₹
2012				2012				
Jan 25	To Cash a/c		2,500	Jan 30	By Balance c/d			2,500
			2,500					2,500
Feb 1	To Balance b/d		2,500					

Trial Balance

Particulars	Debit ₹	Credit ₹
Cash	12,220	
Capital		45,000
Bank	14,000	
Purchases	22,000	
Furniture	5,000	
Sales		12,500
Return inwards	200	

Particulars	Debit ₹	Credit ₹
Return outwards		1,000
Discount a/c (Cr)		20
Drawings	1,000	
Postge & Telephone a/c	400	
Printing & Stationary	200	
Rent	1,000	
Salary	2,500	
TOTAL	**58,520**	**58,520**

Illustration 33: From the following transactions are as on 31ˢᵗ March 2013 of Mr. Anil, pass journal entries, prepare ledger accounts and also prepare Trial Balance under (i) Balance Method (ii) Total Method.

		₹
1.3.2013	Anil started business with	8,000
2.3.2013	Purchased furniture	1,000
3.3.2013	Purchased goods	6,000
4.3.2013	Sold goods	7,000
5.3.2013	Purchased from Raja	4,000
6.3.2013	Sold to Somu	5,000
7.3.2013	Paid to Raja	2,500
8.3.2013	Received from Somu	3,000
9.3.2013	Paid rent	200
9.3.2013	Received commission	100

In the books of Mr. Anil's Journal entries as on 31ˢᵗ March 2013

Month of March	Particulars	L.F.	Debit ₹	Credit ₹
1	Cash a/c		8,000	
	To Capital a/c			8,000
	(Being capital introduced)			
2	Furniture a/c		1,000	
	To cash a/c			1,000
	(Being furniture bought)			
3	Purchase a/c		6,000	
	To cash a/c			6,000
	(Being cash purchase)			
4	Cash a/c		7,000	
	To sales a/c			7,000
	(Being cash sales)			
5	Purchase a/c		4,000	
	To Raja a/c			4,000
	(Being credit purchase)			
6	Somu a/c		5,000	
	To Sales a/c			5,000
	(Being credit sales)			
7	Raja a/c		2,500	
	To Cash a/c			2,500
	(Being cash received from raja)			
8	Cash a/c		3,000	
	To Somu a/c			3,000
	(Being cash received from somu)			

Month of March	Particulars	L.F.	Debit ₹	Credit ₹
9	Rent a/c		200	
	To Cash a/c			200
	(Being rent paid)			
9	Cash a/c		100	
	To Commission received a/c			**100**
	(Being commission received)			

Cash Account

Particulars	₹	Particulars	₹
To Capital a/c	8,000	By Furniture a/c	1,000
To Sales a/c	7,000	By Purchase a/c	6,000
To Somu a/c	3,000	By Raja a/c	2,500
To Commission a/c	100	By Rent a/c	200
		By Balance c/d	8,400
	18,100		18,100
To Balance b/d	8,400		

Capital Account

Particulars	₹	Particulars	₹
To Balance c/d	8,000	By Cash a/c	8,000
	8,000		8,000
		By Balance b/d	8,000

Purchase Account

Particulars	₹	Particulars	₹
To Cash a/c	6,000		
To Raja a/c	4,000	By Balance c/d	10,000
	10,000		10,000
To Balance b/d	10,000		

Sales Account

Particulars	₹	Particulars	₹
To Balance c/d	12,000	By Cash a/c	7,000
		By Somu a/c	5,000
	12,000		12,000
		By Balance b/d	12,000

Raja Account

Particulars	₹	Particulars	₹
To Cash a/c	2,500	By Purchase a/c	4,000
To Balance c/d	1,500		
	4,000		4,000
			1,500
		By Balance b/d	

Furniture Account

Particulars	₹	Particulars	₹
To Cash a/c	1,000		
		By Balance c/d	1,000
	1,000		1,000
To Balance b/d	1,000		

Somu Account

Particulars	₹	Particulars	₹
To Sales a/c	5,000	By Cash a/c	3,000
		By Balance c/d	2,000
	5,000		5,000
To Balance b/d	2,000		

Rent Account

Particulars	₹	Particulars	₹
To Cash a/c	200	By Balance c/d	200
	200		200
To Balance b/d	200		

Commission Received Account

Particulars	₹	Particulars	₹
To Balance c/d	100	By Cash	100
	100		100
		By Balance b/d	100

Balance Method

Trial Balance as on 31ˢᵗ March 2013

Particulars	Debit ₹	Credit ₹
Cash a/c	8,400	
Capital a/c		8,000
Furniture	1,000	
Purchases	10,000	
Sales		12,000
Raja a/c		1,500
Somu a/c	2,000	
Rent a/c	200	
Commission received a/c		100
	21,600	21,600

Total Method

Trial Balance as on 31ˢᵗ March 2013

Particulars	Debit ₹	Credit ₹
Cash a/c	18,100	9,700
Capital a/c		8,000
Furniture	1,000	
Purchases	10,000	
Sales		12,000
Raja a/c	2,500	4,000
Somu a/c	5,000	3,000
Rent a/c	200	
Commission received a/c		100
	36,800	36,800

QUESTIONS

FILL IN THE BLANKS

1. Ledger is the book of account

2. c/d means ____________

3. c/f means ____________

4. b/d means ___________

5. b/f means ___________

6. L.F column in the journal is filled at the time of _______________

7. Real account cannot have_______________balance

8. Trial balance should be tallied by the following rules of ______ ___________

9. Suspense account having debit balance will be shown on the __________side of balancesheet

10. The journal is a book of _______________

11. In journal transactions are recorded on __________________

12. Books of primary entry is better known as _____________

13. Assets are held in business for the purpose of ___________________

14. Rent payable to the landlord ₹5,000 is credited to _____________

15. Patterns and trade mark is_______________a/c

> [**Ans:** 1. Principal, 2. Carried down, 3. Carried forward 4. Brought down, 5. Brought forward, 6. Posting, 7. Credit, 8. Double entry system, 9. Asset, 10 Original entry, 11. Chronological order, 12. Journal, 13. Earning revenue, 14. Land lord account, 15.Real account]

CHOSE THE CORRECT ANSWER

1. Ledger is a book of
   a) Original entry
   b) Final entry
   c) Cash transaction
2. Real account always shown
   a) Debit balance
   b) Credit balance
   c) Nil balance
3. Personal and real accounts are
   a) Closed
   b) balanced
   c) Closed & transferred
4. The column of ledger which links the entry with journal is
   a) L.F column
   b) J.F column
   c) Particulars column
5. Nominal account having credit balance represents
   a) Income / gain
   b) Expenses / losses
   c) Assets
6. The balances of personal and real accounts are shown in the
   a) Profit and loss account
   b) Balance sheet
   c) Both.
7. Trial balance is prepared to find out the
   a) Profit or loss
   b) Financial position
   c) Arithmetic accuracy
8. Suspense account in the trial balance is entered in the
   a) Trading A/c   b) Profit and loss A/c   c) Balance sheet
9. The origin of a transaction is derived from the
   a) Source document
   b) Journal
   c) Accounting equation
10. Amount owned by the proprietor is called
   a) Assets   b) Liabilities   c) Capital

11. Which of the following is correct?
    a) Capital = Assets + Liabilities
    b) Capital = Assets – Liabilities
    c) Assets = Liabilities – Capital
12. Withdrawals of cash from bank by the proprietor for office use should be credited to
    a) Drawings A/c   b)   Bank A/c   c)   Cash A/c
13. An entry is passed in the beginning of each current year is called
    a) Original entry   b) Final entry   c)   Opening entry
14. The liabilities of a business are ₹ 3,000, the capital of the proprietor is ₹ 7,000. The totalassets are:
    a) ₹ 7,000   b)   ₹ 10,000   c)   ₹ 4,000
15. Ledger records transactions in
    a)   Chronological order   b)   Analytical order
    c)   Both (a) and (b)

> [**Answer:** 1 (b), 2 (a), 3 (b), 4(b), 5 (a), 6 (b), 7 (c), 8 (c), 9 (a),
> 10 (c), 11 (b),12 (b), 13 (c), 14 (b), 15 (b)]

OTHER QUESTIONS

---

1. What is a journal?
2. What is narration?
3. What is meant by Cheque?
4. Define ledger?
5. Explain the utilities of a ledger
6. What is a loose – leaf ledger?
7. Why a trial balance is prepared?
8. What is posting?
9. What are the steps in posting?
10. What is a combined trial balance?

11. What is debit balance?
12. What is credit balance?
13. Distinguish Journal with ledger
14. What is trial balance?
15. What are the objectives of a trial balance?
16. Explain the methods of preparing a trial balance.
17. State the features of trial balance.
18. What are the golden rules of Accounting?

EXERCISE PROBLEMS

1. Journalise the following Opening Entry:

Cash in hand	2,000
Plant	50,000
Furniture	5,000
Creditors	13,000
Debtors	18,000

2. Journalise the following transactions in the books of Tmt.Amutha
   2014,

Jan. business with cash	1 Tmt. Amutha commenced 50,000
2 Purchased goods for cash	10,000
5 Purchased goods from Mohan on credit	6,000
7 Paid into Bank	5,000
10 Purchased furniture	2,000
20 Sold goods to Suresh on credit	5,000

25 Cash sales   3,500

26 Paid to Mohan on account   3,000

31 Paid salaries   2,800

3. Journalise the following transactions of Mrs.Rama 2014, Jan 1 Mrs.Rama commenced business with cash 30,000

2	Paid into bank	21,000
3	Purchased goods by cheque	15,000
7	Drew cash from bank for office use	3,000
15	Purchased goods from Siva	15,000
20	Cash sales	30,000
25	Paid to Siva	14,750
	Discount Received	250
31	Paid rent	500
	Paid Salaries	2,000

4. Journalise the following transactions of Mr.Moorthy 2014,

June	3	Received cash from Ramkumar	60,000
	4	Purchased goods for cash	15,000
	11	Sold goods to Damodaran	22,000
	13	Paid to Ramkumar	40,000
	17	Received from Damodaran	20,000
	20	Bought furniture from Jagadeesan	5,000
	27	Paid rent	1,200
	30	Paid salary	2,500

5. Enter the following transactions in journal, post them and prepare trial balance.2014,

Oct.	1	Received cash from Siva	75,000
	7	Paid cash to Sayeed	45,000
	10	Bought goods for cash	27,000
	12	Bought goods on credit from David	48,000
	15	Sold goods for cash	70,000

6. Find out the accounts involved in the following transactions and say which account is to be debited and which account is to be credited.

2014

Feb.	3	Bought goods for cash ₹ 84,500
	7	Sold goods to Dhanalakshmi on credit ₹ 55,000
	9	Received commission ₹ 3,000
	10	Cash Sales ₹ 1,09,000
	12	Bought goods from Mahalakshmi ₹ 60,000
	15	Received five chairs from Revathi & Co. at ₹ 400 each
	20	Paid Revathi & Co.cash for five chairs
	28	Paid Salaries ₹ 10,000
		Paid Rent ₹ 5,000

7. Journalise the following transactions in the books of Thiru. Kalyanasundaram. 2014,

> March 10   Sold goods on credit to Mohanasundaram ₹ 75,000.
>
> 12   Purchased goods on credit from Bashyam ₹ 70,000.
>
> 15   Sold goods for cash to David ₹ 50,000.
>
> 20   Received from Mohanasundaram ₹ 70,000.
>
> 25   Paid to Bashyam ₹ 50,000.

8. Journalise the following transactions and prepare ledger accounts. 2011

> January 1   Babu started business with cash ₹ 5,000, Bank balance ₹ 80,000
>
> 2   Bought of Tamil ₹ 50,000
>
> 3   Sold goods to Gopu ₹ 12,000
>
> 4   Purchase from Pream and paid by cheque ₹ 500
>
> 5   Defective goods returned to Tamil ₹ 5,000
>
> 7   Received goods retunred by Gopu ₹ 2,000
>
> 9   Received cheque from Gopu ₹10,000
>
> 11   Paid Gopu cheque into bank
>
> 12   Commission received ₹ 3,000
>
> 15   Purchased machinery ₹10,000 andFan ₹ 2000 paid by cheque
>
> 18   Withdraw from bank ₹ 2,000
>
> 21   Sold goods to Vimal and cheque received ₹ 2,000
>
> 22   Paid into bank ₹ 3000
>
> 23   Borrowed from Ananth ₹ 20,000
>
> 24   Took for personal use goods ₹ 1,000
>
> 25   Sales ₹ 250

26   Commission paid to broker ₹ 500

30   Paid advertisement ₹ 250

     Postage ₹ 150

     Rent ₹ 1,000

9. From the following transactions prepare journal entries and Trial balance of Mr. Rajesh as on year ended 31st December 2013.

2013

Dec	1	Rajesh commenced business with ₹ 1,000
	2	Opened current account with Indian bank ₹ 600
	4	Purchased goods from Lara ₹ 400
	5	Sold goods to Bharathi ₹ 500
	6	Bought 3 tables and three chairs ₹ 250
	8	Returned goods to Lara ₹ 50
	11	Purchased stationery ₹ 250
	12	Paid Lara ₹ 3,500 by cheque
	14	Bhartathi returned goods worth ₹ 200
	18	Cash sales ₹ 150
	19	Bought of Gokul ₹ 1,000
	20	Sales to Liberty & Co ₹ 6,000
	22	Cash purchase ₹ 300
	22	Returned goods to Gokul ₹ 200
	24	Paid Gokul by cheque ₹ 800
	26	Received cheque from Liberty & Co ₹ 6,000
	27	Drawings ₹ 250

30	Sold goods to Ashok and cash received ₹ 150
30.	Paid rent by cheque ₹ 150
30	Paid salary ₹ 200

10. Journalise the following transactions and Post them in relevant ledger accounts:2015

Jan.1. Bought from Das	1,000	
Jan. 2. Sold to Ravi		400
Jan. 3. Sold to Ramesh	250	
Jan. 4. Purchased from Suresh	200	
Jan. 5. Sales returns by Ravi		50
Jan. 10. Bought from Shyam		600
Jan. 12. Returned to Suresh		100
Jan. 15. Sold to Roy		800
Jan. 16. Roy returned goods		200
Jan. 17. Sold goods to Ram		300
Jan. 19. Bough from Naresh		650
Jan. 21. Sold to Bhatanger		750
Jan. 22. Returned to Naresh		50
Jan. 25. Bought from Kamali	850	
Jan. 27. Sold to Dheeran	260	
Jan. 29. Returns from Bhatanger	100	
Jan. 30. Dheeran Returned	60	
Jan. 31. Returns to Kamali	50	

11. Enter the following transactions in the journal and ledger of Murali in New Delhi:2010

Mar.	1	Murali commenced business with cash	90,000
	4	Purchased goods for cash	6,000
	5	Deposited into bank	40,000
	6	Withdrew from bank for office use	4,500
	8	Sold goods to Raja	4,800
	12	Purchased goods on credit from Kathar	1,380
	15	Received from Raj	4,650
		and allowed him discount	150
	20	Cash sales	7,200
	28	Paid to Kathar in full settlement	1,300
	30	Paid rent	300
		Paid salary	1,600

Accounts are closed on 31st March 2010.

12. Mr. Yuvaraj was carrying business as a cloth dealer. on 1st January 2013 his assets were:

Furniture ₹ 7,500

Stock ₹ 75,000

Cash in hand ₹ 1,500

Bank ₹ 25,500

Amount due from basker ₹ 3,000

Amount due from Gopal ₹ 4,500

His transaction during January were as follows

1. Sold goods on credit to Ganesh ₹ 15,000
2. Purchased goods from Balan ₹ 60,000
3. Paid rent by cheque ₹ 9,000

4. Cash prucahsed by cheque ₹ 24,000
5. Cash sales ₹ 15,500
6. Received cheque from Balan ₹ 36,000
7. Deposited balan cheque deposited into bank
8. Paid for stationery ₹ 1,750
9. Yuvaraj drew cash for personal user ₹ 7,500
11 Purchased goods on credit from Mohan ₹ 75,000
13 Sent cheque to Mohan ₹ 60,000
15 Sold goods to Ganesh ₹ 1,200
16 Cash sales ₹ 9,000
17 Paid for advertising ₹ 3,750
20 Cash purchases ₹ 2,700
22 Purchased computer ₹ 15,000
27 Cash purchased paid by cheque ₹ 65,000
30 Paid salaries ₹ 1,600

Journalise the above transactions and post them into appropriate ledger accounts andalso prepare a Trial balance.

13. From the following ledger accounts of Sathiya, draw Trail Balance as on 31ˢᵗ December 2014.

	₹		₹
House Property	45,000	Repairs	1,200
Furniture	5,000	Rent Received	4,800
Apparatus	6,000	Medical Expenses	1,200
Ornaments	25,000	School Fee	1,800
Cash	630	Conveyance	1,350
Fixed Deposits	20,000	Cosmetics	1,150
Savings Bank	3,500	Interest Received	3,000

Shares & Govt. Securities	12,000	House Building Loan from Govt.	20,000
Interest paid	1,870	Municipal Taxes	3,000
Claims against persons	1,500	Income-tax	2,500
Salary (Income)	24,000	Servants' wages	1,200
Accumulated Fund	88,300	Food and Drink	3,750
Dresses	2,450		

14. The following Trail Balance was extracted from the books of a Merchant, although thecolumns are agreed, yet they are incorrect. You are required to correct and redraft it.

Particulars	Dr ₹	Particulars	Cr ₹
Premises	30,000	Capital	36,800
Machinery	8,500	Fixtures	2,800
Bad debts	1,400	Sales	52,000
Returns outwards	1,300	Debtors	30,000
Cash	200	Interest received	1,300
Discount received	1,500		
Bank overdraft	5,000		
Creditors	25,000		
Purchases	50,000		
	1,22,900		1,22,900

15. From the following ledger accounts of Suriya, draw Trail Balance as on 31st December2014.

Particulars	Debit ₹	Credit ₹
Capital		1,556
Drawings	564	
Leasehold premises	741	
Sales		2,756
Due from customers		560
Purchases	1,268	
Purchase return	264	
Loan from bank		250
Creditors	528	
Trade expenses	784	
Cash at bank	142	
Bills payable	100	
Salaries and wages	598	
Stock 1st January		264
Rent, rates etc	465	
Sales return		98
	5,454	5,454

16. The under mentioned balances were extracted from the books of Mahesh as on 31ˢᵗ March 2005. You are asked to prepare a Trail Balance as on that date.

Particulars	₹	Particulars	₹
Capital	78,000	Stock 1.4.2014	5,000
Leasehold premises	46,000	Furniture and fittings	13,500
Plant and machinery	35,000	Purchases	78,900
Sales	1,30,620	Discount received	470
Discount allowed	540	Carriage inwards	120
Carriage outwards	230	Returns inwards	1,500
Returns outwards	380	Wages and salaries	17,680
Rates and taxes	1,370	Rent received	530
Sundry expenses	1,660	Trade creditors	22,760
Book debts	34,000	Drawings	3,000
Bills payable	1,140	Cash in hand	1,200
Bank loan	5,800	Closing stock	3,900

Chapter 3

SUBSIDIARY BOOKS

In a small business concern, a single journal book is maintained to record all the business transactions. A single accountant can maintain accounts or the owner himself can maintain all the books of accounts. In a large scale business organization or Joint Stock Company, there is an occurrence of number of transactions in a day. Hence, maintaining a single journal book is very difficult. There is a need of several accountants to do accounts work. Such systems of maintaining books of accounts requires many accountants but facilitate ledger work and minimizes the errors, in this way, a new system of books is maintained. This book is called Subsidiary Books.

Business having a large number of transactions it is practically impossible to write alltransactions in one journal. There was need for sub division of the book keeping work leadingto the sub division of the journal in to smaller journals. It was realised that many entries wereof a common recurring type recording transactions of a similar nature.

Moreover, transactions can be classified and grouped conveniently according to their nature, as some transactions are usually of repetitive in nature. Generally, transactions are of two types such as Cash and Credit. Cash transactions can be grouped in one category whereasCredit transactions can be grouped in another category. Thus, in practice, the main journal issub-divided in such a way that a separate book is used for each category or group of transactions.

3.1 SOURCES OF INFORMATION

Invoice: Invoice is prepared by the seller while selling the goods and send the same to the buyer along with goods. Usually, an invoice is prepared in triplicate. One copy is sent to the buyer. These invoices as inward invoice and use this invoice to enter the details in purchase books.

The second copy is sent to the accounts department. The second copy is treated as outward invoice and used for preparing sales book. The third copy is sent to the sales department for collecting the amount from the debtors and send as evidence to answer any point raised by the buyer. Generally, an invoice contains the details like name and address of the seller and buyer, date of transaction, a brief description of goods with quantity and quality, size model, batch number, price, trade discount if any etc.

Debit Note: The purchased goods may be returned to the seller along with a statement. Such a statement contains the details like name and address of the seller, a brief description of the goods to be returned, the reasons for such return, the value of such returned goods etc. This statement is called "Debit Note". This statement informs the seller about the debit given to their accounts. The purchase returned book is prepared with the help of debit note.

Credit Note: The sold goods may be received from the buyer due to defectives or damages. On receipt of goods, a statement is sent to customers with the details like name and address of the customer, invoice No. date of transaction a brief description of goods received, quantity etc. This statement is called "Credit Note". This statement informs the buyer about the credit given to their account. Sales return book is prepared with the help of credit note.

Cash Receipt: A receipt is issued to an individual or corporate that pays cash. Such a receipt is called as cash receipt. Cash receipt is the basis for entries made on the debit side of the cash book.

Voucher: Cash may be paid to an individual or corporate that renders service to the business concern. For which, a receipt is prepared and obtain signature from the party. Sucha receipt is termed as voucher. On the basis of information available from the voucher, the credit side of the cash book is written up.

3.2 ADVANTAGES OF SUBSIDIARY BOOKS

The advantages of maintaining subsidiary books can be summarised as under:

Division of Work: The division of journal, resulting in division of work, ensures more clerks working independently in recording original entries in the subsidiary books.

Efficiency: The division of work also helps the reduction in work load, saving in timeand stationery. It also gives advantages of specialisation leading to efficiency.

Prevents Errors and Frauds: The accounting work can be divided in such a mannerthat the work of one person is automatically checked by another person. With the use of internal check, the possibility of occurrence of errors and frauds may be avoided.

Easy Reference: It facilitates easy references to any particular item. For instance totalcredit sales for a month can be easily obtained from the Sales Book.

Easy Postings: Posting from the subsidiary books are made at convenient intervals depending upon the nature of the business.

3.3 TRADE DISCOUNT

Trade discount is an allowance or concession granted by the seller to the buyer, if thecustomer purchases goods above a certain quantity or above a certain amount. The amount of the purchase made, is always arrived at after deducting the trade discount, **Trade discount isnot recorded in the books**. They are used for determining the net price.

3.4 CASH DISCOUNT

When goods are sold on credit the customers enjoy a facility of making payment on some date in the future. In order to encourage them to make the payment before the expiry ofthe credit period a deduction is offered. The deduction is known as cash discount.

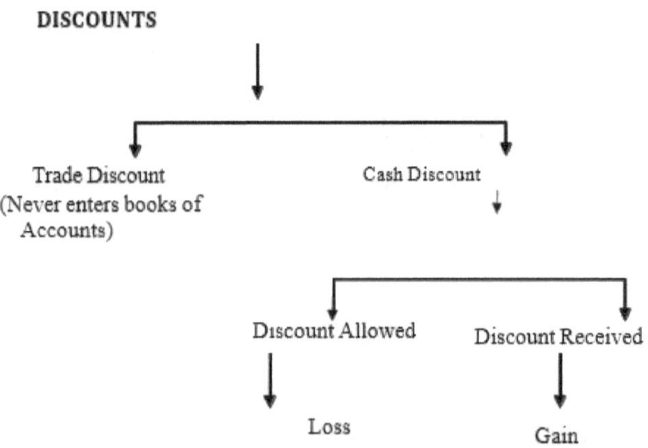

3.5 DISTINCTION BETWEEN CASH DISCOUNT AND TRADE DISCOUNT

Trade Discount	Cash Discount
It is allowed at the time of sales or Purchase	It is allowed at the time of Payment
It is given to promote sales	It is allowed to encourage early cash payment
It is shown as a deduction in the invoice	It had nothing to do with the invoice
Entry is not made in the account book	Entry is made in the account book. Separate ledger accounts are opened for discount received and for discount allowed

Trade Discount	Cash Discount
The object is to enable the buyer to sellat the catalogue price	The object is to induce the debtors to paytheir dues promptly
It is allowed or not allowed according tosales policy followed by a business concern	It is allowed only on a condition. The duesshould be paid within the stipulated time. If not the debtors are not eligible for cash discount.
It is usually given in percentage. It is given on the list price or catalogue priceor retail price.	It may be given in percentage or in absolute figure.

3.6 TYPES OF SUBSIDIARY BOOKS

The number of subsidiary books may vary according to the requirements of each business. The following are the special purpose subsidiary books.

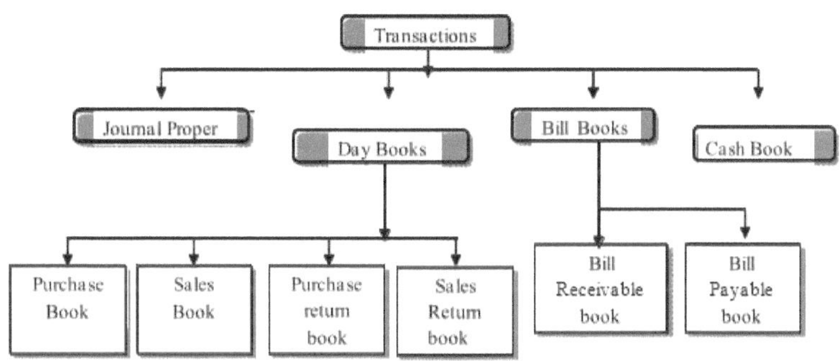

Purchase Book records only credit purchases of goods by the trader. **Cash purchasesnot recorded in the purchase book.**

Sales Book is meant for entering only credit sales of goods by the trader. **Cash sales,cash and credit sales of assets are not recorded in the sales book.** They are dealt with in the cash book.

Purchase Return Book records the goods returned by the trader to suppliers.

Sales Return Book deals with goods returned (out of previous sales) by the customers.

Bills Receivable Book records the receipts of bills (Bills Receivable).

Bills Payable Book records the issue of bills (Bills Payable).

Cash Book is used for recording only cash transactions i.e., receipts and payments of cash.

Journal Proper is the journal which records the entries which cannot be entered inany of the above listed subsidiary books.

Purchase Book

Date	Name of the Sellers	L.F	Inward Invoice No	Amount ₹

- L.F – Page number of the suppliers / sellers account in the ledger account
- Inward invoice no - Reveals the serial number of the inward invoice
- Amount – The amount shows the total goods or materials purchased on credit.

Sales Book

Date	Name of the Customer	L.F	Outward Invoice No	Amount ₹

- L.F – Page number of the customers account in the ledger account
- Outward invoice No - Reveals the serial number of the outward invoice
- Amount – The amount shows the total goods or materials sales on credit.

Purchase Return Book

Date	Name of the Suppliers	L.F	Debit Note	Amount ₹

Debit Note: When goods are returned to sellers, a statement is sent to them informing them about the debit given to their accounts. This statement is called Debit Note.

Sales Return Book

Date	Name of the Customer	L.F	Debit Note	Amount ₹

L.F: Stands for ledger folio which means page of the ledger. This column are entered the page number on which the various counts appear in the ledger.

Credit Note: Customers may return goods when they are damaged or defective on receipt of the goods returned by customers. A Credit Note is sent to them intimating the credit given to their accounts.

3.7 CASH BOOK

In any business, large number of transactions are relating to cash receipts and payments. If journal entries are passed for each transaction, there is a need of more labor and requires more time to post the journals in the ledger accounts. Therefore, it is convenient to have a separate book, to record such transactions. There is no need of maintaining cash account and bank account in the ledger book if cash book is maintained. The maintenance of cash book is highly useful in find the balance of cash in hand and cash at bank at any point of time.

Cash book is the only book which serves the dual purpose of the journal and ledger. The business transactions involving cash receipt and payments directly recorded in the cash book without passing journal enters. Moreover, there is non cash account and bank account inthe ledger book. Hence, cash book is treated as a book of original entry and cash and bank transactions are not recorded in any other subsidiary book.

Posting: Entries on the debit side of cash book are posted to the credit side of accountnamed in cash book by entering "By cash". Likewise, entries on the credit side of cash book are posted to the debit side of account named in cash book by entering "To cash".

Balancing: Always, debit side of cash book is more than credit side. The reason is that there is no possibility of excess payment of cash what one has. The closing balance of cash book is shown as cash in hand in the asset side of the Balance Sheet.

3.8 TYPES OF CASH BOOK

The nature and requirements of the business concern are the factors that determine thetype of cash book maintained. There are four types of cash book. They are listed below.

1. Single Column Cash Book (Cash column only)
2. Double Column Cash Book (Cash and Discount column)
3. Triple Column Cash Book (Cash, Bank and Discount column)
4. Bank Cash Book (Bank and Discount column)

In addition to any one of the above cash book, each business has to maintain petty cash book. The petty cash book is maintained on memorandum basis or imprest system.

1. Single Column Cash Book

Cash book is not only a book of original entry but also a ledger account for cash transactions. Hence, single column cash book has only one column on each side for amount.The cash book is written up just like a cash account in the ledger book, being cash book is areal account, all cash receipts are recorded on debit side as debit what comes in and all cash payments are recorded on credit side as credit what goes out.

2. Double Column Cash book

As the terms indicate, there are two columns on each side of the cash book. One column is meant for cash and another column is meant for discount on each side. On the debit side, cash received from debtors in cash column and discount allowed in discount column are recorded. Likewise, on the credit side, cash paid to creditors in cash column and discount received in discount column are recorded.

3. Triple Column Cash Book

There are three columns on each side of the cash book. One column is meant for cash,another column is meant for bank and next column is meant for discount. All the cash receipts and payments are recorded on the debit side and credit side of the cash book respectively. Both cash deposits and cheque or demand draft deposits into the bank are recorded on the debit side of the cash book. Likewise, payment through a cheque and cash withdrawn from a bank are recorded on the credit side of the cash book. In the cash of discount columns, discount allowed is shown on the debit side of cash book and discount received is shown on the credit side of the cash book.

4. Bank Cash Book

There are two columns on each side of the cash book. One column is meant for bankand another column is meant for discount. On the debit side, both cash deposits and cheque ordemand draft deposits are record. Likewise payment through a cheque and cash withdrawn from a bank are recorded on the credit side. In the case of discount column discount allowedis shown on the debit side and discount received is shown on the credit side. It may also be called as "Cash Book without cash column" or "Bank Book Cash".

3.9 SPECIAL ITEMS OF CASH BOOK

Contra Entries: If a transaction affects cash account and bank accounts only. Entry for recording the transaction is called Contra Entry. Some transaction affects both cash account and bank accounts. This transaction is recorded on the debit side and entered the amount in the bank column.

At the same time, this transaction is recorded in the credit side and entered the amount in the cash column. Therefore, no ledger posting is required in cash of a contra entry. This fact is mentioned in cash book by wetting "C" in LF column.

Endorsement: Sometimes, the received cheque may be endorsed in favour of a creditorin full settlement or partly settlement of account. The cheque received may be recorded on debit side in cash column at the time of receipt. If so, at the time of endorsement, it should berecorded on credit side on cash column.

Bank Overdraft: Sometimes a business concern may arrange the overdraft facility witha bank. If so, the business concern can draw amount more than the amount deposited into the bank. An amount withdrawn in excess of the balance appearing in bank is called bankoverdraft.

In case of bank overdraft the total of bank column of debit side is less than the total ofbank column of credit side. It is shown as "To Balance c/d" at the end of the accounting period while balancing the cash book and shown as "By balance b/d" at the beginning of thesucceeding accounting year.

Bank Charges: A bank renders services to the business concern. Hence, the bank charges some amount for rending services. The bank charge is recorded on the credit side inbank column of cash book.

Received Cheque Dishonoured: It is recorded on the credit side of the cash book in bank column to indicate decrease in bank balance. Besides, and equal amount is credited to creditors account.

Issued Cheque Dishonoured: It is recorded on the debit side of the cash book in bank column to indicate increase in bank balance. Besides, an equal amount is credited to creditorsaccount.

Receipt of other Cheque: The term other cheques include account payee or crossed cheque or bearer or order cheques. All these cheques are received and deposited into the bankon different date, it is treated as cash received and is only entered in the debit side of the cashcolumn. If the cheque is received and deposited into the bank on the same day, it is treated asbank receipt and is entered in the debit side of the bank column. If nothing is mentioned in the problem it is presumed that the cheque is sent to the bank on the same day.

3.10 JOURNAL PROPER

This book is also called General Journal. All those business transactions which cannotbe recorded in any one of the above mentioned books are recorded as in the form of journal entries in this journal proper and such journal entries are posted to ledger. The journal entriesare passed in the journal proper.

3.10.1 Importance of Journal Proper:

Opening Entry: Opening entry is passed in the beginning of an accounting period toopen new set of books and record therein opening balances of assets, liabilities and capital.

Transfer Entry: Some accounts are opened for specific transaction. These accountsare not balanced at the time of balancing of ledger. But, an entry is passed to close these specific accounts. Such journal entry is called transfer entry.

Closing Entry: Some more accounts are not balanced at the time of balancing of ledger but the balance amount is transferred to either trading account or profit and loss account. A journal entry is passed for transferring the balance amount in the ledger account to financial statements. Such an entry is called closing entry.

Rectification Entries: A journal entry is passed to rectify errors in recording transactions in the books of original entry. Such a journal entry is called rectification entry.

Adjusted Entries: At the end of the accounting period, some entries are passed to update the ledger accounts on accrual basis. Such journal entries are called adjustment entries.

Accuracy: The division of work leads to specialization in work. Hence, the subsidiarybooks can be maintained with accuracy.

Time saving: As the recording is done simultaneously in a number of books, the workis complete quickly and independently.

Complete information: The full detail of a business transaction is available in the subsidiary books.

Easy edger posting: At the end of the specific period, consolidated posting is carriedon. Hence, it is more convenient to the very nature of business.

Three column cash book: The maintenance of three column cash book avoids the opening of bank account and discount account separately. Moreover, the cash book takes theplace of journal and ledger account.

Readymade information: Subsidiary books are maintained in group wise business transaction and with complete details. Hence, any class of information is obtained without much difficultly.

Savings in stationary cost: The use of subsidiary books results in economical and limited use of stationary materials.

3.11 DIFFERENCE BETWEEN SUBSIDIARY BOOKS AND LEDGER

S.No	Subsidiary Books		Ledger
1	Subsidiary books are books of original entry or prime entry	1	Ledger is the book of secondaryor final entry
2	Financial statements cannot bedirectly prepared from subsidiary books	2	Financial statements are preparedfrom the balances of ledger accounts.
3	Transactions are recorded in chronological order	3	Transactions are recorded in ananalytical way.

S.No	Subsidiary Books		Ledger
4	It provides complete information ofa transaction	4	It does not provide complete information of a transaction. Butdebit and credit aspects of transactions are given in ledger accounts.
5	Recording of business transactionsin subsidiary books is called journalising	5	Recording of business transactions in the ledger accounts is called posting
6	These books are useful to prepare the ledger accounts, hence, these books are called subsidiary books	6	Ledger book helps to prepare financial statements. i.e. final accounts. Therefore, it is called principal book.

Problem: 1 Enter the following transactions in proper subsidiary books and post to ledger.

2014 March	1	Bought goods from Mohamed	2,000
	2	Sold goods to Nazer	1,000
	5	Charles sold goods to us	1,000
	8	Moses bought goods from us	500
	10	Received goods returned by Nazer	50
	12	We return goods to Mohamed	50
	15	Moses returned goods	100
	18	Sold goods to Hamed	750
	20	Purchased goods from Joseph	600
	25	Returned goods to Charles	150
	30	Sold goods to Antony	700

Solution:

Purchase Book

Date	Name of the Sellers	L.F	Inward Invoice No	Amount ₹
2014 March 1	Mohamed			2,000
5	Charles			1,000
20	Joseph			600
	Total			**3,600**

Sales Book

Date	Name of the Buyers	L.F	Outward Invoice No	Amount ₹
2014 March 2	Nazer			1,000
8	Moses			500
18	Hamed			750
30	Antony			700
	Total			**2,950**

Purchase Return Book

Date	Name of the Sellers	L.F	Debit Note	Amount ₹
2014 March 12	Mohamed			50
25	Charles			150
	Total			200

Sales Return Book

Date	Name of the Buyers	L.F	Credit Note	Amount ₹
2014 March 10	Nazer			50
15	Moses			100
	Total			200

Problem 2: Enter the following transactions for the month of April 2015 in the purchasebooks of M/s. Anbu Traders and post them to ledger.

2015

April   1   Purchased from M/s.Swetha Traders

                     30 Scooters @ ₹ 20,000 per scooter, trade discount at 5%

        12   Purchased from Balraj & Co

                     50 Motor Cycles @ ₹ 40,000 per motor cycle at a trade discount of 10%

        15   Purchases from Indu Motors

                     60 Motor cycles @ ₹ 50,000 per motor cycle

                     Accessories worth ₹ 10,000

Solution:

Books of M/s Anbu Traders Purchase Book

Date	Name of the supplier	L.F	Inward invoice No.	Details ₹	Amount ₹
1.4.2015	M/s Swetha Traders			6,00,000	
	30 Scooters @ ₹ 20,000 per unit			30,000	5,70,000
12.4.2015	Less: Trade Discount @ 5%				
	Balraj & Co			20,00,000	
	50 Motor Cycles @ ₹ 40,000			2,00,000	18,00,000
15.4.2015	Less: Trade Discount 10%			30,00,000	
	Indu Motors			10,000	30,10,000
30.4.2015	60 Motor cycles @ ₹ 50,000				
	Accessories				
	Total				**53,80,000**

| Dr | | | | Ledger Account | | Cr |

Purchase A/c

Date	Particulars	L.F	₹	Date	Particulars	L.F	₹
30.04.2015	To Sundries (as per purchase book)		53,80,000				

Dr				Swathi Traders		Cr		
Date	Parti culars	L.F	₹	Date	Parti culars	L.F	₹
				1.4.2015	By Purchase a/c		5,70,000

Dr				Balraj & Co		Cr		
Date	Parti culars	L.F	₹	Date	Parti culars	L.F	₹
				12.4.2015	By Purchase a/c		18,00,000

Dr	Indu Motors		Cr					
Date	Parti culars	L.F	₹	Date	Parti culars	L.F	₹
				15.4.2015	By Purchase a/c		30,10,000

Problem 3 Record the following transactions in the sales book of M/s Siva & Sons and postthem ledger.

2014

March 5	Sold to M/s Rajesh

300 Shirts at ₹ 150 per unit;

400 towels at ₹ 200 per unit

11	Sold to M/s Ramani

800 shirts at ₹ 300 per unit 1,000 Blankets at ₹ 400 per unit

28   Sold Modern Stores

         500 shirts @ ₹ 75 per unit for cash

30   Old furniture sold to Sami & Sons on credit at ₹ 5,000

It is the practice of M/s Siva & Sons to allow 10% trade discount

Solution:

Books of M/s Siva & Sons Sales Book

Date	Name of the supplier	L.F	outward invoice No.	Details ₹	Amount ₹
5.3.2014	M/s Rajesh				
	300 shirts @ ₹ 150 per unit			45,000	
	400 towels @ ₹ 200 per unit			80,000	
				1,25,000	
	Less: Trade discount @ 10%			12,500	1,12,500
11.3.2014	M/s Ramani				
	800 shirts at ₹ 300 per unit			2,40,000	
	1,000 blankets at ₹ 400			4,00,000	
				6,40,000	
	Less: Trade discount 10%			64,000	5,76,000
30.3.2014	Total				6,88,500

Note: Cash sales and sale of furniture are not entered in sales book. Only credit sale ofgoods are recorded in sales book

Dr   **Ledger Account**   **Cr**

Sales A/c

Date	Parti culars	L.F	₹	Date	Parti culars	L.F	₹
				31.3.2014	By Sundries (as per sales Book)		6,88,500

Dr   **M/s Rajesh**   **Cr**

Date	Parti culars	L.F	₹	Date	Parti culars	L.F	₹
5.3.2014	By Sales a/c		1,12,500				

Dr   **M/s Ramani**   **Cr**

Date	Parti culars	L.F	₹	Date	Parti culars	L.F	₹
11.3.2014	By Sales a/c		5,76,000				

Problem 4: Prepare Purchases Returns book of Mr.Nambiraj

2010

Sept	1	Purchased goods from Suresh	205
	2	Received goods returned by Natarajan	300
	5	Goods returned to Kannan	500
	7	Sales returns by Madhavan	1,260
	15	Returned defective goods to Raju	1,280

23	Outward returns to Kumar	275	
25	Inwards returns by Somu	750	
29	Returned goods to Sankar	890	

Solution:

PURCHASE RETURN BOOK

Date	Particulars	Debit Note	L.F	₹
2010				
Sep 5	Kannan a/c			500
15	Raju a/c			1,280
23	Kumar a/c			275
29	Sankar a/c			890
	Purchase Returns a/c			**2,945**

3.12 CASH BOOK

A cash book is a special journal which is used to record all cash receipts and cash payments. The cash book is a book of original entry or prime entry since transactions are recorded for the first time from the source documents. **Cash Book will always show debit balance**, as cash payments can never exceed cash available. In short, cash book is a special journal which is used for recording all cash receipts and cash payments.

Kinds of Cash Book

The various kinds of cash book from the point of view of uses may be as follow:

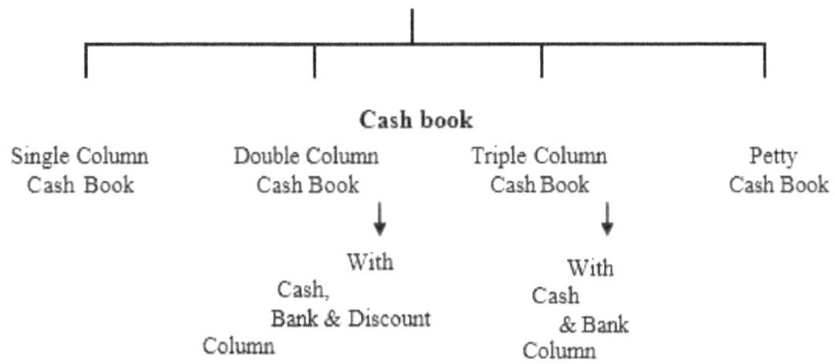

Problem 5: Anbalagan began his business on January 1, 2007. Enter the followingtransactions in his Cash book.

2014	January 1	Started business with cash	₹ 10,000
	3	Purchased goods for cash	₹ 5,000
	4	Sold goods	₹ 17,000
	6	Cash received from Siva	₹ 2,000
	10	Paid Balan	₹ 1,500
	15	Bought furniture	₹ 2,000
	16	Purchased goods from Kala on credit	₹ 200
	25	Paid electric charges	₹ 2,250
	28	Paid salaries	₹ 2,500
	28	Received commission	₹ 750

Solution:

Dr	Cash Book of Mr. Anbalangan (Single Book)				Cr		
Date	**Parti culars**	**L.F**	**₹**	**Date**	**Parti culars**	**L.F**	**₹**
2014				2014			
Jan1	To Capital a/c		10,000	Jan 5	By Purchase a/c		5,000
4	To Sales a/c		17,000	10	By Balan a/c		1,500
6	To Siva a/c		2,000	15	By Furniture a/c		2,000
28	To Commission a/c		750	25	By Electric Charges		2,250
				28	By Salaries		2,500
					By balance c/d		16,500
			29,750				29,750
Feb 1	To Balance b/d		16,500				

Note: The transaction dated January 16th will not be recorded in the cash book as it is a credittransaction.

Problem: 6. Enter the following transactions of Akbar in a Single column cash book.

2012	Jan 1	Commenced business with	₹ 15,000
	2	Paid into bank	₹ 13,000
	3	Purchased goods for cash	₹ 1,500

4	Sold goods for cash	₹ 1,100
5	Paid for stationary	₹ 60
6	Received from Nagaraj	₹ 1,500
7	Paid to Gopu	₹ 800
8	Purchased office furniture	₹ 600

Solution:

CASH BOOK (Single Book)

Date	Particulars	L.F	₹	Date	Particulars	L.F	₹
2012				2012			
Jan1	To Capital a/c		15,000	Jan 2	By Bank a/c		13,000
4	To Sales a/c		1,100	3	By Purchase a/c		1,500
6	To Nagaraj a/c		1,500	5	By Stationary a/c		60
				7	By Gopu a/c		800
				8	By Furniture a/c		600
					By balance c/d		1,640
			17,600				17,600
Jan 9	To Balance b/d		1,640				

Problem: *7* Prepare cash book from the following transactions of Babar in a single columncash book.

2015

Jan   1   Cash in hand ₹ 2,200

           5   Received from Kanmani ₹ 1300

           7   Paid rent ₹ 130

           8   Sold goods ₹ 1,200

           10   Paid Rajesh ₹ 1,700

           27   Purchased furniture ₹ 1,200

           30   Paid salaries ₹ 1,100

Solution:

Single Column Cash Book

Date	Particulars	L.F	Amount ₹	Date	Particulars	L.F	Amount ₹
2015 Jan 1	To Balance b/d		2,200	2015 Jan 7	By Rent a/c		130
5	To Kanmani a/c		1,300	10	By Rajesh a/c		1,700
8	To Sales a/c		1,200	27	By Furniture a/c		1,200
				30	By Salaries a/c		1,100
				31	By Balance c/d		570
			4,700				4,700
Feb 1	To Balance b/d		570				

***Problem:* 8** From the following transactions prepare a cash book under single column cashbook.

2014

May 1   Cash balance ₹ 500

May 2   Goods sold for cash ₹ 850

May 4   Purchases (Cash) ₹ 300

May 5   Received from Sham ₹ 350

May 7   Paid cash to Nalan ₹ 125

May 10   Received cash from Arjun ₹ 400

May 15   Deposited into bank ₹ 600

May 19   Withdraw from bank ₹ 200

May 22   Received dividend on shares ₹ 300

May 30   Paid rent ₹ 200

Single Column Cash Book

Date	Parti culars	L.F	Amount ₹	Date	Parti culars	L.F	Amount ₹
2014				2014			
May1	To Balance b/d		500	May4	By Purchase a/c		300
2	To Sales a/c		850	7	By Nalan a/c		125
5	To Sham a/c		350	15	By Bank a/c		600
10	To Arjun a/c		400	30	By Rent a/c		200
19	To Bank a/c		200	31	By Balance c/d		1,375
22	To Dividend a/c		300				
			2,600				2,600
Jun1	To Balance b/d		1,375				

Problem: 9. Enter the following transactions in the double column cash book of Mr.Moorthy and balance it.

2011

August 1	Opening Balance:	Cash in Hand ₹ 4,250;
		Cash at Bank ₹13,750
2	Paid to petty cashier ₹ 2,500	
2	Cash sales ₹ 1,750	
3	Paid to Arun by cheque ₹ 3,750	
3	Received a cheque from Mr.Ram Babu ₹ 4,500 paid into bank.	
5	Received cheque from Mr.Jayaraman ₹ 6,000 paid into bank	
8	Cash Purchases ₹ 2,500	
8	Paid rent by cheque ₹ 2,500	
9	Cash withdrawn from bank for office use ₹ 2,500	
10	Cash sales ₹ 3,750	
14	Stationery purchased ₹ 1,000	
20	Cash sales ₹ 6750	
21	Paid into bank ₹ 10,000	
23	Withdrew cash for personal use ₹ 1,000 from Bank	
25	Salaries paid by cheque ₹ 9,000	

Solution:

Double Column Cash book of Mr. Moorthy
(Cash & Bank Column)

Date	Particulars	L.F	Cash ₹	Bank ₹	Date	Particulars	L.F	Cash ₹	Bank ₹
2011					2011				
Aug 1					Aug 2			2,500	
	To Balance b/d		4,250	13,750		By Petty cash a/c			
2	To Sales a/c		1,750		3	By Arun a/c			3,750
3	To Ram babu a/c			4,500	8	By Purchase a/c		2,500	
5	To Jayaraman a/c			6,000	8	By Rent a/c			2,500
9	To Bank a/c	C	2,500		9	By Cash a/c	C		2,500
10	To Sales a/c		3,750		14	By Stationary a/c		1,000	
20	To Sales a/c		6,750		21	By Bank a/c	C	10,000	
21	To Cash a/c	C		10,000	23	By Drawings a/c			1,000
					25	By Salary a/c			9,000
					31	By Balance c/d		3,000	15,500
			19,000	34,250				19,000	34,250
Sep 1	To Balanceb/d		3,000	15,500					

Problem: 10: Compile three column cash book of Mr.Sundarm from the following transactions:

2012

August 1   Sundarm started business with cash ₹ 2,00,000.

      2   Deposited into Bank ₹ 50,000.

      4   Cash purchases ₹ 5,000.

      5   Purchases by cheque ₹ 6,000.

      6   Goods sold to Nathan on credit ₹ 5,000.

      8   Received cheque from Mano ₹ 490, Discount allowed ₹ 10.

     10   Paid carriage ₹ 1,000.

     12   Withdrew from Bank for office use ₹ 10,000.

     15   Paid to Sundari ₹ 4,960, Discount allowed by her ₹ 40.

     20   Received a cheque for ₹ 4,950 from Nathan in full settlement of his account,which is deposited into Bank.

Solution:

Triple Column Cash book of Mr. Sundaram

					Dr	Cr						
Date	Particulars	L.F	Disc.	Cash ₹	Bank ₹	Date	Particulars	L.F	Disc.	Cash ₹	Bank₹
2012						2012					
Aug1	To Capitala/c			2,00,000		Aug	By Bank a/c	C		50,000	
						2					
2	To Cash a/c	C			50,000	4	By Purchasea/c			5,000	
8	To Mano a/c		10	490		5	By Purchasea/c				6,000
12	To Bank a/c	C		10,000		10	By Carriagea/c			1,000	
20	To Nathana/c		50		4,950	12	By Cash a/c	C			10,000
						15	By Sundari a/c		40	4,960	
						31	By Balancec/d			1,49,530	38,950
			60	2,10,490	54,950				40	2,10,490	54,950
Sep 1	To Balanceb/d			1,49,530	38,950						

Note : Transaction dated 6th August will not appear in the cash book as it is a credittransaction

Problem: 11 From the following information show how Mr. Venu Gopal's triple column cash book would appear for the week ended 7th October 2012 and close the cash book for the day.

2012

Oct 1   Cash in hand ₹ 30,000 ; Bank balance ₹ 1,000

2   Sivan, our customer has paid directly into our bank account ₹ 5,000.

3   Paid rent by cheque ₹ 500.

4   Cheque issued in favour of Bharathi for purchase of furniture ₹ 2,400.

5   Received from Vinoth ₹ 2,225 Discount allowed ₹ 75.

6   Paid into bank ₹ 4,000

7   Cash withdrawn from bank ₹ 2,000.

Bharathi, to whom we have issued a cheque of ₹ 2,400 has reported that our cheque isdishonoured.

Solution:

Triple Column Cash book of Mr. VenuGopal

| Dr | | | | | | | Cr | | | | |
Date	Particulars	L.F	Disc. Allow ed	Cash ₹	Bank ₹	Date	Particulars	L.F	Disc. Recei ved	Cash ₹	Bank ₹
2012						2012					
Oct1	To Balanceb/d			30,000	1,000	Aug 3	By Rent a/c				500
2	To Sivan a/c				5,000	4	By Furniturea/c				2,400
5	To Vinoth a/c		75	2,225		6	By Bank a/c	C		4,000	
6	To Cash a/c	C			4,000	7	By Cash a/c	C			2,000
7	To Bank a/c	C		2,000		7	By Balancec/d			30,225	7,500
7	To Furniture a/c				2,400						
			75	34,225	12,400					34,225	12,400
Oct8	To Balanceb/d			30,225	7,500						

Problem: 12 Enter the following transactions in three column cash book

Date	Particulars	₹
2004	Balance of cash	600
Jan 1	Bank	7,300
3	Cash sales	2,000
5	Withdrew from bank	5,000
5	Paid wages	6,000
6	Paid in to bank	1,000
10	Received from Geo	8,000
	Discount allowed	50
12	Withdrew from bank	800
15	Purchases paid by cheque	200
31	Paid Managers salary by cheque	1,500

Solution:

Three Column Cash Book

Date	Particulars	LF	Discount	Cash ₹	Bank ₹	Date	Particulars	LF	Discount	Cash ₹	Bank ₹
2004						2004					
Jan1	To Balance b/d			600	7,300	Jan 5	By Cash a/c	C			5000
3	” Sales a/c			2,000	-	5	” Wages a/c			6000	
5	” Bank a/c	C		5000		6	” Bank a/c	C		1000	
6	” Cash a/c	C			1000	12	” Cash a/c	C			800
10	” Geo a/c		50	8000		15	” Purchases				200
12	” Bank a/c	C		800		31	” Salary a/c				1500
						31	” Balance c/d			9400	800
			50	16400	8300					16400	8300
Feb1	To Balance b/d			9400	800						

Problem: 13. From the following transactions in Abi & Abi cash book with cash and discountcolumns.

2015

April 1	Cash balance ₹ 11,000
May 2	Goods sold to Amali ₹ 6,000
May 3	Cash sales ₹ 20,000
May 4	Purchases from Semalar ₹ 13,500
May 5	Bought goods for ₹ 9,000
May 8	Amalai paid his dues @ 1% Cash discount
May 9	Paid to Semalar 13,365 and settled their account
May 15	Cash Withdraw for personal expenses ₹ 2,000
May 18	Draw a cheque for office use ₹ 7,500
May 25	Paid office rent ₹ 3,750
May 28	Paid into the bank ₹ 12,500
May 29	Received from Balan ₹ 2,400 in settlement of his account ₹ 2,500
May 30	Paid Salaries ₹ 2,000

Double Column Cash Book (Cash & Discount)

Date	Particulars	L.F	Discount	Amount ₹	Date	Particulars	L.F	Discount	Amount ₹
2015					2015				
Apr 1	To Balance b/d			11,000	Apr 5	By Purchase ac			9,000
3	To Sales a/c			20,000	9	By Semalar a/c		135	13,365
8	To Amali		60	5,940	15	By Drawings			2,000
18	To Bank a/c			7,500	25	By Rent a/c			3,750
29	To Balan a/c		100	2,400	28	By Bank a/c			12,500
					30	By Salaries a/c			2,000
					31	By Balance c/d			4,225
			160	46,840				135	46,840
May1	To Balance b/d			4,225					

Problem: 14: From the following particulars prepare Triple Column Cash book of Mr.John

2015

Jan 1		Cash in hand ₹ 450
		Cash at Bank ₹ 6,500
3		Cash sales ₹ 2,500
4		Paid for advertising by cheque ₹ 350
5		Withdraw from bank for office use ₹ 600
	8	Received cheque from Neema ₹ 620 (debt ₹ 650)
	10	Withdraw from bank for domestic use ₹ 200
	18	Purchased goods by cheque ₹ 1,000
	20	Paid into Bank ₹ 800
	25	Sale of machinery, received cheque ₹ 2,500
	31	Paid salaries by cheque ₹ 500

Triple Column Cash Book of Mr. John (Cash & Discount)

Date	Particulars	L.F	Discount	Bank ₹	Cash ₹	Date	Particulars	L.F	Discount	Bank	Cash ₹
2015						2015					
Jan 1	To Balance b/d			6500	450	Jan 4	By adv a/c			350	
3	To Sales a/c				2500	5	By Cash a/c	C		600	
5	To Bank a/c	C			600	10	By Drawings			200	
8	To Neema a/c		30	620		18	By Purchase			1,000	
20	To Cash a/c	C		800		20	By Bank a/c	C			800
25	To Machinery			2,500		31	By Salaries			500	
						31	By Balance c/d			7770	2750
			30	10420	3550					10420	3550
Feb 1	To Balance b/d			7770	2750						

3.13 PETTY CASH

The word "Petty" is derived from French word "PETIT" which means small. Hence, it is treated as small cash book. The petty cash book is maintained along with main cash book. This type of cash book is maintained in the large size business concern. These small and recurring expenses are recorded in a separate cash book called "**Petty Cash Book**" and the person who maintains the petty cash is called the "**Petty Cashier**".

Petty cash book is the record of petty (small) payments which have no significant on the expenses of the business concern. Petty cash is given to the petty cashier for payments relating to postage, cartage, stationary, conveyance, telecommunication etc. sometimes a journal entry is passed in general journal debiting various petty expenses and crediting pettycash. Then, posting is done into ledger accounts. In such case, petty cash book is not treated as a subsidiary book. It is referred to as a memorandum book which is not a part of double entry system but prepared to develop specific information. In this way, the petty cash booksnot only records petty payments but also analyse and classified the payments made under different heads. The cash given to petty cashier is recorded on the credit side of the cash bookas "By Petty Cash a/c" and posted to the debit side of petty cash account in ledger book.

3.14 IMPRESET SYSTEM OF PETTY CASH BOOK

At the beginning of the period a specified amount is given to the petty cashier to meetpetty expense for a specific period. The duration of a period may be a week or a fortnight or amonth or a quarter and so on. At the end of the specific period, the petty casher can get an equal amount of what he spends from the main cashier or head cashier or chief casher so thatin the beginning of the succeeding period, cash available with petty cashier remains constant. This system is called impreset system of petty cash. Generally sufficient cash is given to thepetty cashier to meet petty expenses. However, if cash falls short during the period, an additional amount is given to the petty cashier by the chief cashier. Imprest means 'money advanced on loan'. Under this system the amount required to meet out various petty expensesis estimated and given to the petty cashier at the beginning of a month. At the end of the given period, when the petty cashier has spent the petty cash amount, he closes the petty cash book for the period and balances it. Then submits the accounts to the cashier. He verifies the pettycash book with the vouchers. After satisfying himself as to the correctness and genuiness of the payments an amount equal to the cash spent is given to the petty cashier. This amount together with the unspent amount will bring up the cash in hand to the amount with which heoriginally started i.e., the imprest amount. Thus the system of reimbursing the amount spent by the petty cashier at fixed period is known as the **imprest system of petty cash**.

3.15 ANALYTICAL PETTY CASH BOOK (OR) COLUMNAR PETTY CASH BOOK

Analytical petty cash book system is maintained for controlling the petty expenses. Ifnot so, petty cash payments may lead to uncontrolled expenses. This system is more convenient to record the petty expenses in group wise, separate columns are opened for eachgroup in the petty cash book with a column for overall total expenditure. The left hand side shows the opening balance and the amount received from the main cashier. The right hand side shows total payments and analytical column for different groups of expenses.

At the end of the specific period, total payments column and analytical columns for each group are separately totaled. The total payments column is equal to the total of analytical column. Thus, the receipts and total payments columns are balanced and the balance is carried forward to the succeeding period. As in the case of any other cash book, petty cash book also has the debit side and the credit side. The debit side is smaller and has very infrequent entries because cash receipt by the petty cashier is mainly from the cashier atthe beginning or close of a specified period. The credit side is bigger and thus has many columns. For each important petty expenses there is a separate column, and therefore columnar cash book is another name for this petty cash book.

These analytical columns helps to know the actual amount spent on each and every type of petty expenses for the specified period. Each petty payment is first entered in the totalpayments column, and then recorded in the respective analytical column.

3.16 ADVANTAGES OF PETTY CASH BOOK

Generally petty cash book is maintained on imprest system with analytical columns.

Hence, the following advantages are available.

1. The work load of main cashier is reduced to some extent
2. There is a control over the small payments
3. Petty cashier is working under the control of main cashier
4. The imprest system provides a sort of ceiling on petty payments
5. A single journal is passed for recording four or five nominal accounts instead of passing separate entry.

Problem: 15 Petty cashier received ₹ 600 on April 2009 from the head cashier. Prepare a petty cash book on the impreset system for the month of April 2009 from the following items:

Date	Particulars	₹	Date	Particulars	₹
3	Stamps	50	15	Refreshment	55
5	Taxi fare	100	16	Auto fare	20
6	Pencil & pads	75	19	Printing paper	60
7	Registry	25	20	Bus fare	15
10	Speed post	45	22	Mobile calls	43
12	E-mail	35	25	Office cleaning	18
			30	Courier services	17

Show the analysis of payments as postage and stamps, E-mail, telephone conveyance, stationery and sundry expenses. Assume imprest amount of ₹ 600.

Solution:

Petty Cash Book

Amount Received	Date	Particulars	Total Amount	Postage Stamps	E- mail	Tele phone	Conve yance	Stati onary	S.Exp
600.00	2009								
	April 1	Cash Received							
	3	Stamps	50.00	50					
	5	Taxi fare	100.00				100		
	6	Pencil & Pads	75.00					75	
	7	Registry	25.00	25					
	10	Speed post	45.00	45					
	12	E- mail	35.00		35				
	15	Refreshment	55.00						55
	16	Auto fare	20.00				20		

Amount Received	Date	Particulars	Total Amount	Postage Stamps	E- mail	Tele phone	Conve yance	Stati onary	S.Exp
	19	Printing Paper	60.00					60	
	20	Bus fare	15.00				15		
	22	Mobile calls	43.00			43			
	25	Office cleaning	18.00						18
	30	Courier service	17.00	17					
			558.00	137	35	43	135	135	73
	30	Balance c/d	42.00						
600.00			600.00						
	May 1								
42.00		Balance b/d							

Problem: 16 Write the analytical petty cash book from the following transactions (on imprest system)

Jan.		₹	Jan.		₹
1	Opening Balance	100	22	Paid tips to office peons	9
2	Bought postage	20	27	Paid stationary	10
10	Paid for stationary	29	30	Paid for tea to agent	3
15	Paid for Carrage	4			
20	Taxi Hire	20			

Solution:

Petty Cash Book

Amount Received	Date	Particulars	Total Amount	PostageStamps	Traveling& Cartage	Stationary	S.Exp
100.00	Jan 1	By Bank					
	2	Postage Stamps	20.00	20.00			
	10	Stationary	29.00			29.00	
	15	Cartage	4.00		4.00		
	20	Taxi hire	5.00		5.00		
	22	Tips to peons	9.00				9.00
	27	Stationary	10.00			10.00	
	31	Tea exp	3.00				3.00
			80.00	20.00	9.00	39.00	12.00
	31	Balance c/d	20.00				
100.00			100.00				
20.00	Feb 1	Balance b/d	100.00				

Problem:17 Record the following transactions in the analytical petty cash book of Mr.Mano. Balance the book on 6th May, 2013.

2013

May 1.   Received for petty cash payment ₹1,500

2   Paid taxi hire ₹ 250

3   Bought stamps ₹ 75

4   Paid for carriage ₹ 120

4 Paid for Courier charges ₹ 75

4   Paid for auto ₹ 125

5   Paid for carriage ₹ 300

6   Bought revenue stamps ₹ 50

Solution:

Analytical Petty Cash Book Analysis of Payments

AmountReceived	Date	Particulars	Total Amount	PostageStamps	Traveling	Carriage	S. Exp
1,500.00	2003	To Balance b/d					
	May 1						
	2	By Taxi Hire	250.00		250.00		
	3	By Stamps	75.00	75.00			
	4	By Carriage	120.00			120.00	
	4	By Courier	75.00	75.00			
	4	By Auto fare	125.00		125.00		
	5	By Carriage	300.00			300.00	
	6	By Revenue stamp	50.00	50.00			
			995.00	200.00	375.00	420.00	
	6	By Balance c/d	505.00				
1,500.00			1500.00				
505.00	7	To Balance b/d					
995.00	7	To Cash a/c					

Problem: 18: From the following particulars prepare Petty Cash Book

2016		₹
April 1	Received cheque for petty expenses	200.00
2	Purchased stamps	11.00
3	Postage	4.00
5	Wages to workers	15.00
6	Bus fare	16.00
7	Postage	3.50
8	Wash equipments	5.00
10	Miscellaneous	2.00
12	Postage	14.00
14	Stationary	15.00
16	Travelling expenses	7.00
18	Proprietor personal expenses	10.00

Petty Cash Book

Amount Received	Date	Particulars	Amount Paid	Postage	Conve-yance	Stationary	Wages	Misce-llaneous
200.00	1.4.16	To Bank						
	2.4.16	By Stamps	11.00	11.00				
	3.4.16	By Postages	4.00	4.00				
	5.4.16	By Wages	15.00				15.00	
	6.4.16	By Bus fare	16.00		16.00			
	7.4.16	By Postage	3.50	3.50				
	7.4.16	By Postage	3.50	3.50				
	8.4.16	By Wash equipment	5.00					5.00
	10.4.16	By Miscellaneous	2.00					2.00
	12.4.16	By Postage	14.00	14.00				
	14.4.16	By Stationary	15.00			15.00		
	16.4.16	By Travelling expenses	7.00		7.00			

Amount Received	Date	Particulars	Amount Paid	Postage	Conve-yance	Stationary	Wages	Misce-llaneous
	18.4.16	By Drawings	10.00					10.00
			102.50	32.50	23.00	15.00	15.00	17.00
	31.4.16	By Balance c/d	97.50					
200.00			200.00					
97.50	1.5.16	By Balance b/d						
102.50	1.5.16	To Cash						

QUESTIONS

Fill in the blanks:

1. Sub division of the journals into various books for recording transactions of similar natureare called________.
2. The total of the______book is posted to the debit of purchases account.
3. Discount allowed column appears in__side of the cash book.
4. In the triple column cash book, when a cheque is received the amount is entered in the______ column.
5. Discount received column appears in__side of the cash book.
6. A cheque received and paid into the bank on the same day is recorded in the ______column of the three column cash book.
7. When a cheque received from a customer is dishonoured, his account is__.
8. Cash Book is one of the______books.

> [**Answers:** 1. Subsidiary books, 2. Purchases, 3. Debit, 4. Bank,
> 5. Credit, 6. Bank, 7. Debited, 8. Subsidiary]

CHOOSE THE CORRECT ANSWER

---

1. Purchase of machinery is recorded in
   a) Sales book   b) Journal proper
   c) Purchases book
2. Purchase book is kept to record
   a) All purchases   b) Only cash purchases
   c) Only credit purchases

3. Credit sales are recorded in
   a) Sales book
   b) Cash book
   c) Journal proper
4. Goods returned by customers are recorded in
   a) Sales book
   b) Sales return book
   c) Purchases return book
5. The cash book records
   a) All cash payments
   b) All cash receipts
   c) All cash receipts & payments
6. When goods are purchased for cash, the entry will be recorded in the
   a) Cash book
   b) Purchases book
   c) Journal
7. The balance of cash book indicates
   a) Net income
   b) Cash in hand
   c) Difference between debtors and creditors
8. In triple column cash book, cash withdrawn from bank for office use will appear in
   a) Debit side of the cash book only
   b) Both sides of the cash book.
   c) Credit side of the cash book only.
9. If a cheque sent for collection is dishonoured, the debit is given to
   a) Suppliers A/c
   b) Bank A/c
   c) Customers A/c
10. If a cheque issued by us is dishonoured the credit is given to
   a) Supplier's A/c
   b) Customer's A/c
   c) Bank A/c

[**Answers:** 1. (b), 2. (c), 3. (a), 4.(b), 5. (c), 6. (a), 7. (b), 8. (b), 9. (c), 10.(a)]

OTHER QUESTIONS:

1. What are the various types of subsidiary books?
2. What are the advantages of subsidiary books?
3. What is cash discount?
4. What are the differences between Trade Discount and Cash Discount?
5. What is Purchases Book?
6. What is Sales Returns Book?
7. What is cash book? What are its features?
8. What are the advantages of cash book?
9. What are the various kinds of cash book?
10. What is single column cash book?
11. What is double column cash book?
12. What is triple column cash book?
13. Write notes on 'contra entry'.
14. Give the specimen of 'triple column cash book'.
15. What are the rules for making entries in the double column cash book with cash and bankcolumn?
16. How the postings are made from the cash book?

EXERCISE

1. From the below transactions prepare Cash Book.

2010	May 1	Cash balance in hand	₹ 1,000
	4	Cash sales	₹ 2,500
	5	Purchases	₹ 400
	7	Amount paid to Suresh	₹ 500

9	Paid into bank	₹ 350
14	Paid Salaries	₹ 450
25	Withdrawn from Bank	₹ 200
30	Rent paid	₹ 150

(Answer: ₹ 2,650)

2. Enter the following transactions in Purchase book and post them into Ledger.

2000	Jan 1	Purchased goods from Kannan	₹ 500
	7	Purchased goods from Somu	₹ 100
	10	Ram Sold goods to us	₹ 750
	15	Purchased from Kumaran	₹ 1,000
	20	Purchased goods from Manimaran	₹ 650
	25	Purchased goods from Jasmin	₹ 1,250

(Answer: ₹ 5,150)

3. Enter the following transactions in Proper subsidiary books.

2011	Mar 1	Purchased goods from Amaran	₹ 2,000
2		Sold goods to Babu	₹ 1,000
5		Chidamparam sold goods to us	₹ 1,000
8		Draviam purchased goods from us	₹ 7,000
10		Returned goods from Babu	₹ 180
15		Returned goods to Amaran	₹ 150
20		Returned goods from Draviam	₹ 9,00
25		Sold goods to Mullai	₹ 5,000

27	Purchased goods from Madhan	₹ 6,000
29	Returned goods to Chidamparam	₹ 100
30	Sold goods to Salesman	₹6,000

(Answer: Purchase ₹ 9,000: Purchase Returns ₹ 250: Sales ₹ 19,000: Sales returns ₹ 1,080)

4. Enter the following transactions in Purchase book, Sales book, Return inward book,Return outward book of Mr.Mahesh.

2013		₹
Jan 1	Bought goods from Aruna	6,000
2	Sold goods to Banu	3,000
3	Hema sold goods to us	3,000
5	Jamuna bought goods from us	1,800
10	Received goods returned by Banu	240
11	We returned goods to Aruna	200
15	Dhanush returned goods	300
20	Sold goods to Vembu	1,400
25	Returned goods to Hema	200
30	Sold goods to Premnath	2,400

(Answer: Purchase ₹ book ₹ 10,600; Sales book 8,600; Return inward book ₹ 540; Return outward book ₹ 400)

5. Record the following transaction in the proper subsidiary books.

2012

March 1	Bought from Kumaresan & Co 40 tables @ ₹ 150 trade discount of 15%
2	Sold to Ramesh & Sons 25 wooden chair @ ₹ 150 trade discount of 5%
5	Mukesh & Co sold us 40 tables @ ₹ 120 less a trade discount of 15%
5	Damaged tables returned to Kumaresan & Co 5 tables
8	Ramesh & Sons returned 5 chair
11	Mukesh & Co received 6 tables returned by us
12	Rasu & Brothers sold us 30 dinning tables @ ₹ 250, less trade discountof 2%
13	Sold 15 dinning tables @ ₹250 to Jaya & Co, trade discount of 2%
15	Purchased from Suriya 40 stools @ ₹ 20, trade discount of 5%
20	Sold 20 stools to Rani @ ₹ 20
25	Returned 3 dinning tables to Rasu & Brothers
28	Jaya & Co returned 5 dinning tables
30	Returned 5 stools to Suriya
30	Sold 5 dinning tables to Dinesh & Sons@ ₹ 250, less trade discount of5%

(Answer: Purchase book ₹ 16,960; Purchase return book ₹ 2,019.50; Sales book ₹ 8,825; Sales return book ₹ 1,937.50)

6. Prepare two column cash book from the following.

2009			₹
March 1		Brindha started business with cash	10,000
	2	Opened current account with the bank	4,000
	3	Paid to Krishnan by cheque	2,000
	7	Cash sales	5,000
	8	Ashok paid into our account directly	2,000
	15	Paid wages	500
	20	Draw from bank	500
	25	Cash sales received in cheque	800
	27	The above cheque deposited into bank	
	30	Drew from bank for personal use	200

(Answer: Cash balance (Dr) ₹ 12,100; Bank balance(Dr) ₹ 3,300)

7. Record the following in a double column cash book

2007		₹
Jan 1	Cash balance	3000
3	Received from Sathish	780
	Discount allowed	20
7	Paid Prakesh	285
	Discount received	15
11	Cash purchases	1500
15	Cash sales	1000

20	Paid Rajan	290
	Discount received	10
26	Cash withdrawn for personal use	370
28	Paid wages	600

8. From the following transactions, prepare three column cash book and balance the same.

2013		₹
Jan 1	Muthuraja commenced business with	10,000
2	Remitted into current account with bank	9,000
3	Paid to Kannan by cheque	4,000
	Discount allowed to Kannan	100
10	Cash sales	4,000
11	Paid into bank	3,000
15	Manickam paid into our bank account	1,000
20	Issued cheque to Neelakandan	2,000
22	Received from Nandakumar	500
	Discount allowed to Nandakumar	50
25	Withdraw from bank	200
28	Cash purchased paid by cheque	800
30	Paid salaries by cheque	1,200

(Answer: Discount (Dr) ₹ 50 (Cr) ₹ 100; Cash a/c(Dr) 2,700; Bank a/c (Dr) ₹ 4,800)

9. From the following transaction write up the cash book.

2003			₹
July 1	Commenced business with cash		15,000
2	Paid into bank		13,500
3	Paid Ramu by cheque		3,450
	Discount allowed by him		50
5	Paid carriage on goods		85
8	Bought furniture by cheque		700
12	Received cheque from Kumaran		3,300
	Discount allowed		60
22	Cash sales		2,500
23	Deposited into bank		2,400
25	Purchases		5,000
26	Received commission		150
27	Advertising expenses		120
28	Withdrew cash from bank		500
28	Received cheque from Murugan		1,250
	Discount allowed		50
29	Drew for private use		500
29	Office expenses		125
30	Salaries by cheque		500
30	Office rent		250

(Answer: Discount (Dr) ₹ 50 (Cr) ₹ 50; Cash (Dr) ₹ 1,230;
Bank a/c (Dr) ₹ 10,300)

10. From the following information, you are required to write the petty cash book (on imprestsystem) for the month of October 2012.

2012			₹
Oct 1		Amount of imprest received from cashier	100.00
	2	Typing papers	4.00
	3	Office cleaning	2.00
	5	Postage	5.00
	6	Cartage	1.00
	8	Ink	1.50
	12	Computer Print out	5.00
	15	Courier	3.50
	20	Cleaning	1.00
	23	Window planes	13.00
	25	Postage	12.70
	30	Stationary	15.00

(Answer: Balance ₹ 33.30)

11. Write out an analytical petty cash book from the following

2011

May 1	Gave an imprest cheque for ₹ 100
2	Bought postage stamps ₹ 20
5	Paid to stationary ₹ 6.75
7	Paid for carriage ₹ 7.50
10	Paid for taxi hire to sales manager ₹ 15.50
22	Sent a courier to Delhi ₹ 35.00
25	Bought ink and paper ₹ 2.25
27	Paid for Coolie ₹ 25
31	Cash purchase from stationary Mart ₹ 9.25

Chapter 4

RECTIFICATION OF ERRORS

The arithmetical accuracy of recording of journal posting to ledger and balancing of ledger accounts is verified through preparation of trial balance. If trial balance agrees, it is presumed that recording of journal posting to ledger and balancing of ledger accounts has no errors. Even though, an agreement of trial balance is not a conclusive proof of arithmetical accuracy of records. There may be some errors even if their trial balance agrees. For example, credit purchase may be totally omitted to record in the books of accounts. In this case, both debit and credit aspects of purchase are not recorded, even though, the trial balance agrees. Hence errors whether affecting the trial balance or not, are to be corrected. The procedure followed to remedy the errors committed and to set right accounting records is called rectification of errors.

A commitment of mistake knowingly or unknowingly in the books of accounts without any intention is called error. Likewise, a commitment of mistake knowingly in the books of accounts with any intention is called fraud. Hence, error is differing from fraud.

4.1 ERRORS IN ACCOUNTING

The fundamental principle of the double-entry system is that every debit has a corresponding credit of equal amount and vice-versa. The total of all debit balances in different accounts must be equal to the total of all credit balances in different accounts, i.e., the total of the two columns should equal.

Debit balances and credit balances of the trial balance ensures only arithmetic accuracy but not accounting accuracy. The two totals do not tally, it implies that some errors have been committed while recording the transactions in the books of accounts. The following are the various kinds of errors.

4.2 KINDS OF ERRORS

Keeping in view the nature of errors, all the errors committed in the accounting process can be classified into two.

    i   Errors of Principle and

    ii   Clerical Errors

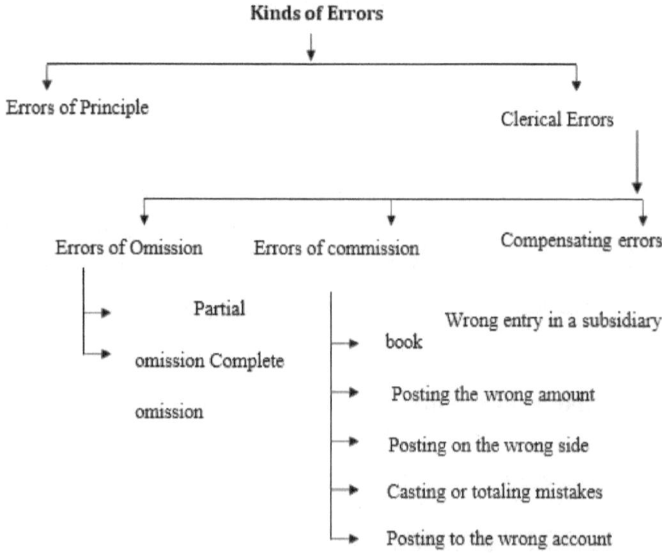

I   **Errors of Principle**

Transactions are recorded as per generally accepted accounting principles. If any of these principles is violated or ignored, errors resulting from such violation are known as **errors of principle**. In other words error of principle is the occurrence of an error due to improper application of accounting rules and principles. Errors of principle are occurred in the following manner. Capital items are treated as revenue items and vice versa.

Ex. Purchase of assets recorded in the purchases book. A trial balance will not disclose errors of principle.

II Clerical Errors

These errors arise because of mistakes committed in the ordinary course of accounting work. These can be further classified into three types.

a) ***Errors of Omission:*** *Err*ors of omission means non recording of any transaction either whole or part in the journal or subsidiary books or in the ledger. Error of complete or full omission means non recording of any transaction in the journal and thereby no posting in the ledger accounts. This error arises when a transaction is completely or partially omitted to be recorded in the books of accounts. Errors of omission may be classified as below.

> *i)* ***Error of Complete Omission:*** This error arises when a transaction is totally omitted to be recorded in the books of accounts. This error does not affect the trial balance.

> *ii)* ***Error of Partial Omission:*** This error arises when only one aspect of the transaction either debit or credit is recorded. This error affects the trial balance.

b) ***Error of Commission:*** This error arises due to wrong recording, wrong posting, wrong casting, wrong balancing, wrong carrying forward etc. errors of commission are committed while preparing ledger accounts and subsidiary books. Errors of posting and errors of balancing are the errors which are committed while preparing ledger accounts. Errors of posting may be recording of right amount in the right side of wrong account, recording of right amount in the wrong side of right account, recording of wrong amount in the right side of right account, recording of wrong amount in the wrong side of right account recording of wrong amount in the wrong side of wrong account, recording of wrong amount in the right side of wrong account and the like, error of balancing is committed in one or more ledger accounts while balancing one ledger account.

Some errors of commission are committed while preparing the subsidiary books, such errors may be wrong entry, entry in wrong book and wrong casting. Errors of commission may be classified as follows:

i)   ***Error of Recording:*** This error arises when a transaction is wrongly recorded in the books of original entry. This error does not affect the trial *balance.*

ii) ***Error of Posting:*** This error arises when information recorded in the books of original entry are wrongly entered in the ledger.

iii) ***Error of Casting (Totaling):*** This *error* arises when a mistake is committed while totaling the subsidiary book. For example, instead of ₹15,000 it may be wrongly totaled as ₹16,000. This is called **overcasting**. If it is wrongly totaled as ₹14,000, it is called **undercasting**.

iv) ***Error of Carrying Forward:*** This error arises when a mistake is committed in carrying forward a total of one page to the next page.

c) ***Compensating Errors:*** The errors arising from excess debits or under debits of accounts being neutralized by the excess credits or under credits to the same extent of some other account is compensating error. Since the errors in one direction are compensated by errors in another direction.

Errors disclosed and not disclosed by trial balance

If the impact of the errors on trial balance is considered, errors may be classified into two categories – Errors disclosed by trial balance, and Errors not disclosed by trial balance.

Errors Disclosed by Trial balance	Errors not Disclosed by Trial balance
• Errors of partial omission	• Errors of complete omission
• Errors of casting	• Errors of recording
• Errors of carrying forward	• Errors of principle
• Errors of posting in the wrong side of the correct account	• Errors of posting to wrong account in the right side with the correct amount
• Errors of posting to correct account with wrong amount	• Compensating Errors
• Double posting in the same account	

4.3 RECTIFICATION OF ERRORS

Correction of errors in the books of accounts is not done by erasing, rewriting or striking the figures which are incorrect. Correcting the errors that has occured is called **Rectification**. Appropriate entry is passed or suitable explanatory note is written in the respective account or accounts to neutralise the effect of errors. From the point of rectification, errors may be classified as follows:

Single sided errors are errors which affect one side of an account.

Double sided errors are errors which affect both the accounts in a transaction.

4.4 RECTIFICATION ENTRY

Some errors affect any one side of the account either debit side or credit side. It is called a "One side error". Generally one side errors results disagreement of trial balance. Some errors affect both sides of one or more accounts, such errors can be called "Two side errors". The correction of one side error does not require the passing of journal entry. Sometimes, if suspense account is opened, a journal entry is passed to rectify the errors. Hence, the one side error is rectified by means of noting the correction on the appropriate side in the ledger accounts. In the case errors which affect two sides of one or more accounts, there is a need of passing journal entry for rectification. This type of journal entry is called "Rectification entry". It is necessary to understand the nature of error. i.e. whether it is a one sided error or a two sided error before deciding to rectifying.

4.5 SUSPENSE ACCOUNT

When it is difficult to locate the mistakes before preparing the final accounts, the difference in the trial balance is transferred to newly opened imaginary and temporary account called '**Suspense Account**'.

Suspense account is prepared to avoid the delay in the preparation of final accounts. If the total debit balances of the trial balance exceed the total credit balances, the difference is transferred to the credit side of the suspense account. On the other hand, if the total credit balances of the trial balance exceeds the total debit balances the difference is transferred to the debit side of the suspense account.

Such balance will be shown in the balance sheet. Debit balance will be shown on the asset side and the credit balance will be shown on the liability side.

4.6 BASIC PRINCIPLES FOR RECTIFICATION OF ERRORS

All errors, whatever may be their kind or nature, result in one of the following four positions in one or more accounts.

Excess debit in one or more accounts: This must be rectified by *'Crediting'* the excess amount to the respective account or accounts.

Short debit in one or more accounts: This must be rectified by a *'Further debit'* to the respective account or accounts involved.

Excess credit in one or more accounts: This can be rectified by *'Debiting'* the respective account with the excess amount involved.

Short credit in one or more accounts: This can be rectified by a *'Further credit'* to the respective account or accounts involved.

Problem 1: The following errors were found in the books of Mr. Prbakaran. Give the necessary entries to correct them.

a) Salary of ₹ 10,000 paid to Murali has been debited to his personal account.

b) ₹ 3,500 paid for a typewriter was charged to office expenses account.

c) ₹ 8,000 paid for furniture purchased has been charged to purchases account.

d) Repairs made were debited to building account for ₹ 500.

e) An amount of ` 5,000 withdrawn by the proprietor for his personal use has been debited to trade expenses account.

f) ₹ 2,000 received from Shanthi & Co. has been wrongly entered as from Shakila & Co.

Solution:

In the Books of Mr. Prabakaran Rectifying Journal Entries

Errors	Particulars		LF	Debit ₹	Credit ₹
a)	Salaries a/c	Dr		10,000	
	To Murali a/c				10,000
	(Being wrong debit to Murali's a/c corrected)				
b)	Typewriter a/c	Dr		3,500	
	To Office expenses a/c				3,500
	(Being Correction of wrong debit to office expenses a/c for purchase of typewriter)				

Errors	Particulars		LF	Debit ₹	Credit ₹
c)	Furniture a/c	Dr		8,000	
	To Purchases a/c				8,000
	(Being Correction of wrong debit to purchases account for furniture purchased]				
d)	Repairs a/c	Dr		500	
	To Building a/c				500
	(Being Correction of wrong debit to building Account for repairs made]				
e)	Drawings a/c	Dr		5,000	
	To Trade expenses a/c				5,000
	(Being Correction of wrong debit to Trade Expenses a/c for cash withdrawn by the proprietor for his personal use)				
f)	Shakila & Co a/c	Dr		2,000	
	To Shanthi & Co a/c				2,000
	(Being Correction of wrong credit to Shakila & Co. instead of Shanthi & Co.)				

Workings:

	Correct entry		Wrong entry		Rectify entry	
a)	Salary a/c	Dr	Murali a/c	Dr	Salary a/c	
	To Cash a/c		To Cash a/c		To Murali a/c	
b)	Type writer a/c	Dr	Office expenses a/c	Dr	Type writer a/c	Dr
	To Cash a/c		To Typewriter a/c		To Office expenses a/c	
c)	Furniture a/c	Dr	Purchase a/c	Dr	Furniture a/c	Dr
	To Cash a/c		To Cash a/c		To Purchase a/c	
d)	Repairs a/c	Dr	Building a/c	Dr	Repairs a/c	Dr
	To Cash a/c		To Cash a/c		To Building a/c	
e)	Drawings a/c	Dr	Trade expenses a/c	Dr	Drawings a/c	Dr
	To Cash a/c		To Cash a/c		To Trade expenses a/c	
f)	Cash a/c	Dr	Cash a/c	Dr	Shakila a/c	Dr
	To Shanthi & Co		To Shakila a/c		To Shanthi a/c	

Problem 2: Give journal entries to rectify the following errors:

i   Credit sale of goods ₹ 30,000 to Rajan has been wrongly passed through the purchases book.

ii   Sold old furniture for ₹ 3,500 passed through the sales book.

iii   Paid wages for the construction of Building debited to wages account ₹ 1,00,000.

iv   Paid ₹10,000 for the installation of Machinery debited to wages account.

v   On 31st Dec. 2013 goods worth ₹ 5,000 were returned by Manjula and were taken into stock on the same date, but no entry was passed in the books.

vi   Purchase of goods from Devi amounting to ₹ 25,000 has been wrongly passed through the sales book.

Solution:

Rectifying Journal Entries

Errors	Particulars		LF	Debit ₹	Credit ₹
(i)	Rajan a/c	Dr		60,000	
	To Purchase a/c To Sales a/c				30,000
					30,000
	(Being Correction of wrong entry in purchases book for credit sale to Rajan)				
(ii)	Sales a/c	Dr		3,500	
	To Furniture a/c				3,500
	(Being Correction of wrong credit to sales account for sale of old furniture)				
(iii)	Building a/c	Dr		1,00,000	
	To Wages a/c				1,00,000
	(Being Correction of wrong debit to wages account for wages paid for construction of building)				
(iv)	Machinery a/c	Dr		10,000	
	To Wages a/c				10,000
	(Being Correction of wrong debit to wages account for wages paid for installation of machinery)				

Errors	Particulars		LF	Debit ₹	Credit ₹
(v)	Sales return a/c	Dr		5,000	
	To Manjula a/c				5,000
	(Being entry for goods returned and taken into stock]				
(vi)	Purchase a/c	Dr		25,000	
	Sales a/c	Dr		25,000	
	To Devi a/c				50,000
	(Being Correction of wrong entry in sales book for a credit purchase from Devi)				

Workings:

	Correct entry		Wrong entry		Rectify entry	
i	Rajan a/c	Dr	Purchase a/c	Dr	Rajan a/c	Dr
	To Sales a/c		To Rajan a/c		To Purchase a/c	
					To Sales a/c	
ii	Cash a/c	Dr	Cash a/c	Dr	Sales a/c	Dr
	To Furniture a/c		To Sales a/c		To Furniture a/c	
iii	Building a/c	Dr	Wages a/c	Dr	Building a/c	Dr
	To Cash a/c		To Cash a/c		To Wages a/c	
iv	Machinery a/c	Dr	Wages a/c	Dr	Machinery a/c	Dr
	To Cash a/c		To Cash a/c		To Wages a/c	
v	Sales return a/c	Dr			Sales return a/c	Dr
	To Manjula a/c		----		To Manjula a/c	
vi	Purchase a/c	Dr	Purchase a/c	Dr	Sales a/c	Dr
	To Devi a/c		To Devi a/c		Purchase a/c	Dr
					To Devi a/c	

Problem 3: How will you rectify the following mistakes?

i)   Goods worth ₹ 58 returned by Raja, a customer was entered in the books of a/c as ₹ 85

ii) ₹ 150 paid to Rani towards his salary debited to his personal account.

iii) Goods worth ₹120 used by proprietor was not recorded in the books.

iv) Goods sold to Shri for ₹ 350 was debited to Ram.

v)   Sales return book was under cost by ₹ 50

Solution:

Rectifying entries

	Particulars		Debit ₹	Credit ₹
(i)	Raja a/c (85 -58)	Dr	27	
	To Sales return a/c			27
	(Being returned goods value rectified)			
(ii)	Salary a/c	Dr	150	
	To Rani a/c			150
	(Being rani account now rectified)			
(iii)	Drawings a/c	Dr	120	
	To Purchase a/c			120
	(Being goods brought into recorded)			
(iv)	Shri a/c	Dr	350	
	To Ram a/c			350
	(Being sold goods error rectified)			
(v)	Sales return a/c	Dr	50	
	To Suspense a/c			50
	(Being sales return rectified)			

Workings:

	Correct entry	**Wrong entry**	**Rectify entry**
i	Sales return a/c Dr 58 To Raja a/c 58	Sales return a/c Dr 85 To Raja a/c 85	Raja a/c Dr 27 To Sales return a/c 27
ii	Salary a/c Dr To Cash a/c	Rani a/c Dr To Cash a/c	Salary a/c Dr To Rani a/c
iii	Drawings a/c Dr To Purchase a/c	---	Drawings a/c Dr To Purchase a/c
iv	Shri a/c Dr To Sales a/c	Ram a/c Dr To Sales a/c	Shri a/c Dr To Ram a/c
v	Sales return a/c Dr To Suspense a/c		Sales return a/c Dr To Suspense a/c

Problem 4: Correct the following errors before preparation of Trial Balance.

i)   An amount of ₹ 600 withdrawn by the proprietor for his personal use, it is posted to travelling expenses account.

ii) ₹ 900 spent in the extension of Machinery are posted to wages account.

iii) A sales of ₹ 344 was recorded in Sales account as ₹ 434.

iv) Sharmila's cheque of ₹ 500 was dishonored, its amount was posted to allowance account.

v) Depreciation of ₹ 200 was not recorded.

Solution:

Rectifying entries

	Particulars		**Debit ₹**	**Credit ₹**
(i)	Drawings a/c	Dr	600	
	To Travelling expenses a/c			600
	(Being travelling expenses a/c rectified)			
(ii)	Machinery a/c	Dr	900	
	To Wages a/c			900
	(Being wages account rectified)			
(iii)	Sales a/c (434 -344)	Dr	90	
	To Suspense a/c			90
	(Being wrong posting to sales account rectified)			
(iv)	Sharmila a/c	Dr	500	
	To Allowance a/c			500
	(Being allowance a/c rectified)			
(v)	Depreciation a/c	Dr	200	
	To Asset a/c			200
	(Being depreciation recorded)			

Problem 5: The following mistakes were located in the books of a concern. You are required to pass rectifying journal entries.

1. A purchase of goods from Devaraj ₹ 500 has been wrongly passed through the sales book

2. A credit sale of goods ₹ 600 to Rajesh has been wrongly passed through the purchase book

3. Sold old furniture for ₹ 750 passed through the sales book

4. Paid wages for the construction of building debited to wages account ₹ 10,000

5. A cheque for ₹ 500 received from Manohar wad dishonoured and has been posted to the debit of sales returns account
6. Paid ₹ 1,000 for the installation of machinery debited to wages account
7. On 31st December 2015 goods of the value of ₹ 250 were returned   by Shankar and were taken into stock on the same date, but no entry was passed in the books.

Solution:

Rectifying Journal Entries

	Particulars		LF	Debit ₹	Credit ₹
(1)	Purchase a/c	Dr		500	
	Sales a/c	Dr		500	
	To Devaraj a/c				1,000
	(Being sales book correction made)				
(2)	Rajesh a/c	Dr		1,200	
	To Purchase a/c				600
	To Sales a/c				600
	(Being credit sales amount rectified)				
(3)	Sales a/c	Dr		750	
	To Furniture a/c				750
	(Being correction of wrong credit to sales)				
(4)	Building a/c	Dr		10,000	
	To Wage a/c				10,000
	(Being correction of wrong debit to wages account)				

	Particulars		LF	Debit ₹	Credit ₹
(5)	Manohar a/c	Dr		500	
	To Sales return a/c				500
	(Being correction of sales return account)				
(6)	Machinery a/c	Dr		1,000	
	To Wages a/c				1,000
	(Being correction of wrong debit to wages)				
(7)	Sales return a/c	Dr		500	
	To Shankar a/c				500
	(Being entry of goods returned by him)				

Workings:

	Correct entry		Wrong entry		Rectify entry	
1	Purchase a/c	Dr	Devaraj a/c	Dr	Purchase a/c	Dr
	To Devaraj a/c		To Sales ac		Sale a/c	Dr
					To Devaraj a/c	
2	Rajesh a/c	Dr	Purchase a/c	Dr	Rajesh a/c	Dr
	To Sales a/c		To Rajesh a/c		To Purchase a/c	
					To Sales a/c	
3	Cash a/c	Dr	Cash a/c	Dr	Sales a/c	Dr
	To Furniture a/c		To Sales a/c		To Furniture a/c	
4	Building a/c	Dr	Wages a/c	Dr	Building a/c	Dr
	To Cash a/c		To Cash a/c		To Wages a/c	
5	Manohar a/c	Dr	Sales return a/c	Dr	Manohar a/c	Dr
	To Bank a/c		To Bank a/c		To Sales return a/c	

	Correct entry		Wrong entry		Rectify entry	
6	Machinery a/c	Dr	Wages a/c	Dr	Machinery a/c	Dr
	To Cash a/c		To Cash a/c		To Wages a/c	
7	Sales		No entry made		Sales Return a/c	Dr
	returned a/c	Dr			To Shankar a/c	
	To Shankar a/c					

Problem 6: The following errors were discovered by a trader, you are required to pass rectifying entries.

1. Sale of old machinery ₹ 500 has been entered in the sales book
2. The total of discount column debit side of the cash book is ₹ 10 short
3. A sale of ₹ 250 to Moorthy has been debited to him as ₹ 520
4. Hariharan pays of ₹ 200. This amount has been credited to Harikanth
5. A purchase of computer from Computer point for ₹ 25,000 on credit has not been entered in the books
6. ₹ 210 received from the estate of Gopal has been credited to his account. His account written off last year as bad.

Solution:

Rectifying Journal Entries

	Particulars		LF	Debit ₹	Credit ₹
(1)	Sales a/c	Dr		1,000	
	To Machinery a/c				1,000
	(Being error rectified)				
(2)	Discount a/c	Dr		10	
	To Suspense a/c				10
	(Being debiting the discount account)				

	Particulars		LF	Debit ₹	Credit ₹
(3)	Sales a/c (520 -250)	Dr		270	
	To Moorthy a/c				270
	(Being over costing the amount rectified)				
(4)	Harikanth a/c	Dr		200	
	To Hariharan a/c				200
	(Being wrong credited amount rectified)				
(5)	Computer a/c	Dr		25,000	
	To Computer point a/c				25,000
	(Being computer purchase entered)				
(6)	Gopal a/c	Dr		210	
	To Bad debts recovered a/c				210
	(Being bad debts recovered amount entered)				

Workings:

	Correct entry			Wrong entry			Rectify entry		
1	Cash a/c	Dr		Debtors a/c	Dr		Sales a/c		Dr
	To Machinery a/c			To Sales ac			To Machinery a/c		
2	Discount a/c	Dr		Not entered			Discount a/c		Dr
							To Suspense a/c		
3	Moorthy a/c	Dr	250	Moorthy a/c	Dr	520	Sales a/c	Dr	270
	To Sales a/c			To Sales a/c			To Moorthy a/c		
4	Cash a/c	Dr		Cash a/c	LDr		Harikanth a/c		Dr
	To Hariharan a/c			To Harikanth a/c			To Hariharan a/c		

	Correct entry		Wrong entry		Rectify entry	
5	Computer a/c	Dr	No entry made		Computer a/c	Dr
	To Computer point a/c				To Computer point a/c	
6	Cash a/c	Dr	Cash a/c	Dr	Gopal a/c	Dr
	To Bad debts recovered		To Gopal a/c		To Bad debts recovered	

Problem 7: An accountant could not tally the Trial balance. The difference of ₹ 5,180 was temporarily placed to the credit of suspense account for preparing the final accounts. The following errors were later located.

1. Commission of ₹ 500 paid, was posted twice, once to discount allowed account and once to commission account.
2. The sales book was under cost by ₹ 1,000.
3. A credit sale of ₹ 2,780 to Roja though correctly entered in sales book, was posted wrongly to her account as ₹ 3,860.
4. A credit purchase from Nataraj of ₹ 1,500, though correctly entered in purchases book, was wrongly debited to his personal account.
5. Discount column of the payments side of the cash book was wrongly added as ₹ 2,800 instead of ₹ 2,400.

You are required to pass the necessary rectifying entries. And Prepare Suspense Account.

Solution:

Rectifying Journal Entries

	Particulars		LF	Debit ₹	Credit ₹
(1)	Suspense a/c	Dr		500	
	To Discount allowed a/c				500
	(Being amount wrongly debited to discount account, now rectified)				
(2)	Suspense a/c	Dr		1,000	
	To Sales a/c				1,000
	(Being Sales book undercost by ₹ 1000, now rectified)				
(3)	Suspense a/c (3860 -2780)	Dr		1,080	
	To Roja a/c				1,080
	(Being wrong posting of sale of ₹ 2,780 to Roja as ₹ 3,860, now rectified)				
(4)	Suspense a/c	Dr		3,000	
	To Nataraj a/c				3,000
	(Being Credit purchase of ₹ 1,500 from Nataraj wrongly debited to his personal account now rectified)				
(5)	Discount Received a/c	Dr		400	
	To Suspense a/c				400
	(Being Excess credit in discount account, now rectified)				

Dr				Suspense Account			Cr
Date	Parti culars	L.F	₹	Date	Parti culars	L.F	₹
	To Discount allowed		500		By Balance b/d		5,180
	To Sales a/c		1,000		By Discount received		400
	To Roja a/c		1,080				
	To Nataraj a/c (1500+1500)		3,000				
			5,580				5,580

Workings:

	Correct entry		Wrong entry	Rectify entry	
i	Commission a/c Dr		Discount allowed a/c Dr	Suspense a/c Dr	
	To Cash a/c		To Cash a/c	To Discount allowed	
ii	Cash a/c	Dr		Suspense a/c Dr	
	To Sales a/c		Under costing	To Sales a/c	
iii	Roja a/c	Dr	Roja a/c (over casting)	Suspense a/c Dr	
	To Sales a/c		To Sales a/c	To Roja a/c	
iv	Purchase a/c	Dr	Nataraj a/c Dr	Suspense a/c Dr	
	To Nataraj a/c			To Nataraj a/c	
v	Cash a/c	Dr		Discount received a/c Dr	
	To Discount a/c		Under casting	To Suspense a/c	

Problem 8: Mr.Gopu failed to balance his trial balance, the credit side exceeding the debit side by ₹ 1,270. This amount was entered in a suspense account. Later the following errors were discovered.

1. The sales day book is totaled ₹ 50 short

2. Payment of trade expenses ₹ 275 entered on the payment side of the cash book is omitted to be posted.

3. Commission ₹ 125 paid has been posted twice to commission account

4. A sale to Palaniappan for ₹ 195 though correctly entered in the day book is debited to Palaniappan account as ₹ 465

5. Goods bought from Lalitha for ₹ 500 though correctly entered in the invoice book is debited to lalitha personal account instead of being credited to him.

6. Discount column on the receipts side of cash book, totaling ₹ 615 has been added up to show ₹ 715

Give the journal entries to rectify the above errors and prepare the suspense account.

Solution:

Rectifying Journal Entries

Errors	Particulars	LF	Debit ₹	Credit ₹
(1)	Suspense a/c	Dr	50	
	To Sales a/c			50
	(Being short total of sales book is rectified)			
(2)	Trade Expenses a/c	Dr	275	
	To Suspense a/c			275
	(Being omission of payment of trade expenses, now rectified)			

Errors	Particulars		LF	Debit ₹	Credit ₹
(3)	Suspense a/c	Dr		125	
	To Commission a/c				125
	(Being twice posting to commission account is rectified)				
(4)	Suspense a/c (465-295)	Dr		270	
	To Palaniappan a/c				270
	(Being excess debit account is rectified)				
(5)	Suspense a/c	Dr		1,000	
	To Lalitha a/c				1,000
	(Being wrong debit of amount rectified)				
(6)	Suspense a/c	Dr		100	
	To Discount a/c				100
	(Being excess totaling of discount is rectified)				

Dr			Suspense Account			*Cr*		
Date	**Parti culars**	**L.F**	**₹**	**Date**	**Parti culars**	**L.F**	**₹**
	To Sales a/c		50		By Difference in book		1,270
	To Commission		125		By Trade expenses		275
	To Palaniappan		270				
	To Lalitha		1,000				
	To Discount		100				
			1,542				1,542

Workings:

	Correct entry		Wrong entry	Rectify entry	
1	Cash a/c	Dr		Suspense a/c	Dr
	To Sales a/c		Under costing	To Sales a/c	
2	Trade Expenses a/c	Dr	Entry omitted	Trade expenses a/c	Dr
	To Cash a/c			To Suspense a/c	
3	Commission a/c	Dr	Entry twice	Suspense a/c	Dr
	To Sales a/c			To Commission a/c	
4	Palanaiappan a/c	Dr	Palanaia ppan a/c Dr	Suspense a/c	Dr
	To Sales a/c		To Sales a/c (over costing)	To Palani appan a/c	
5	Purchase a/c	Dr	Lalitha a/c Dr	Suspense a/c	Dr
	To Lalitha a/c			To Lalitha a/c	
6	Discount a/c	Dr	Dis count a/c Dr	Suspense a/c	Dr
	To Sales a/c		To Sales a/c (over costing)	To Discount a/c	

QUESTIONS

FILL IN THE BLANKS

1. Suspense account having debit balance will be shown on the ____ side of balance sheet.

2. Suspense account having credit balance will be shown on the ____ side of the balance sheet.

3. When errors are located and rectified _ automatically gets closed.

4. Journal entries passed to correct the errors are called ___.

5. Excess debit of an account can be rectified by _ the same account.

6. Short debit of an account can be rectified by _ of the same account.

   [**Answer:**   1.   Assets,   2.   Liabilities,   3. Suspense account
   4. Rectifying entries, 5. Credit, 6. Further debit]

CHOOSE THE CORRECT ANSWER:

1. Suspense account in the trial balance is entered in the
   a)   Trading A/c   b)   Profit and loss A/c
   c)   Balance sheet
2. Suspense account having credit balance will be shown on the
   a) Credit side of the profit and loss A/c
   b) Liabilities side of the balance sheet
   c) Assets side of the balance sheet

3. State which of the following errors will not be revealed by the Trial Balance.

    a)   Errors of complete omission.

    b)   Error of carrying forward.

    c)   Wrong totaling of the purchases book.

4   Errors which affect one side of an account are called

    a)   Single sided errors   b)   Double sided errors

    c)   None of the above.

5. Amount spent on servicing office typewriter should be debited to

    a)   Miscellaneous Expenses Account.

    b)   Typewriter Account.

    c)   Repairs Account.

6. Wages paid to workers for the installation of new Machinery should be debited to

    a)   Wages Account   b)   Machinery Account

    c)   Factory Expenses Account

7. Salary paid to Manager must be debited to

    a)   Manager's Account

    b)   Office Expenses Account   c) Salary Account.

[**Answer:** 1 (c), 2 (b), 3 (a), 4(a), 5 (c), 6 (b), 7 (c)]

OTHER QUESTIONS

---

1. Name the different kinds of errors?

2. Write short notes on

    i   Error of Principle

    ii   Compensating error

    iii Error of casting.

    iv   Error of Posting

3.   What are the errors disclosed by the Trial Balance?
4.   What are the errors not disclosed by the Trial Balance?
5.   What is a Suspense Account? When is it opened?
6.   What do you mean by Rectification of Errors?
7.   In what ways may the errors be rectified?

EXERCISE

---

1.   Give journal entries to rectify the following errors
   a)   A purchase of goods from Deva ₹ 250 has been wrongly passed through the sales book
   b)   Sale of old furniture ₹ 1,500 passed through the sales book
   c)   Sales to Vijay ₹ 1,520 has been posted to his credit as ₹ 1,250

2   Rectify the following errors
   a)   Sales to Z ₹ 400 posted to A's account
   b)   Furniture purchased on credit from Narayanan for ₹ 300 posted as ₹ 30
   c)   Sales to Xavier ₹ 250 was recorded as ₹ 205
   d)   Sales to Balaji ₹ 200 was not recorded
   e)   Purchases from Mururgan ₹ 1,002 was omitted from the book.

3   Write down the rectifying journal entries for the following
   a)   The sales returns book has been under cost by ₹ 500
   b)   Goods worth ₹ 1,500 sold to Bharath has been credited to his account
   c)   Purchase of furniture ₹ 5,000 has been entered in the purchases account
   d)   Cash ₹ 2,500 received from Sekar has been posted to his account as ₹ 5,200
   e)   A bill received from Suman for ₹ 4,000 has been posted to bills payable account
   f)   Received ₹ 3,000 as advanced for sale, from a customer has not yet been recorded in the account books

4. Rectify the following errors
   a) A total of ₹ 798 in the purchase book has been carried forward as ₹ 897
   b) The total of the sales book ₹ 968 on page 15 was carried forward to page 16 as ₹ 698
   c) Purchase return book was carried forward as ₹ 3,280 instead of ₹ 2,380
   d) Sales book total is carried forward as ₹ 450 more
   e) Purchase book is carried forward ₹ 100 less

5. Rectify the following errors
   a) Machinery sold for ₹ 1,000 was credited to sales account
   b) Furniture purchased for ₹ 5,000 was debited to purchases account
   c) Goods sold to Rajan ₹ 2,000 was debited to Raju account
   d) Purchase returns book under cost by ₹ 100
   e) ₹ 6,000 paid to Mullai as salary debited to his personal account
   f) Discount received ₹ 500 was credited to interest account.

6. Pass rectification entries for the following transaction
   a) Purchase book is overcost by ₹ 500
   b) Sales book has under cost by ₹ 300
   c) Purchase returns book has been overcost by ₹ 50
   d) Sales returns book has been under cast by ₹ 75
   e) Purchase from Ram for ₹ 300 has been omitted to be recorded to personal account
   f) Sales to Anand for ₹ 650 has been posted to his account as ₹ 560
   g) Purchase from Vijay for ₹ 750 has been posted to the debit of his account.

7 Rectify the following errors

    a) Furniture purchased for ₹ 700 was taken to the purchase account

    b) Goods sold on credit to A for ₹ 6,000 where debited to B's account

    c) Goods worth ₹ 100 returned by C were not passed through the sales return book

    d) Purchased goods worth ₹ 100 from D was entered in the purchase book as ₹ 1000

    e) An amount of ₹ 2,600 incurred for repaired to Machinery were debited to Machinery account

Chapter 5

BANK RECONCILIATION STATEMENT

A business concern can prepare three column cash book. If so, one is cash column, another one is bank column and third one is discount column on both sides. The transactionswhich increase bank balance are recorded on debit side of cash book in bank column and a transaction which decreases bank balance are recorded on credit side of cash book in bank column. The balance of bank column is called bank balance as per cash book. Generally, bank column of cash book shows debit balance, it means the balance of deposit at the bank. Sometimes, the bank column of cash book shows credit balance, it means, bank overdraft. Bank overdraft is the excess of withdrawals over deposits.

Bank maintains accounts of customers in its ledger. In this ledger, the transactions which increase balance are recorded on the credit side and the transactions which decrease balance are recorded on the debit side. Balance of customers account in ledger book of the bank as shown by pass book is called bank balance as per pass book. If customers account shows debit in the ledger book it is bank overdraft. On the contrary, if customers account shows credit balance in the ledger book. It is a balance of deposit at a particular point of time.

It is clear from the above explanation that deposits in bank are recorded on the debit side of cash book and on the credit side of pass book. Likewise, the withdrawals from the bank are recorded on the credit side of cash book and on the debit side of pass book. If all thetransactions are recorded correctly in the pass book and cash book, certainly, the pass book balance must tally with the balance of cash book.

The nature of balance shown by pass book and cash book is entirely different. It means that if pass book shows debit balance of one amount an equal amount shows as creditbalance in the cash book. It means that the relationship between the business concern and thebank is that a debtor and a creditor.

5.1 MEANING

'**Bank Reconciliation Statement** is a list in which the various items that cause a difference between bank balance as per cash book and pass book on any given date are indicated'.

It is simply says, Bank reconciliation statements is a list of items that cause a difference between the bank balance as per cash book and pass book on any given date.

Cash book is a book of original entry in which all the deposits and withdrawals enteredday by day in a chronological order.

Pass book is a copy of details of customers' account which is given by a bank to its customers in the form of a statement of a book.

5.2 BANK PASS BOOK

Bank Pass Book (statement of account) is merely a copy of the customer's account in the books of a bank. It shows all the deposits, withdrawals and the balance available in the customer's account. The main point to be remembered is that entries are made only after cashis received or paid, except in the case of interest and bank charges. Interest and bank charges are mere book adjustments and in these, there are neither receipt of cash nor payment of cash.

Bank Pass Book

Date	Particulars	Dr. Withdrawals ₹	Cr. Deposits ₹	Balance Dr/Cr ₹	Initials

5.3 BANK RECONCILIATION STATEMENT

The balance of the bank column in the cash book represents the customers cash balance at bank. It should be the same as shown by his bank pass book on any particular day.For every entry made in the cash book if there is a corresponding entry in the pass book (maintained by the banker) or vice versa, the bank balance will be the same in both the books.

But in practice, the balances generally differ. In case of disagreement in the balance ofthe cash book and the pass book, the need for preparing Bank Reconciliation Statement arises.

5.4 CAUSES OF DISAGREEMENT BETWEEN THE BALANCE SHOWN BY CASHBOOK AND PASS BOOK

1. **Cheques paid into bank but not yet collected**
   The cheques paid into bank for collection but not credited into the account of thecustomer, because the cheque is
   i. Not collected and credited till that date.
   ii. Collected but the bank staff has forgotten to make entry.
   iii. Collected but credited to wrong account.
   iv. Dishonoured.
      As soon as the cheques are sent to the bank, entries are made in the debit side of the cash book (bank column). But, usually bank credit the customer's account only when they have received payment from the bank.
2. **Cheques issued but not yet presented for payment**
   The cheques issued but not debited customers account may be because the cheque is:
   i.) Not cashed till date.
   ii.) Not presented till date.
   iii.) Presented but dishonoured for some reasons or others.
   iv.) Lost by the party to whom the cheque was issued.

In all of the above cases, the entry in the cash book is made immediately on the issue of cheque but naturally the entry will be made by bank only when the cheque ispresented for payment. Thus, there will be a gap of some days between the entry for issue of cheque in the cash book and the entry for payment made in the pass book.

3. **Amount credited in the pass book without knowledge of the customer**

   The following are some of the examples for the above statement.

   i.) The bank might have collected rent, dividend, bills of exchange, interest etc.,

   ii.) Some debtors might have directly paid into bank.

   iii.) Bank credits interest on the credit balance of the customer's account.

   iv.) The banker has wrongly credited this account instead of some other account.

   In all the above cases, the entry will be first entered in the pass book. The customer will know this only after verifies the entries in the pass book. So there may be a timegap of some days before the customer includes entries made in the pass book.

4. **Amounts debited in the pass book without knowledge of the customer**

   The following are some of the examples for this.

   i.) The banker has recorded bank charges, interest on overdraft etc.

   ii.) The banker has paid insurance premium, subscription for periodicals, etc.

   iii.) The banker has wrongly debited this account instead of some other account.

   iv.) The banker has paid the bills payable of the customer.

   v.) Dishonour of a cheque deposited and discounted bills receivable

In all the above cases, the entry will be first entered in the pass book of the customer. And the customer will know only after verifies the entries in the pass bookor statement of account. So there may be a time gap of some days before the customerincludes the entries made in the pass book.

5.5 BANK OVERDRAFT

Bank overdraft is an amount drawn over and above the actual balance kept in the bank account. This facility is available only to the current account holders. Interest will be charged for the amount overdrawn i.e., overdraft. The Cash book will show a credit balance i.e., unfavourable balance. The pass book will show a debit balance.

For easy reference the table given below will be useful.

Book	Favourable Balance	Unfavourable Balance (Overdraft)
Cash	Debit	Credit
Pass	Credit	Debit

Favourable balance means the cash book will have a debit balance and the passbookwill have a credit balance.

Unfavourable balance or Bank **overdraft** means cash book will have a credit balanceand passbook will have debit balance.

5.6 ADVANTAGES OF BANK RECONCILIATION STATEMENT

After tracing the various items of differences bank reconciliation statement is prepared. The following are the advantages in which lies its importance.

- The errors that right have taken place in the cash book in correction with banktransactions can be easily found.
- Regular preparation of bank reconciliation statement prevents frauds.

- It indirectly imposes moral check on the accounting staff.
- By the preparation of BRS uncredited cheques can be detected and steps can betaken for their collection.

5.7 DIFFERENCES BETWEEN CASH BOOK AND PASS BOOK

Basis of Distinction	Cash Book	Pass Book
1. Maintained by	Cashier	Banker
2. Deposits of cash	Entered on the debit side ofthe cash book	Entered on the credit column of the pass book
3. Withdrawals of cash	Entered on the credit of thecash book	Entered on the debit column of the pass book
4. Cheques deposited for collection	Entered on the debit side ofthe cash book on the date ofdepositing the cheques intothe bank	Entered in the passbook only on the date of therealization of the cheque.
5. Cheqes issued	Entered on the credit side ofthe cash book on the date ofissuing the cheque to the creditors	Entered on the debit column of the pass book only which they arepresented and paid.
6. Collections and paymentsas per customer standing instruction	Entered in the cash bookafter seeing the pass	Entered in the pass bookfirst
7. Signature	It is not signed by thecashier	It is signed by the bank official after each transaction.

Basis of Distinction	Cash Book	Pass Book
8. Balancing	It is balanced at the end of aspecified period	It is balanced after eachtransaction.

Proforma

BRS AS ON ....

Cash Book

	Bank balance as per Cash book	xxx		Bank over draft as per Cashbook	xxx
1	Cheque deposited but not yetcleared / credited/ collected	xxx	1	Cheque issued but not yetpresented for payment	xxx
2	Cheque entered in cash book butnot yet deposited	xxx			
3	Cheque deposited but not yetentered in cash book	xxx			

Pass Book

	Bank overdraft as per Passbook	xxx		Bank over draft as per Cash book	xxx
1	Interest on over draft	xxx	1	Interest on deposits / investment	xxx
2	Bank charges	xxx	2	Direct present by customer	xxx

	Bank overdraft as per Passbook	xxx		Bank over draft as per Cash book	xxx
3	Dishonoured cheque / bill	xxx	3	Interest collected on behalf of customers	xxx
4	Insurance premium paid onbehalf of customers	xxx	4	Dividend collected on behalf of customers	xxx
5	Electricity bill paid on behalfof customers	xxx	5	Rent collected on behalf of customers	xxx
6	Amount is wrong debited inthis book	xxx	6	Amount is wrong credited in thisbook	xxx

Specimen

Bank Reconciliation Statement

Particulars	₹	₹
Bank balance as per Cash book		xxx
Add: Opposite side items:		
(1)	xxx	
(2)	xxx	
(3)	xxx	xxx
		xxx
Less: Same side items		
(1)	xxx	
(2)	xxx	
(3)	xxx	xxx
Bank balance as per Pass book		xxx

Problem 1: From the following details, make out a bank reconciliation statement for M/s.Mukesh & Company as on December 31, 2013 to find out the balance as per pass book.

1. Cheques deposited but not yet collected by the Bank ₹1,500
2. Cheque issued to Mr.Raju has not yet been presented for payment ₹ 2,500
3. Bank charges debited in the pass book ₹ 200
4. Interest allowed by the bank ₹ 100
5. Insurance premium directly paid by the bank as per standing instructions ₹ 500
6. Balance as per cash book ₹ 200

Solution:

Bank Reconciliation Statement as on December 31, 2013

Particulars	₹	₹
Balance as per Cash Book		200
Add: Cheques issued to Mr.Raju but not presented for payment	2,500	
Interest allowed by bank but not recorded in cash book	100	2,600
		2,800
Less: Cheques deposited but not credited by the bank	1,500	
	500	
Bank has paid insurance premium	200	2,200
Bank charges as per pass book		600
Balance as per Pass Book		

Problem 2: From the following particulars of Mr. Suman, prepare a bank reconciliation statement as on 31.12.2015.

1.   Balance as per cash book on 31.12.2015 was ₹ 15,000

2.   Cheque for ₹ 8,000 were deposited on December out of which only cheques for ₹2,000 were presented for payment in December 2015

3.   Banker has debited bank charges of ₹ 25 for which no entry has been made in cashbook.

4.   Cheque issued but not presented for payment of ₹ 1000

Solution:

Bank Reconciliation Statement of Mr. Suman as on December 31, 2015

Particulars	₹	₹
Balance as per Cash Book		15,000
Add: Cheques issued but not presented for payment	1,000	1,000
		16,000
Less: Cheques deposited but not collected by the bank	6,000	
Bank charges as per pass book	25	6,025
Balance as per Pass Book		9,975

Problem 3: From the under mentioned particulars of Mr.M.Mohan prepare a BankReconciliation Statement on 31st July, 2014.

1.   Cheques paid into Bank on the 28th July 2014 but credited to Mohan's A/c in thefirst week of Aug.2014.

K.Kalyan ₹ 1,000   J.Joy ₹ 800   R. Raghul ₹ 1200

2.   The following cheques were issued by Mohan on 30th July 2014 but presented toBank for payment after the close of the year.

D.David ₹ 1,200   H.Hari ₹ 1,000   L.Lal ₹ 800

3. A cheque for ₹ 300 was credited directly to the account and was not passed through the cash book.

4. The Bank balance as per cash book on 31st July 2014 amounted to ₹ 30,000

Solution:

Bank Reconciliation Statement as on July 31, 2014

Particulars		₹	₹
	Balance as per Cash Book		30,000
Add:	Cheques issued to but not Collected		
	D.David	1,200	
	H.Hari	1,000	
	L.Lal	800	3,000
	Cheques directly deposited to bank		300
			33,300
Less:	Cheques deposited but not collected		
	K.Kalyan	1,000	
	J.Joy	800	
	R.Raghul	1,200	3,000
	Balance as per Pass Book		30,300

Problem 4: Mrs.Jame's pass book showed a balance of ₹ 25,000 on June 30, 2013. Her cashbook shows a different balance. On examination, it is found that

1. No record has been made in the cash book for a dishonour of a cheque for ₹ 250
2. Cheques paid into bank amounting to ₹ 3,500 were paid into the bank on June 28,2013 and the same had not been entered in the pass book.
3. Bank charges of ₹ 300 have not been entered in the cash book.
4. Cheques amounting to ₹ 9,000 issued to Ms.Devi has not been presented forpayment till.
5. Mr. Balu who owed ₹ 3,000 has directly paid the sum into the bank account

You are required to prepare a Bank reconciliation statement and ascertain the balanceas per cash book.

Solution:

Bank Reconciliation Statement as on June 30, 2013

Particulars	₹	₹
Balance as per Pass Book		25,000
Add: Dishonour of cheque not recordedin cash book	250	
Cheques paid into bank, not collected	3,500	
Bank charges as per pass booknot entered in the cash book	300	4,050
		29,050
Less: Cheques issued but not presentedfor payment	9,000	
Amount directly paid by Mr.Baluinto the bank	3,000	12,000
Balance as per Cash Book		17,050

Problem 5: On 31st March 2014 the Pass book showed the credit balance of ₹ 10,500 giventhat:

a) Cheques amounting to ₹ 2,520 was deposited in the bank but only cheques for ₹ 750 had not been cleared up to 31st March.

b) Cheques amounting to ₹ 3,500 were issued, but cheques for ₹ 1,200 has not beenpresented for payment in the bank upto 31st March

c) Bank had given the debit of ₹ 35 for sundry charges

d) Bank had received directly from customer ₹ 800 and dividend of ₹ 130 upto 31stMarch.

Solution:

Bank Reconciliation Statement as on 31st March 2014

Particulars	₹	₹
Balance as per Pass Book		10,500
Add: Cheques paid into bank, not collected	750	
Bank charges debited in the pass book	35	785
		11,285
Less: Cheques issued but not presented for payment	1,200	
Amount directly deposited by customer	800	
Dividend collected by bank	130	2,130
Balance as per Cash Book		9,155

Problem 6: Prepare a Bank Reconciliation Statement as at June 30, 2012 for M/s.Jothi Sales Private Limited from the information given below.

1. Bank overdraft as per Cash book ₹ 1,10,450

2. Cheques issued on June 20, 2012 but not yet presented for payment ₹ 15,000

3. Cheques deposited but not yet credited by bank ₹ 22,750

4. Bills receivable directly collected by bank ₹ 47,200

5. Interest on overdraft debited by bank ₹ 12,115

6. Amount wrongly debited by bank ₹ 2,400

Solution:

Bank Reconciliation Statement as on June 30, 2012

Particulars	₹	₹
Overdraft balance as per Cash book		1,10,450
Add: Cheques deposited but not yet credited	22,750	
Interest on overdraft debited by bank	12,115	
Wrong debited by bank	2,400	37,265
		1,47,715
Less: Cheques issued but not presented for payment	15,000	
Bills receivable collected by bank	47,200	62,200
Overdraft balance as per Pass Book		85,515

Problem 7: From the following particulars ascertain the bank balance as per pass book ofMr.Ramayan as on 31st December 2015

1. The bank overdraft (Cr) as per cash book on 31st December 2015 was ₹15,000

2. Interest on overdraft for six months ending 31st December 2015, debited in thepass book ₹ 600

3. Bank charges for the above period also debited in the pass book amounted to ₹ 150

4. Cheques issued but not cashed before 31st December 2015, ₹ 4,000

5. Cheques paid into bank but not cleared and credited before 31st December 2015,were for ₹ 5,000

6. Interest on investments collected by the banker and credited in the pass bookamounted to ₹ 3,500

Solution:

Bank Reconciliation Statement as on 31.12.2015

Particulars	₹	₹
Overdraft balance as per Cash book		15,000
Add Interest on overdraft not entered in the cash book	600	
Bank charges debited in the pass book	150	
Cheques paid into bank but not yet cleared	5,000	5,750
		20,750
Less Cheques issued but not cashed	4,000	
Interest on investments credited by the bank but not entered in the cash book	3,500	7,500
Over draft as per Pass Book		13,250

Problem 8: Ms.Haritha gives you the following information regarding her bank account. It shows an overdraft balance of ₹ 6,500 on March 31, 2010. This does not agree with the cashbook balance.

1. Cheques amounting to ₹ 15,000 were paid into bank out of which, only chequesamounting to ₹ 4,500 were credited by the bank.

2. Cheques issued during March amounted in all to ₹ 11,000, out of these, chequesamounting to ₹ 3000 were unpaid till March 31, 2003.

3. The bank has wrongly debited account No.1 with ₹ 500 in respect of a chequedrawn on account No.2.

4. The account stands debited with ₹ 150 for interest and ₹ 30 for bank charges.

5. The bank has paid the annual subscription of ₹100 to club according to instructions.

    You are required to ascertain balance as per cash book

Solution:

Bank Reconciliation Statement as on March 31, 2010

Particulars	₹	₹
Overdraft balance as per Pass book		6,500
Add Cheques issued but not presented for payment	3,000	3,000
		9,500
Less Cheques paid into bank but not collected (₹15000- ₹ 4,500)	10,500	
Wrong debit in pass book in account No.1 instead of account No.2	500	
Interest and bank charges not entered in the cash book (₹ 150+ ₹ 30)	180	
Subscription paid as per standing Instruction	100	11,280
Balance as per Cash Book (Favourable)		(1780)

Problem 9: From the following particulars prepare a reconciliation statement as on 31.12.2013. Balance as per pass book on 31.12.2013 overdrawn ₹ 10,260

- a) Cheques drawn on 31.12.2013 but not cleared till January, 2014 ₹ 3,225, ₹ 775 and ₹ 926
- b) Bank overdraft interest charged on 20.12.2013 not entered in the cash book ₹ 1,610
- c) Cheque received on 29.12.2013 entered in the cash book but not deposited to banktill 2nd January 2014 ₹ 11,322 and 1,730
- d) Cheque amounting to ₹ 30 entered in the cash book twice
- e) Bills receivable due on 28.12.2013 was sent to the bank for collection on 27.12.2013 and was entered in the cash book

forthwith, but the proceeds were notcredited in the bank pass book till 1.1.2014 ₹ 2,980

f)   A periodic payment by bank of ₹ 40 understanding instructions not entered in cashbook

g)   Cheque deposited on 30th November 2013 dishonoured, but the entry there of notmade in cash book ₹ 1,890

Solution:

Bank Reconciliation Statement as on 31st December 2013

Particulars		₹	₹
	Overdraft balance as per Pass book		10,260
Add	Cheques drawn but not cleared till January2013:	3,225	
		775	
		926	
		30	4,956
	Cheque entered in the cash book twice		15,216
Less			
		1,610	
	Interest on overdraft not entered in the cashbook	11,322	
		1,730	
	Cheque received but not deposited in to bank:	2,980	
		40	
	Proceeds of bill receivables entered in the cash book but not in the pass book		
	Periodic payment understanding instructionnot entered in the cash book	1,890	19,572
			(4,356)
	Dishonor entry in respect of a cheque not made in the cash book		
	Balance as per Cash Book (Favorable)		

QUESTIONS

FILL IN THE BLANKS:

1. The bank statement is sent by_to the customer.
2. Overdraft means credit balance as per_book.
3. When cash is withdrawn from the bank, the bank_______________ the customer's account.
4. ____ balance in pass book shows bank overdraft.
5. For the purposes of reconciliation only the_____column of the cash book are to beconsidered.
6. A bank reconciliation statement is prepared by the_____.

> [**Answers:** 1. Bank,   2. Cash,   3. Debit,
>   4. Debit,   5. Bank,   6. Customers]

CHOOSE THE CORRECT ANSWER:

1. Bank Reconciliation statement is prepared by the
   a)   Bank   b) Creditor of a business
   c)   Customer of a bank
2. Debit balance in the Cash Book means
   a)   Overdraft as per Pass Book
   b)   Credit balance as per Pass Book
   c)   Overdraft as per Cash Book
3. When balance as per Cash Book is the starting point, to ascertain balance as per pass book interest allowed by Bank is
   a) Subtracted   b) Added   c) Not adjusted
4. When balance as per Cash Book is the starting point, to ascertain the balance as per pass book interest charged by Bank is:
   a) Added   b) Subtracted   c) Not adjusted

5. When the balance as per Cash Book is the starting point to ascertain balance as per pass book, direct deposits by customers are

   a) Added   b) Subtracted   c) Not adjusted

6. When the balance as per Cash Book is the starting point to ascertain balance as per pass book, direct payment by bank are:

   a) Added   b) Subtracted   c) Not adjusted

7. A bank pass book is a copy of

   a) The cash column of a customer's cash book.

   b) The bank column of a customer's cash book.

   c) The customer's account in the bank's ledger.

8. Bank reconciliation statement is

   a) a part of cash book   b) a ledger account

   c) a part of transaction

9. Favourable balance as per cash book means

   a) Debit balance in the bank column of the cash book

   b) Debit balance in the pass book

   c) Neither of the two

10. Unfavourable bank balance means

   a) Credit balance in the cash book

   b) Credit balance in the pass book

   c) Debit balance in the pass book

[Answers: 1. (c), 2. (b), 3. (b), 4. (b), 5. (a), 6. (b), 7. (c),8 (a), 9 (a), 10 (a)]

OTHER QUESTIONS

---

1. What is a Bank Pass Book?
2. What is a BRS?
3. When can bank reconciliation be prepared?
4. Who prepares a bank statement?

5. Why is the preparation of Bank Reconciliation Statement necessary?
6. List the five items having the effect of higher balance in the Cash Book.

EXERCISES

---

1. From the following particulars prepare a Bank Reconciliation Statement.

   Balance on 31.12.2005 as per pass book ₹ 4,500

   Four cheques drawn on 31st December 2005 but not cleared till January the followingamount ₹ 150, ₹ 1,000, ₹ 100, ₹ 250

   Interest on investments not entered in cash book ₹ 500 Bank charges ₹ 50 debited in the pass book

   Chamber of Commerce subscription ₹ 100 paid by bank on 31.12.2005 but not enteredin cash book.

   Cheques for ₹ 4,000 sent for collection not entered in the pass book

   (Answer: Balance as per Cash Book ₹ 6,650)

2. From the following particulars, prepare the Bank Reconciliation Statement of Mr. Aravinth as on 30th September 2000.

   Balance as per cash book ₹ 6,000

   Cheque issued to a creditor but not presented for payment ₹1,500

   Cheque is presented but not collected by bank ₹ 400

   The bank debited ₹ 100 for bank charges

   An amount of ₹ 250 credited in the pass book only for dividends.

   (Answer: Balance as per Pass Book ₹ 7,250)

3. On checking the bank pass book it was found that is showed an overdraft of ₹ 5,200 as on31.12.2004 while as per ledger it was ₹ 150 to bank's debit.

   a) Cheques deposited but not yet credited by bank ₹ 6,000

b) Cheques dishonoured and debited by bank but not given effect to in the ledger ₹ 800

c) Bank charges debited by bank but debit memo not received from bank ₹ 50

d) Interest on overdraft excess credited in the ledger ₹ 200

e) Wrongly credited by the bank to the account deposit of some other party ₹ 900

f) Cheques issued but not presented for payment ₹ 400

   You are required to prepare a Bank Reconciliation Statement as on 31.12.2004

4. From the following particulars prepare a bank reconciliation statement as on 31st March1992

   1. Balance as per pass book ₹ 10,500
   2. Cheques deposited but not cleared upto 31st March ₹ 750
   3. Cheques issued but not presented for payment ₹ 1,200
   4. Sundry charges debited by the bank ₹ 35
   5. Bank received deposits directly from customers ₹ 930

(Answer: Balance as per Cash Book ₹ 9,155)

5. Prepare Bank Reconciliation Statement

   Overdraft as per Pass book ₹ 2000

   Two cheques from Prasanth for ₹ 200 and ₹ 400 were deposited with the bank butwere still not collected by the bank.

   A cheque for ₹ 1,000 issued to Mr. Z not yet presented to the bank for paymentInterest on overdraft ₹100 appears in the pass book.

(Answer: Over draft as per Cash Book ₹ 2,300)

6. From the following particulars, prepare Bank Reconciliation Statement as on 31.3.2010

   a) Overdraft balance as per pass book ₹ 8000
   b) Cheques issued but not enchased ₹ 3100
   c) Cheques deposited into bank but yet collected ₹ 1800

d) The debit of ₹ 950 in pass book for interest is not entered in cash book

e) ₹ 1750 paid into bank by customers directly is not entered in the cash book

f) Dividend collected by the bank ₹ 500

(Answer: Over draft balance as per Cash Book ₹ 10,600)

7. From the following particulars ascertain the balance by means of a statement that wouldappear in the pass book of Mr. Abishek as on 31st December 2005

   a) Overdraft balance as per cash book ₹ 4,558

   b) Interest on overdraft for six months ending 31st December 2005 ₹ 120

   c) Bank charges debited in the pass book ₹ 24

   d) Cheques drawn but not cashed by the customers prior to 31st December 2005 ₹ 1,326

   e) A bills receivable originally discounted with the bank in November 2005 is dishonored ₹ 800

(Answer: Overdraft balance as per Pass Book ₹ 6,588)

8. From the following information, prepare Bank Reconciliation Statement and find the balance as per pass book.

   1. Overdraft balance as per Cash book ₹ 12,000

   2. Interest on overdraft ₹ 400 recorded and debited only in pass book

   3. Bank charges ₹ 100 debited in pass book

   4. Cheques issued but not presented for payment ₹ 3,000

(Answer: overdraft balance as per Pass Book ₹ 9,500)

9. Draw up a Bank Reconciliation Statement from the following particulars of Mr.Ganapathy as on 31.12.2015

   Balance as per cash book on 31.12.2015 was ₹10,000

   Cheques of ₹10,000 were paid on 25th December but collected in January 2016

Cheques of ₹ 4,000 were issued in December out of which only cheques of ₹ 2,500 were presented for payment in December 2015

Bank charged ₹ 15 as incidental charge for which no adjustment was made in the cashbook.

(Answer: Balance as per Pass Book ₹ 1,485)

10. From the following details prepare a Bank Reconciliation Statement

Over draft as per cash book ₹ 2,000

A cheque deposited into bank but not collected by bank ₹ 560

A cheque issued to the customer but not presented for payment ₹ 1,350

An amount of ₹ 905 directly credited in the pass book for interest on investment

The bank debited customer's account for ₹ 80 as bank charges. This fact not yet entered in cash book.

(Answer: Overdraft balance as per Pass Book ₹ 385)

Chapter 6

FINAL ACCOUNTS

6.1 INTRODUCTION

The main aim of accounting is to supply maximum accounting data through financialstatements or final accounts. The final accounts consist of two statements. They are Profit and Loss Account and Balance Sheet. The Profit and Loss Account is otherwise called income Statement. Both manufacturing concerns and trading concerns are preparing profit and loss account. This account is prepared to know the operating results of the business concern during a specific period.

Nonprofit organization and charitable institutions are preparing income and expenditure account in the case of joint stock Company, the profit and Loss account should show true and fair view of the profit earned or loss suffered during the specific period. Trading account is the part of Profit and Loss account.

All the manufacturing concerns, trading concerns nonprofit organizations and charitable trust are required to prepare Balance Sheet. The balance sheet should be preparedto give a true and fair view of the financial position at the end of the specific period.

The Profit and Loss Account gives the information of operating results of the business concern as profit earned or loss suffered for a specific period. The revenues or incomes earned and other gains made by the business concern are recorded on the credit side of the profit and loss account. The amount spent to earns the revenues or incomes and other lossessuffered by the business concern are recorded on the debit side of the Profit and Loss Account. If credit side of Profit and Loss account is more than the debit side, the difference isthe profit earned by the business concern for a specific period. If debit side of profit and lossaccount is more than the credit side, the difference is loss suffered by the business concern fora specific period.

The balance sheet is prepared to show assets and properties of the business concern onone side and show capital and liabilities on the other side. In other words, the sources of finance and liabilities of third parties are showing on one side of Balance Sheet and ways ofutilizing the sources of finance are showing on the other side of Balance Sheet. The financial position of the company is disclosed in the balance sheet as on a specified date.

The financial position of the business concern is affected by its operating results. If abusiness concern suffers a loss, the loss amount is deducted from the balance of capital account. If so, the capital account balance is reduced. Likewise, if a business concern earnsprofit, it is added with capital account balance. If so, the balance of capital account is increased. Hence, it is assured that there is a matching of revenues and expenses. If revenue ismore than expense, it is profit. If expense is more than revenue, it is loss. Therefore, it is future proved that matching principle is followed to prepare final accounts.

6.2 STEPS IN PREPARATION OF FINAL ACCOUNTS

The following steps are taken by an accountant while preparing final accounts.

   i   **Preparation of Trial balance:** Trial balance should be prepared before preparing trading and profit & loss account and balance sheet. If the trial balance do not get tally, the difference is provisionally transferred to suspense account. If debit balance of trial balance is more than credit balance, the difference is transferred to suspenseaccount and shown in the liabilities side of the balance sheet and vice versa.

ii   Showing of Trial Balance items: All the items of trial balance are showing in only one place of finance accounts i.e. either in trading account or profit and loss account or balance sheet.

iii   Posting of Trial balance: Accounts appearing at the debit side of trial balance are shown at the debit side of trading and profit & loss account or at the asset side of the balance sheet and vice versa.

iv   Posting of expenses: All the **direct expenses** are posted on the **debit side** of manufacturing account and trading account. All the **indirect expenses** are posted on the **debit side** of profit and loss account. All the factory expenses are direct expenses. All the office expenses are indirect expenses.

v   Personal accounts: Some personal expenses are showing debit balance and some more personal expenses are showing credit balances. If personal accounts are showing debit balances, these are recorded on the asset side of the balance sheet and vice versa.

vi   Real Account: All the real accounts are showing debit balance. If so, these are recorded on the asset side of balance sheet. Sometimes, cash at bank may show credit balance. This is possible if Overdraft (O.D) arrangement is made by the business concern. It is shown on liabilities side of the balance sheet.

vii   Treatment of rent discount, interest and commission: Rent, discount, interest and commission may be expenses, if so, there are sowing debit balance. In this case, these are recorded on the debit side of profit and loss account. Sometimes, rent, discount, interest and commission may be an income of the business concern. If so, these are showing credit balance. In this case, these are recorded on the credit side of profit and loss account. If the trial balance is not given any specific word as allowed or received, these items should be treated as expenses and posted to the debit side of the profit and loss account.

6.3 MANUFACTURING ACCOUNT

Manufacturing account is prepared to know the cost of production of finished goods. Hence, the value of raw materials utilized is taken into account along with the expenses incurred for the conversion of raw materials into finished goods. Manufacturing companies are preparing manufacturing account.

Dr	Cash		Cr
Particulars	₹	**Particulars**	₹
To Opening stock of raw materials	xxx	By Closing stock of raw materials	xxx
To Purchase of raw materials	xxx	By Closing stock of work in progress	xxx
To Direct wages	xxx	By Sales of scrap	
To Direct expenses	xxx	By Sales of scrap	xxx
To Carriage on purchase	xxx	By Cost of goods manufacturing	xxx
To Factory lighting	xxx	(b/f)	
To Factory rent	xxx		
To Factory wages	xxx		
To Depreciation on factory plant	xxx		
To Factory Supervisor salary	xxx		
To Opening work in progress	xxx		
	xxx		xxx

6.4 TRADING ACCOUNT

Trading accounting is prepared for a specific period to know the operating results of the business. Trading account is prepared by the trading concern. Sometimes, a business concern is doing both manufacturing function and trading function. If so, such business concern is also preparing trading account.

Some business concerns are buying goods and selling the same to customers withoutmaking any modifications in the goods. Such types of business concerns are also preparingthe trading account. It is prepared to find the gross profit or loss. In the trading account, thecost of goods sold and sales revenue is taken into considered to find the gross profit or loss. If cost of goods sold is more than the sales revenue, the difference is gross loss and vice versa.

The term cost of goods sold refers to the value of goods purchased which are sold along with the direct expenses incurred for maintaining goods in saleable condition.

i Preparation of Trading Account

Trading account is a ledger account. Hence, this account is prepared according to thedouble entry principles. Moreover, this account discloses the operating results of one business concern. Hence, the opening stock, purchase less returns and all direct expenses are recordedon the debit side of trading account. Both sales less returns and closing stock are recorded onthe credit of the trading account. The trading result may be either gross profit or gross loss.

ii Valuation of closing stock

Closing stock refers to the stock lying as unsold in the godown or shop on the last dateof accounting period. Generally, the value of closing stock is given outside the trial balance,in that case it is shown on the credit side of trading account and asset side of balance sheet. Sometimes, the value of closing stock is given inside the trial balance, it is not to be shown onthe credit of trading account but appears only on the balance sheet as asset. Closing stock should be valued at cost price or market price whichever is less.

To ascertain the value of closing stock it is necessary to appoint an individual to prepare complete inventory list kept in the godowns together with quantities. On the basis of physical observation and verification, the stock lists are prepared and the total value is calculated on the basis of unit value. The cost price remains constant. At the same time, each item of stock is valued on the basis of may valuation methods.

6.5 TRADING ACCOUNT CLOSING ENTRIES

The following closing entries are passed to transfer various accounts in the tradingaccount.

1. For transferring all accounts shown on the debit side of trading account

    Trading a/c   Dr
        To Opening Stock a/c
        To Purchase a/c
        To Sales Returns a/c
        To Wages a/c
        To Fright and Octroi a/c

2. For transferring all accounts shown on the credit side of trading account

    Sales a/c   Dr
        To Trading a/c

3. For bringing closing stock into books

    Closing stock a/c   Dr
        To Trading a/c

4. If trading account shows gross profit, the following closing entry is passed

    Trading a/c   Dr
        To Profit and Loss a/c

5. If trading account shows gross loss, the following closing entry is passed.

    Profit and Loss a/c   Dr
        To Trading a/c

CLOSING ENTRIES

All the expenses, revenues, loss, incomes and gains are not carried over to the succeeding accounting year. Hence, these accounts should be closed at the end of the each accounting year. These accounts are transferred to either trading account or profit and loss account by passing a journal entry. A journal entry is required to transfer the balance and ledger account into trading account or profit and loss account. Such journal entries are called closing entries.

Closing entries are passed to close the accounts which are of revenue nature and theseaccounts are not carried over to the succeeding accounting year. Both gross profit or loss andnet profit or loss is ascertained with the help of passing closing entries. Other than nominal accounts are not closed at the end of the accounting year personal accounts is closed only when actual receipts or payments of money are made. The real accounts such as land and building account, plant and machinery account, furniture and fittings account etc are not closed but balance. Hence, the balances of personal account and real accounts are shown in the balance sheet. No closing entry is required to close the accounts of assets and liabilities.

6.6 PARTS OF FINAL ACCOUNTS

The final accounts include two parts. The first part is Trading and Profit & Loss Account. This is prepared to find out the net result of the business. The second part is BalanceSheet which is prepared to know the financial position of the business.

i   **Trading Account**

This account is prepared to know the trading results of the business. Trading means buying and selling. The trading account shows the result of buying and selling during a particular period. At the end of each year, it is necessary to ascertain the net profit or net loss. The difference between the sales and cost of goods sold is Gross Profit. For this purpose, it is first necessary to know the gross profit or gross loss. The balance of this account represents gross profit or gross loss and is to be transferred to the profit and loss account.

Proforma

Dr	Trading Account of_____		Cr	
	for the year ended______			
Particulars	₹	**Particulars**		₹
To Opening stock	xxx	By Sales	xxx	
To Purchase	xxx	Less: Sales returns	xxx	xxx
Less: Purchase return	xxx xxx	(or) Return inwards	xxx	
(or) Return outwards	xxx	Less: Sales Tax	xxx	xxx
To Manufacturing Wages	xxx	By Sale of Scrap		xxx
To Freight	xxx	By fire / theft – (related to		
To Carriage inwards	xxx	Insurance claim)	xxx	
To Carriage on purchase	xxx	By Any other **Direct Income**	xxx	
To Fuel and Power	xxx	By Closing stock	xxx	
To Cartage	xxx	By Gross Loss c/d	xxx	
To Import duty / Excise	xxx	(Carried to P & L a/c)		
To Local Taxes	xxx			
To Royalties	xxx			
To Oil	xxx			

To Customs duty	xxx		
To Consumable stores	xxx		
To Cleaning Charges	xxx		
To Coal, gas, water	xxx		
To Royalty on Production	xxx		
To Excise duty	xxx		
To Factory Insurance	xxx		
To Factory Rent	xxx		
To Packing Charges	xxx		
To Dock dues	xxx		
To Power (Factory)	xxx		
To Octroi duty	xxx		
To Any manufacturing exp.	xxx		
To any other **Direct Expenses**	xxx		
To Gross Profit c/d	xxx		
(Carried to P & L a/c)	xxx		xxx

ii. Profit and Loss Account

There are certain revenues, incomes, gains etc, to any business concern. Moreover, some indirect expenses are also incurred by business concern to earn above mentioned revenues, incomes and gains. An account is opened to record all types of indirect expenses and revenues, incomes and gains and find the results for a specified period. Such type of account is called Profit and Loss account. According to Prof. Carter. "Profit and Loss account is an account into which all gains and losses are collected in order to ascertain the excess of gains over the losses or vice versa. The Profit and Loss account is opened by recording the gross profit or gross loss. Allthe indirect expenses and losses of business concern for a specific period are deducted from the gross profit or added with gross loss. Then all the operating and noncompeting incomesare added with gross profit or deducted from gross loss to find out either net profit or not lossas the case may be.

This account is prepared to calculate the net profit or net loss of the business during a particular period. A trader has to incur many expenses apart from those spent for purchases and manufacturing of goods. Such expenses are less than gross profit, the result will be net profit and all expenses are more than gross profit the result will be net loss.

The Profit and Loss account is started with recording of either gross profit or gross loss which is transferred from trading account. Both profits earned and losses suffered by a business concern are recorded in one account. Hence, this account heading is recorded as "Profit and Loss account for the year ending….." The main aim of preparing the profit and loss account is finding either net profit earned or let loss suffered by a business concern for aspecific period. The net profit is transferred to and added with capital account. In other words, the net loss is transferred to and deducted from capital account.

6.7   ADVANTAGES OF TRADING ACCOUNT

1. The result of buying and selling can be ascertained by finding out the gross profit.
2. The percentage of gross profit on sales can be ascertained. This percentage can beusefully compared with the results in the preceding years.
3. The stock at commencement can be compared with the stock at end in order to ascertain whether the purchases have been wise.
4. The trading account affords facilities for comparing the figures of sales and direct expenses with those of previous years and draw useful conclusions for increasing theprofitability of the business.
5. The percentage of gross profit serves as a guide in fixing the selling price of the goodsin future.

Special items of Profit and Loss Account

Some expenses and incomes are having special nature. Hence, the understanding of concepts is highly required for preparing profit and loss account. Such special items of profitand loss account are briefly explained below.

Rent: A rent may be either received or paid. If rent is paid, it is an expenses. Hence, rent account is debited in the profit and loss account. In other words,, if rent is received, it isan income. Hence, rent account is credited in the profit and loss account.

Interest: An interest may be either received or paid. If interest is received, it is an income. Hence, interest account is credited in the profit and loss account. In other words, ifan interest is paid, it is an expense. Hence, an interest account is debited in the profit and lossaccount.

Discount: A discount may be either allowed or received. If discount is allowed, it isan expense. Hence, discount account is debited in the profit and loss account. In other words,if discount is received, it is an income. Hence, discount account is credited in the profit andloss account.

Commission: A commission may be either received or paid. If commission is received, it is an income. Hence, commission account is credited in the profit and loss account. In other words, if commission is paid, it is an expense. Hence commission account is debited in the profit and loss account.

Trade expenses: These are the petty expenses connected with the business. Petty expenses are revenue in nature. Hence, trade expenses are debited in the profit and loss account. But in the trial balance, if trade expenses, general expenses, sundry expenses and office expenses are given than the trade expenses should be debited to trading account and the other expenses should be debited to profit and loss account.

Closing entries of Profit and Loss Account

The following closing entries are passed for closing all indirect expenses accounts, loss accounts, operating and non operating income accounts, gain accounts and transferring them to profit and Loss account.

1. For closing all indirect expenses accounts and loss account

   Profit and Loss a/c   Dr

       To General expenses a/c

       To Office expenses

       To Administrative expenses

       To Selling and Distribution expenses

       To Loss a/c

       To Rent Paid a/c

       To Commission Paid a/c

       To Interest Paid a/c

       To Discount allowed a/c

2. For closing all income accounts and gain accounts

   Income a/c   Dr

       Gains a/c   Dr

       Rent received a/c   Dr

       Interest received a/c   Dr

Commission received a/c   Dr
Miscellaneous receipts   Dr
To Profit and Loss a/c

3. If Profit and Loss account shows net profit, the following closing entry is passed.

Capital a/c   Dr
To Profit &Loss a/c

Cr	Profit & Loss Account offor the year ended_____		Cr
Particulars	₹	**Particulars**	₹
To Gross Loss b/d	xxx	By Gross profit b/d	xxx
To Salaries and wages	xxx	By Commission received/ earned	xxx
Add: Outstanding salary	xxx xxx	By Discount received	xxx
To Rent, Rates & Taxes	xxx	By Interest received	xxx
To Commission paid	xxx	By Provision for discount on	xxx
To Agent's Commission	xxx	creditors	
To Discount allowed	xxx	By Interest on Drawings	xxx
To Insurance	xxx	By Rent received	xxx
Less: Prepaid insurance	xxx xxx	By Income from Investments	xxx
To Advertisement	xxx	By Dividend (Cr)	xxx

Cr		Profit & Loss Account offor the year ended______		Cr
Particulars	₹	**Particulars**		₹
To Printing and stationary	xxx	By Miscellaneous income		xxx
To Heating and lighting	xxx	By Profit on sale of assets		xxx
To Interest on Capital	xxx	By Net Loss		xxx
To Interest on Loan	xxx	(Carried to Balance sheet)		
To Electricity	xxx			
To Trade expenses	xxx			
To Sundry expenses	xxx			
To General expenses	xxx			
To Carriage outwards	xxx			
To Carriage on Sales	xxx			
To Travelling expenses	xxx			
To Repairs	xxx			
To Loss on sale of fixed assets	xxx			
To Audit Fees	xxx			
To Postage and telegram	xxx			
To Repacking Charges	xxx			
To Depreciation on assets	xxx			

Cr	Profit & Loss Account of for the year ended_____		Cr
Particulars	**₹**	**Particulars**	**₹**
To Loss by fire	xxx		
To Discount on bills	xxx		
To Conveyance	xxx		
To Legal Charges	xxx		
To Cash defalcations	xxx		
To Loss by Theft	xxx		
To Loss by embeggelement	xxx		
To Brokerage	xxx		
To Samples	xxx		
To Mobile Charges	xxx		
To Sales Tax	xxx		
To Godown Rent	xxx		
To Bank charges	xxx		
To Bad debts	xxx		
(+) Old Bad debts	xxx		
Add: New provision (adjustment)	xxx		
	xxx		
(-) Old Provision for Bad debts	xxx xxx		

Cr		Profit & Loss Account offor the year ended______		Cr
Particulars	₹	**Particulars**		₹
To Reserve for discount onDebtors	xxx			
To General Expenses	xxx			
To Net profit	xxx			
(Carried to Balance sheet)	xxx			xxx

iii) Balance Sheet

The final account has two parts. The first part contains trading account and profit and loss account. The second part contains balance sheet only. A balance sheet is prepared to know the financial position of the business concern at the end of the accounting year. It is prepared with the help of personal account and real account balances appearing in the trial balance. A debit balance in a personal account or real account represents an asset. Acredit balance in a personal account or real account represents a liability.

A Balance sheet is statement prepared with a view to measure the financial position ofa business on a certain fixed date. The financial position of the concern is indicated by its assets on a given date and its liabilities on that date. It is statement and not an account. It is described as a statement showing the sources and application of capital. This statement also called as **"Mirror"** of a business, since the true position of the business is reflected.

An excess of assets over liabilities represents capital. If capital is high, it is an indication of sound financial position of the business concern and vice versa. Hence, a balance sheet is defined as a statement which sets out the assets and liabilities of business firmand which serves to ascertain the financial position of the same on any particular date.

The left hand side of balance sheet shows capital and liabilities. On the right hand side of balance sheet shows assets and properties. Therefore, both left hand side and right hand side are always equal.

a) **Characteristics of Balance Sheet**

1.   It is a statement but not an account
2.   It is prepared on anyone of one date
3.   It has both sides of debit and credit
4.   It shows the financial position of the business concern
5.   It shows what the firm owes to others and also what others owe to the firm
6.   Both sides of balance sheet are always equal
7.   The assets and liabilities are shown either in the order of liquidity or performance

6.8 CLASSIFICATION OF ASSETS

Various assets are held by the business concern. These assets are always showing debit balances. Hence, these are appearing on the assets and properties side of balance sheet.Assets are classified on the following ways.

i   **Fixed assets:** An asset purchased for utilizing for business purpose and not for resale is called fixed assets. They are a permanent nature and are used for effective functioning of business. The maintenance of fixed assets is highly useful for maintaining ad or increasing the profitability of business concern. The fixed assets can be classified as tangible assets and intangible assets.

ii   **Tangible Assets:** An asset can be seen, touch and has a value referred as Tangible assets. For example Plant and Machinery, Furniture and Fittings.

iii   **Intangible Asset:** An asset has no physical existence but has a value. Such type of an asset is called intangible asset. For example goodwill, patents, Trademarks and copyrights.

iv   **Current assets:** It is otherwise called as circulating assets and floating assets. Current assets are those assets which are converted into cash from any form of asset within one year. For example cash in hand, cash at bank, marketable securities, sundry debtors, bills receivable, stock etc.

v   **Liquid assets:** Liquid assets are those assets which are very easily converted into cash at short notice without any risk of loss. For example: Cash in hand, Cash at bank, Marketable securities, Sundry debtors and Bills Receivable.

vi   **Fictitious Assets:** Fictitious assets are those assets which are not having any value at all any benefit are derived from these assets in further operation. Hence, really speaking, these are not assets. But, these are recorded in the books of accounts as assets for the sack of accounting conventions and convenience. Moreover, these balances are written off over a stipulated period of time with the help of profits earned by the company. These assets are shown on the assets and properties side of balance sheet to the extent of balances not written off. Fictitious assets examples are preliminary expenses, expenses on issue of shares and debentures, discount on issue of shares and debentures, debit balance of P & L a/c, advertisement and goodwill.

vii   **Wasting assets:** An asset which has value for a limited period or short period termed as Wasting asset. Hence, high rate of depreciation is provided within the life period of an asset. Generally wasting assets are losing their values with the extraction or removal of a natural product. For example Oil, well, Gas, Mines, Quaries, Gold, Granites, Marbles.

viii   **Contingent Assets:** Contingent assets are those assets which are having existence and value but ownership of such assets is clearly knows on the date of the balance sheet. The ownership is decided in the court of law or happening of a certain event which may or may not take place. According to Kohlar, "Contingent asset refers to an asset the existence, value and ownership of which depends upon the occurrence or nonoccurrence of a specific event or upon the performance or nonperformance of a specified act". For example claim of income tax refund, uncalled share capital ofpublic limited company, bills receivable discounted in a bank, claims by the company for infringement of trademarks or patent or copy right etc. by others and the like. Contingent assets are not shown in the balance sheet but shown as foot note to the balance sheet.

6.9 CLASSIFICATION OF LIABILITIES

Liability is a claim by an outsider against the assets of the business. As per the separate legal entity concept, proprietor of a business concern is also treated as an outsider. Hence, the contribution of proprietor is recorded as capital and shown credit balance in ledger.In this way, the business concern owes to the proprietor up to the balance shown in the capital account. Liabilities are classified in the following ways.

i) **Capital / Net worth:** Capital refers to an amount contributed by the proprietor to starta business unit. Subsequently, proprietor contribute further if need arises and withdrawn if requires. Capital account is credited whenever further contribute in made by the proprietor and debited withdraws amount from the business.

Net worth means an amount of capital outstanding on the particular date plus any profits retained in the business. In other words, total amount belongs to the proprietor, hence, this is shown on the liabilities side of the balance sheet. In the case of a company, equity share holders are contributing capital to start and run a business.

Here, net worth refers to an amount which is to be payable to the equity share holder, reserves and surplus and undistributed profits minus any losses. Preference capital is not included in the net worth, moreover, preference capital is the amount contributedby preference share holders and separately shown on the liabilities side of the balancesheet.

ii) **Long term liabilities:** It is otherwise called fixed liabilities. The liabilities which arerepayable after a long period of time, say, not less than one year. Moreover, these liabilities are not repayable during ordinary course of the business, for example longterm loans, debentures.

iii) **Secured liabilities:** Loans and advances are received from the banks and financial institutions either through mortgage or hypothecation. These types of liabilities are known as secured liabilities. In other words, a charge is created on the assets of the business while receiving loans and advances.

iv) **Unsecured liabilities:** Sometimes, a business concern may obtain loans and advances from outsiders on the basis of goodwill. In this case, there is no mortgage or hypothecation. If so, these types of liabilities are known unsecured liabilities. But, generally no such practice is followed in the business world.

v) **Current liabilities:** An amount is payable within a year or during general operationof the business termed as current liability. The existing resources are used for payingcurrent liabilities. Besides, one more current liability is created to pay off existing current liability.

vi) **Contingent liability:** An amount which may or may not be payable to outsiders during the normal course of the business termed as contingent liability. One cannot predict definitely whether an amount is payable or not. These types of liabilities aregiven below:

   (i)   Bills receivable discounted in a bank and if dishonoured

   (ii) Bills receivable endorsed to creditor or the company and if dishonoured

   (iii) A claim of outsiders pending in a court of law

   (iv) Investments made in the partly paid up equity shares.

Balance Sheet of_as on _________________

Liabilities	₹	Assets	₹
Trade / Sundry Creditors(-)	xxx	Cash in HandCash at Bank	xxxxxx
Discount on CreditorsLoan from Bank	xxx	Trade/ sundry Debtors	xxx
	xxx	(-) Bad debts	xxx
(+) Interest on loan	xxx		
	xxx		xxx
Bank Overdraft	xxxxxx	(-) Provision for Bad debts	xxx
Bills Payable	xxx		xxx
Outstanding expenses	xxx		xxx
Prepaid income Capital			xxxxxx
(+) Additional Capital(+) Net Profit	xxx	(-) Discount on debtorsBills receivable	xxx
	xxx		xxx
	xxx	Land and Building (-) Depreciation Plant & Machinery	xxxxxx
	xxx		xxxxxx
(-) Net Loss	xxx	Freehold Premises	xxxxxx
	xxx	Leasehold premises	xxxxxx
	xxx	Furniture & Fixtures Patents & Copy rights	xxx
(-) Drawings	xxx	Goodwill	xxx
(-) Interest on drawings	xxx	(-) Written off Stock at the end Prepaid expenses Accrued income	
	xxx		
	xxx		
(-) Income Tax	xxx		xxx
(-) Loss if any	xxx		xxx

Hint: Income tax as a Personal expense.

6.10 IMPORTANT TERMS

Operating income: This refers to the incomes which are earned by a businessoperation, such as interest, discount, commission received etc.,

Non Operating Income: This refers to income not earned by business operation, suchas any profit on sale of fixed assets, tax refund etc.

Dock Charges: These are charges levied on ships and their cargoes when entering andleaving docks.

Freight: Refers to transportation cost by Rail, Air or Sea freight inwards.

Carriage: It refers to transportation charge by road particularly by motor lorrytransport.

Cartage: These are expenses incurred in the goods from seller's to the buyer's placeor vice versa.

Customs duty: Paid on goods purchased from foreign country

Excise duty: On goods manufactured in the country is debited to trading account.

Royalty: Is the amount paid by a publisher to the author of a book.

Factory expenses: All direct expenses incurred in the factory e.g. factory rent, motivepower, coal, gas, water, electricity, fuel, heating and lighting etc.

Packing materials: Required for bringing the finished product in a saleable condition.

Loss by fire: If the item is found in the Trial Balance, it is dealt with only once depending on the fact whether the loss is covered by insurance or not.

Consumable stores: Refers to engine oil, cotton waste, grease, soap for washing etc.

Trade expenses: Refers to miscellaneous sundry expenses.

Samples: It means distributed free of charge to push the sales

Income Tax: This is treated as a personal expense and not a business expense, the amount of income tax paid is debited to drawings account and shown as a deduction from capital.

Sales tax: An indirect expense shown on the debit side of profit and loss account.

6.11 DIFFERENCE BETWEEN A TRIAL BALANCE AND BALANCE SHEET

Trial Balance	Balance Sheet
1) A trial balance is a list of all theBalance on the ledger accounts	1) A balance sheet is a statement of Assetsand liabilities of the business.
2) It is prepared before the preparation of the trading and Profit and loss Account	2) A balance sheet is prepared after the preparation of the trading and profit andloss account.
3) The object of trail balance is to test the arithmetical accuracy of Ledger posting	3) The object of the balance sheet is to ascertain the true and fair view of the financial position
4) A trial balance contains the stock atcommencement.	4) The balance sheet includes the closingStock
5) The trial balance is prepared beforeadjusting entries	5) The balance sheet is prepared afteradjusting entries.
6) It contains all kinds of accounts	6) Balance sheet does not contain nominalaccounts

6.12 DIFFERENCE BETWEEN PROFIT AND LOSS ACCOUNT AND BALANCE SHEET

Profit and Loss Account	Balance Sheet
1) It is prepared to find out result of operation of business during an account period	1) It is prepared to portray the financial position of the business at the end of theaccounting period.
2) It records balances of nominalaccounts	2) It shows ledger balances of real, capitalaccounts and personal accounts.
3) Balance of profit and loss account shows net profit or net loss and is transferred to capital account	3) There is no balance in balance sheet. Assets are always equal to capital and liabilities.
4) Principle of double entry is followedto prepare profit and loss account	4) It is a mere statement of assets and liabilities. Hence, principle of double entry is not followed to prepare balance sheet.
5) Closing journal entries are passed toprepare profit and loss account	5) There is no need of passing any journalentry to prepare balance sheet.
6) All revenue accounts are transferredto profit and loss account	6) Only real and personal accounts areused to prepare balance sheet
7) It is prepared for a particular period	7) It is prepared on a particular date.

Problem 1: Prepare a Trading account for the year ended 31st December 2012.

Opening Stock	₹ 5,700	Purchases	₹ 1,58,000
Purchase returns	₹ 900	Sales	₹ 2,62,000
Sales Returns	₹ 600	Closing Stock	₹ 8,800
Wages	₹ 2,000		

Solution:

Trading Account for the year ended 31.12.2012

Particulars		₹	Particulars		₹
To Opening stock		5,700	By Sales	2,62,000	
	1,58,000		Less: Sales return	600	2,61,400
To Purchase	900	1,57,100			8,800
Less: Purchase return		2,000	By Closing stock		
		1,05,400			
To Wages		2,70,200			2,70,200
To Gross Profit c/d					

Problem 2: The following are the balances extracted from the ledger of Mr. Sundaram as on 31st December 2014. Prepare a Trading Account.

	₹		₹
Stock 1.1.2014	12,500	Purchases	78,000
Sales	1,25,000	Returns outwards	3,000
Returns inwards	5,000	Salaries	4,400
Wages	7,500	Rent	2,750
Carriage inwards	3,000	Carriage outwards	750

Closing Stock as on 31.12.2014 was valued at ₹ 14,000.

Solution:

Mr. Sundaram trading Account for the year ended 31.12.2014

Particulars		Amount ₹	Particulars		Amount ₹
To Opening stock (1.1.14)		12,500	By Sales	1,25,000	
To Purchase	78,000		Less: Return inwards	5,000	1,20,000
Less: Return outwards	3,000	75,000	By Closing stock (31.12.2014)		14,000
To Wages		7,500			
To Carriage inwards		3,000			
To Gross Profit c/d		36,000			
		1,34,000			1,34,000

Problem 3: From the following information ascertain gross profit and net Profit.

Stock at opening	₹	2,400	Purchases	₹	15,205
Sales	₹	20,860	Closing stock	₹	3,840
Return outwards	₹	185	Return inwards	₹	860
Carriage inwards	₹	524	Manufacturing wages	₹	2,800
Wages owing	₹	96	Loss due to fire	₹	1,000
Indirect expenses	₹	200			

Solution:

Dr			**Trading Account**		Cr
Particulars		**Amount ₹**	**Particulars**		**Amount ₹**
To Opening Stock		2,400	By Sales	20,860	
To Purchases	15,205		Less: Returns	860	20,000
Less: Returns	185	1,5020	By Closing Stock		3,840
To Carriage inwards		524			
To Manufacturing wages	2,800				
Add: Owing	96	2,896			
To Gross Profit (Transferred to P & L a/c)		3,000			
		23,840			23,840

Dr		**Profit & Loss Account**		Cr
Particulars	**Amount ₹**	**Particulars**		**Amount ₹**
To Loss due to fire	1,000	By Gross Profit (transfer from Trading a/c)		3,000
To Indirect expenses	200			
To Net Profit	1,800			
	3,000			3,000

Problem 4: From the following information ascertain opening stock as on 1.1.2016

Purchase	₹ 2,50,000	Sales	₹ 3,25,000
Stock closing	₹ 60,000	Wages	₹ 3000

Rate of gross profit on cost 25%

Solution:

Dr		Trading Account		Cr
Particulars	**Amount ₹**	**Particulars**	**Amount ₹**	
To Opening Stock	67,000	By Sales	3,25,000	
To Purchases	2,50,000	By Closing Stock	60,000	
To Wages	3,000			
To Gross Profit on cost	65,000			
	3,85,000		3,85,000	

Calculation of Gross Profit

Sales - Cost = Profit

Sales = Profit + Cost

Cost is taken as 100

Sales = 25+100

Sales = 125

If sales is ₹ 125, the profit is ₹ 25

If sales is ₹ 3,25,000, the profit is

25 /125 x 3,25,000

₹ 65,000

Problem 5: Prepare Profit and Loss Account, from the following balances of Mr.Kandan forthe year ending 31.12.2003.

Office rent	₹ 30,000	Salaries	₹ 80,000
Printing expenses	₹ 2,000	Stationeries	₹ 3,000
Tax, Insurance	₹ 4,000	Discount allowed	₹ 6,000
Advertisement	₹ 36,000	Travelling expenses	₹ 26,000
Gross Profit	2,50,000	Discount received	₹ 4,000

Solution:

Profit and Loss account of Mr.Kandan for the year ending 31st Dec.2014

Particulars	Amount ₹	Particulars	Amount ₹
To Salaries	80,000	By Gross Profit	2,50,000
To Office rent	30,000	By Discount received	4,000
To Stationeries	3,000		
To Printing expenses	2,000		
To Tax, Insurance	4,000		
To Discount allowed	6,000		
To Advertisement	36,000		
To Travelling expenses	26,000		
To Net Profit	67,000		
(Transferred to Capital a/c)			
	2,54,000		2,54,000

Problem 6: Prepare a profit and loss account from the following extracted from the trialbalance of Mr.Sri for the year ending 31.12.2013

	₹		₹
Salary	4,000	Discount allowed	400
Insurance	2,000	Bad debts	1,200
Advertisement	1,400	Telephone charges	1,100
Office rent	1,000	Trade expenses	900
Salesmen's salary	3,200	Gross profit	22,000
Carriage inwards	800	Rent received	1,000
Printing & Stationary	1,200		

Solution:

Profit and Loss account of Mr.Sri for the year ending 31ˢᵗ Dec.2013

Particulars	Amount ₹	Particulars	Amount ₹
To Salary	4,000	By Gross Profit	22,000
To Insurance	2,000	By Rent received	1,000
To Advertisement	1,400		
To Office rent	1,000		
To Salesmen's salary	3,200		
To Printing & Stationary	1,200		
To Discount allowed	400		
To Bad debts	1,200		
To Telephone charges	1,100		
To Trade expenses	900		
To Net Profit	6,600		
(Transferred to Capital a/c)			
	23,000		23,000

Problem 7: Prepare Trading and Profit Loss Account for the year ending 31st March 2012 from the books of Mr. Siva Subramanian.

Stock (31.3.2011)	₹ 15,000	Carriage outwards	₹ 4,000
Purchases	₹ 1,65,000	Wages	₹ 30,000
Purchase return	₹ 10,000	Sales return	₹ 5,000
Postage	₹ 3,000	Salaries	₹ 20,000
Discount received	₹ 5,000	Stationeries	₹ 2,000
Bad debts	₹ 1,000	Interest	₹ 8,000
Sales	₹ 3,00,000	Insurance	₹ 4,000
Stock (31.3.2012)	₹ 80,000		

Solution:

Trading and Profit and Loss account of

Mr. Siva Subramanian for the year ended 31st March 2012

Particulars		Amount ₹	Particulars		Amount ₹
To Opening stock		15,000	By Sales	3,00,000	
To Purchases	1,65,000		Less: Sales returns	5,000	2,95,000
Less: Returns	10,000	1,55,000	By Closing Stock		80,000
To wages		30,000			
To Gross Profit		1,75,000			

Particulars	Amount ₹	Particulars	Amount ₹
	3,75,000		3,75,000
To Salaries	20,000	By Gross Profit	1,75,000
To Postage	3,000	By Discount received	5,000
To Bad debts	1,000		
To carriage outwards	4,000		
To Stationeries	2,000		
To Interest	8,000		
To Insurance	4,000		
To Net Profit	1,38,000		
	1,80,000		1,80,000

Problem 8: From the following trial balance of Mr.John, prepare Trading, Profit and LossAccount for the year ending 31.12.2002.

Particulars	Dr ₹	Particulars	Cr ₹
Purchases	5,40,000	Sales	10,40,000
Salaries & wages	3,50,000	Returns outward	12,000
Office expenses	4,000	Discount received	6,000
Trading expenses	8,000	Interest received	3,000
Factory expenses	11,000	Bills Payable	13,000
Carriage inwards	8,000	Sundry Creditors	1,65,000
Returns inward	12,000		
Discount allowed	4,000		
Commission	2,000		

Particulars	Dr ₹	Particulars	Cr ₹
Stock	60,000		
Income tax	40,000		
Cash in hand	2,00,000		
	12,39,000		12,39,000

Closing stock is valued at ₹ 1,35,000

Solution:

Trading and Profit and Loss Account of Mr.John for the year ended 3112.2002

Particulars		Amount ₹	Particulars		Amount ₹
To Stock		60,000	By Sales	10,40,000	
To Purchase	5,40,000		Less: Return outward	12,000	10,28,000
Less: Return inward	12,000	5,28,000	By Closing stock		1,35,000
To Trading expenses		8,000			
To Factory expenses		11,000			
To Carriage inwards		8,000			
To Gross Profit c/d		5,48,000			
		11,63,000			11,63,000
To Salaries & Wages		3,50,000	By Gross Profit b/d		5,48,000
To Office expenses		4,000	By Discount received		6,000
To Discount allowed		4,000	By Interest received		3,000
To Commission		2,000			
To Net Profit		1,97,000			
		5,57,000			5,57,000

Problem 9: Ascertain purchases from the following data.

Cost of goods sold ₹ 80,700

Opening stock ₹ 5,800

Closing stock ₹ 6,000

Solution:

Opening stock + Purchases – Closing stock = Cost of goods sold
Purchases = Cost of goods sold – opening stock + Closing stock
Purchases = ₹ 80,700 – ₹ 5,800 + ₹ 6,000 Purchases = ₹ 80,900

Problem 10: Prepare Trading account of Mr. Xavier for the year ending 31.03.2009

	₹		₹
Sales	8,00,000	Purchases	2,50,000
Stock 1.4.2008	30,000	Wages	20,000
Returns inwards	5,000	Returns outwards	10,000
Carriage inwards	3,000	Octroi	1,000
Freight charges	2,000		

Stock on 31.03.2009 is ₹ 50,000

Solution:

Trading Account of Mr. Xavier for the year ending 31.03.2009

Particulars		Amount ₹	Particulars		Amount ₹
To Opening stock		30,000	By Sales	8,00,000	
To Purchase	2,50,000		Less: Return inwards	5,000	7,95,000
Less: Return outwards	10,000	2,40,000	By Closing stock		50,000
To Wages		20,000			
To Carriage inwards		3,000			
To Octroi		1,000			
To Freight charges		2,000			
To Gross Profit c/d (Transferred to P&L a/c)		5,49,000			
		8,45,000			8,45,000

Problem 11: Prepare Trading and Profit and Loss account of Sri Narayanan Ltd, for the year ending 31st March 2012.

	₹		₹
Stock 1st April 2011	50,000	Sales	2,89,600
Sales returns	9,600	Purchases	2,43,000
Purchase returns	3,000	Freight inwards	4,000
Carriage outwards	6,000	Salaries and wages	30,000

Bank interest paid	2,000	Printing and stationary	7,000
Discount received	900	Discount allowed	600
Audit fee	3,000	Insurance Premium	600
Trade expenses	2,500		

Stock on 31ˢᵗ March 2012 was ₹ 70,000

Solution:

Dr **Trading Account for the year ended 31ˢᵗ March 2012** **Cr**

		₹			₹
To Opening stock		50,000	By Sales	2,89,600	
To Purchases	2,43,000		Less: Sales return	9,600	2,80,000
Less: Purchase returns	3,000	2,40,000	By Closing Stock		70,000
To Fright inwards		4,000			
		56,000			
To Gross Profit (Transferred to P & L a/c)					
		3,50,000			3,50,000

Dr **Profit & Loss Account for the year ended 31ˢᵗ March 2012** **Cr**

	₹		₹
To Carriage outwards	6,000	By Gross Profit	56,000
To Salaries and wages	30,000	By Discount received	900

	₹		₹
To Bank interest paid	2,000		
To Printing and stationary	7,000		
To Discount allowed	600		
To Audit fees	3,000		
To Insurance Premium	600		
To Trade expenses	2,500		
To Net Profit	5,200		
	56,900		56,900

Problem 12: From the following particulars of Joe, prepare a Balance Sheet as on 31.12.2010.

	₹		₹
Capital	1,00,000	Loan to Mr. Johnson	10,000
Building	1,10,000	Investments	6,000
Bills Receivable	7,000	Drawings by Joe	6,000
Furniture	5,000	Cash in hand	7,400
Bills Payable	5,000	Net Profit	77,800
Plant & Machinery	9,000	Sundry Creditors	31,600
Closing stock	14,000	Sundry Debtors	40,000

Solution:

Balance Sheet of Mr.Joe as on 31.12.2010

Liabilities	Amount ₹		Assets	Amount ₹
Capital	1,00,000		Building	1,10,000
(+) Net Profit	77,800		Furniture	5,000
	1,77,800		Plant & Machinery	9,000
(-) Drawings	6,000	1,71,800	Loan to Johnson	10,000
Sundry Creditors		31,600	Investments	6,000
Bills Payable		5,000	Bills receivable	7,000
			Cash in hand	7,400
			Sundry Debtors	40,000
			Closing stock	14,000
		2,08,400		2,08,400

Problem 13: From the following Trial Balance as on 31.12.2014, prepare Profit and Lossaccount and Balance Sheet.

	₹	₹
Capital		1,00,000
Drawings	18,000	
Buildings	15,000	
Furniture	7,500	
Motor van	25,000	
Loan from Mr.Hendry		15,000
Interest paid	900	
Sales		1,00,000

	₹	₹
Purchase	75,000	
Opening stock	25,000	
General expenses	15,000	
Wages	2,000	
Insurance	1,000	
Commission received		7,500
Sundry debtors	28,100	
Cash at bank	20,000	
Sundry creditors		10,000
	2,32,500	2,32,500

Value of closing stock as on 31.12.2014 ₹ 32,000

Solution:

Dr	Trading Account for the year ended 31.12.2014		Cr
Particulars	**Amount ₹**	**Particulars**	**Amount ₹**
To Opening stock	25,000	By Sales	1,00,000
To Purchases	75,000	By Closing Stock	32,000
To Wages	2,000		
To Gross Profit	30,000		
(Transferred to P & L a/c)			
	1,32,000		1,32,000

Dr	**Profit and Loss Account for the year ended 31.12.2014**		**Cr**
Particulars	**Amount ₹**	**Particulars**	**Amount ₹**
To Interest	900	By Gross Profit	30,000
To General expenses	15,000	By Commission	7,500
Particulars	**Amount ₹**	**Particulars**	**Amount ₹**
To Insurance	1,000		
To Net Profit	20,600		
(Transferred to Capital a/c)			
	37,500		37,500

Balance Sheet as on *31.12.2014*

Liabilities		**Amount ₹**	**Assets**	**Amount ₹**
Capital	1,00,000		Buildings	15,000
Less: Drawings	18,000		Furniture	7,500
	82,000		Motor Van	25,000
Add: Net Profit	20,600	1,02,600	Sundry Debtors	28,100
Loan from Mr. Hendry		15,000	Cash at Bank	20,000
Sundry Creditors		10,000	Closing Stock	32,000
		1,27,600		1,27,600

Problem 14: Following is the Trial Balance of Suganthi manufacturing Company on 31ˢᵗ December 2012.

	₹	₹
Capital		43,970
Opening stock	42,800	
Discounts		175
Advertising	2,350	
Goodwill	4,750	
Bills Payable		600
Wages	3,750	
Duty and cleaning charges	600	
Factory rent	800	
Carriage inwards	1,650	
Return inwards	2,250	
Salaries	7,500	
Interest		1,100
Sales		1,80,000
Gas and water	350	
Returns outwards		950
Office rent	750	
Plant and Machinery	10,000	
Purchases	1,31,350	
Bill receivable	1,000	
Cash at bank	3,300	

	₹	₹
Cash in hand	42	
Office furniture	1,250	
Sundry creditors		4,225
Taxes	150	
Printing and stationary	238	
Sundry debtors	9,000	
Drawings	6,250	
General expenses	680	
Insurances	210	
	2,31,020	2,31,020

Closing stock was valued at ₹19,900. You are required to prepare Trading and Profitand Loss Account for the year and the balance sheet as at that date.

Solution:

Dr		**Trading Account for the year ended 31.12.2012**			**Cr**
	₹				₹
To Opening stock		42,800	By Sales	1,80,000	
To Purchases	1,31,350		Less: Returns	2,250	1,77,750
Less: Returns	950	1,30,400	By Closing Stock		19,900

	₹		₹
To wages	3,750		
To Duty and cleaning charges	600		
To Factory rent	800		
To Carriage inwards	1,650		
To Gas and water	350		
To Gross Profit (Transferred to P&L a/c)	17,300		
	1,97,650		1,97,650

Dr	**Profit and Loss Account for the year ended 31.12.2012**		**Cr**
	₹		₹
To Advertising	2,350	By Gross Profit	17,300
To Salaries	7,500	By Discounts	175
To Office rent	750	By Interest	1,100
To Taxes	150		
To Printing and stationary	238		
To General expenses	680		
To Insurance	210		
To Net Profit (Transferred to capital a/c)	6,697		
	18,575		18,575

Balance Sheet as on 31.12.2012

Liabilities	₹		Assets	₹
Capital	43,970		Stock	19,900
Add: Net Profit	6,697		Goodwill	4,750
	50,667		Plant and Machinery	10,000
Less: Drawings	6,250	44,417	Bills Receivable	1,000
Bills Payable		600	Cash at Bank	3,300
Sundry Creditors		4,225	Cash in hand	42
			Office furniture	1,250
			Sundry Debtors	9,000
		49,242		49,242

Problem 15: From the following Trial Balance prepare Profit and Loss account and BalanceSheet.

	₹		₹
Capital	16,800	Furniture	900
Drawings	5,000	Bills receivable	2,300
Stock	21,000	Bills payable	4,200
Purchases	36,000	Wages	1,200
Sales	72,000	Advertisement	600
Purchase returns	2,000	Discount (Dr)	100
Sales returns	3,000	Commission received	600
Debtors	4,500	Machinery	20,000
Creditors	2,500	Cash	3,500

Solution:

Trial Balance

Particulars	₹	₹
Capital		16,800
Drawings	5,000	
Stock	21,000	
Purchases	36,000	
Sales		72,000
Purchase returns		2,000
Sales returns	3,000	
Debtors	4,500	
Creditors		2,500
Furniture	900	
Bills receivables	2,300	
Bills Payable		4,200
Wages	1,200	
Advertisement	600	
Discount (Dr)	100	
Commission received		600
Machinery	20,000	
Cash	3,500	
	98,100	98,100

Dr   **Trading Account for the year ended…**   **Cr**

	₹		₹	
To Opening stock	21,000	By Sales	72,000	
To Purchases 36,000		Less: Returns	3,000	69,000
Less: Returns 2,000	34,000			
To wages	1,200			
To Gross Profit	12,800			
(Transferred to P & L a/c)				
	69,000			69,000

Dr   **Profit and Loss Account for the year *ended…***   *Cr*

	₹		₹
To Advertisement	600	By Gross Profit	12,800
To Discount	100	(Transferred from trading a/c)	
To Net Profit	12,700	By Commission	600
(Transferred to capital a/c)			
	13,400		13,400

Balance Sheet as on ....

Liabilities	₹		Assets	₹
Capital	16,800		Debtors	4,500
Add: Net Profit	12,700		Furniture	900
	29,500		Bills Receivable	2,300
	5,000		Machinery	20,000
Less: Drawings		24,500	Cash	3,500
Creditors		2,500		
Bills Payable		4,200		
		31,200		31,200

Problem 16: From the following information was extracted from the books of Mr.Z as on 31st December 2013.

	₹		₹
Plant & Machinery	20,000	Opening stock	34,200
Manufacturing wages	34,500	Motor car	12,000
Salaries	15,850	Sales return	3,100
Furniture	10,000	Purchases	1,02,000
Freight on purchase	1,860	Bad debts	1,400
Building	2,140	Interest on bank charges	400
Manufacturing expenses	9,500	Cash at bank	4,200
Insurance and taxes	4,250	Cash in hand	1,120
Goodwill	25,000	Capital	56,000
General expenses	8,200	Sundry creditors	44,560

	₹		₹
Factory fuel and power	1,280	Bank loan	15,000
Sundry debtors	78,200	Purchase returns	1,740
Factory lighting	950	Interest received	2,000
Sales	2,50,850		

Prepare Trading and Profit and loss account for the year ended 31st December 2013 and the balance sheet as on that date taking into consideration the following information. Stock on 31st December 2013 was valued at ₹ 30,500.

Solution:

Dr   **Trading Account for the year ended 31st December 2013**   **Cr**

		₹			₹
To Opening stock		34,200	By Sales	2,50,850	
To Purchases	1,02,000		Less: Returns	3,100	2,47,750
Less: Returns	1,740	1,00,260	By Closing Stock		30,500
To Factory fuel & Power		1,280			
To Freight on purchase		1,860			
To manufacturing expenses		9,500			
To Manufacturing wages		34,500			
To Factory lighting		950			
To Gross Profit (Transferred to P & L a/c)		95,700			
		2,78,250			2,78,250

Dr		Profit and Loss Account for the year ended 31st December 2013		Cr
	₹			₹
To Salaries	15,850	By Gross Profit		95,700
To Insurance and taxes	4,250	(Transferred from trading a/c)		
To General expenses	8,200	By Interest received		2,000
To Bad debts	1,400			
To Interest on bank charges	400			
To Net Profit	67,600			
(Transferred to capital a/c)				
	97,700			97,700

Balance Sheet as on 31st December *2013*

Liabilities		₹	Assets	₹
Sundry Creditors		44,560	Plant & Machinery	20,000
Bank Loan		15,000	Furniture	10,000
Capital	56,000		Building	2,140
(+) Net Profit	67,600	1,23,600	Goodwill	25,000
			Sundry Debtors	78,200
			Motor car	12,000
			Cash at bank	4,200
			Cash in hand	1,120
			Stock	
				30,500
		1,83,160		1,83,160

Problem 17: Prepare Trading and Profit and Loss account for the year ended 31ˢᵗ December2011 and Balance sheet on that date.

Particulars	Dr ₹	Cr ₹
Stock	15,000	
Purchases	13,000	
Sales		30,000
Carriage inwards	200	
Salaries	5,000	
Stationary	800	
Drawings	1,700	
Sundry creditors		2,000
Sundry debtors	18,000	
Furniture	1,000	
Capital		25,000
Postage	750	
Interest paid	550	
Machinery	3,500	
Cash	500	
Loan		3,000
	60,000	60,000

Stock on 31st December 2011 was ₹ 12,000/-

Solution:

Trading and Profit and Loss Account for the year ended 31.12.2011

Particulars	Amount ₹	Particulars	Amount ₹
To Opening stock	15,000	By Sales	30,000
To Purchase	13,000	By Closing stock	12,000
To Carriage inwards	200		
To Gross Profit c/d	13,800		
	42,000		42,000
To Salaries	5,000	By Gross Profit b/d	13,800
To Stationary	800		
To Postage	750		
To Interest paid	550		
To Net Profit			
(Transferred to Capital a/c)	6,700		
	13,800		13,800

Balance Sheet as on 31st December 2011

Liabilities	Amount ₹	Assets	Amount ₹
Sundry Creditors	2,000	Cash	500
Loan	3,000	Sundry debtors	18,000
Capital	25,000	Furniture	1,000
(+) Net Profit	6,700	Machinery	3,500

Liabilities		Amount ₹	Assets	Amount ₹
		31,700	Stock (31.12.2011)	12,000
(-) Drawings	1,700	30,000		
		35,000		35,000

Problem 18: From the following trial balance of Mr. Selvam, prepare Trading and Profit andLoss account for the year ending 31.03.2011 and balance sheet as on that date:

	Dr ₹	Cr ₹		Dr ₹	Cr ₹
Stock (1.4.2010)	30,000		Discount received		500
Sales		1,55,000	Telephone charges	500	
Purchases	80,000		Plant and machinery	2,00,000	
Return inwards	5,000		Land and building	2,00,000	
Return outwards		2,000	Sundry debtors	1,30,000	
Trade expenses	1,500		Sundry creditors		20,000
Discount allowed	1,000		Capital		5,00,000
Wages	10,000		Cash in hand	3,700	

	Dr ₹	Cr ₹		Dr ₹	Cr ₹
Salaries	12,000			6,77,500	6,77,500
Carriage outwards	2,000				
Rent, rates and taxes	1,800				

Stock as on 31.12.2010 was valued at ₹ 45,000.

Solution:

Books of Mr.Selvam

Dr		Trading and Profit and Loss Account for the year ended 31.03.2010			Cr
Particulars		**Amount ₹**	**Particulars**		**Amount ₹**
To Opening stock		30,000	By Sales	1,55,000	
To Purchase	80,000		(-) Return inwards		1,50,000
(-) Return outwards	2,000	78,000		5,000	45,000
			By Closing Stock		
To Wages		10,000			
To Gross Profit		77,000			
(Transferred to P&L a/c)		1,95,000			1,95,000
To Trade expenses		1,500	By Gross Profit b/d		77,000
To Discount allowed		1,000	(Transferred from trading a/c)		
To Salaries		12,000			
To Carriage outwards		2,000	By Discount received		500

Particulars	Amount ₹	Particulars	Amount ₹
To Rent, rates and taxes	1,800		
To Telephone Charges	500		
To Net Profit	58,700		
(Transferred to Capital a/c)			
	77,500		77,500

Balance Sheet as on 31.03.2010

Liabilities		Amount ₹	Assets	Amount ₹
Sundry Creditors		20,000	Cash	3,700
Capital	5,00,000		Plant & Machinery	2,00,000
(+) Net Profit	58,700	5,58,700	Land and Building	2,00,000
			Sundry Debtors	1,30,000
			Closing stock	45,000
		5,78,700		5,78,700

Problem 19: The following Trial balance as on 31st March 2013 was extracted from thebooks of Joseph.

Debit Balance	₹	Credit Balance	₹
Drawings	12,000	Capital	3,65,000
Wages	42,000	Sales	7,00,000
Factory expenses	14,500	Returns outwards	7,000
Insurance	5,400	Discounts	1,900
Office expenses	34,600	Creditors	43,600

Debit Balance	₹	Credit Balance	₹
Factory rent	13,000	Bank overdraft	7,000
Office rent	7,000	Loan on Mortgage	2,00,000
Purchases	3,60,000	Commission received	4,000
Advertising	17,000		
Carriage	3,500		
Returns inwards	2,500		
Debtors	98,000		
Salaries	31,000		
Plant	98,000		
Loose tools	10,000		
Premises	4,00,000		
Stock of stationery	5,000		
Stock on 1.4.2012	1,62,000		
Trade expenses	13,000		
	13,28,500		13,28,500

Prepare Trading and Profit and Loss account for the year ended 31st March 2013assuming closing stock on that date ₹ 1,80,000. Also prepare a Balance sheet.

Solution:

Trading and Profit and Loss Account of Mr. Joseph For the year ending 31.3.2013

Particulars	Amount ₹			Amount ₹
To Opening stock		1,62,000	By Sales	7,00,000	
To Purchase	3,60,000		Less: Returns inwards	2,500	6,97,500
Less: Returns inwards	7,000	3,53,000	By Closing stock		1,80,000
To Wages		42,000		
To Factory expenses		14,500		
To Factory rent		13,000		
To Carriage		3,500		
To Gross Profit c/d		2,89,500		
		8,77,500			8,77,500
To Insurance		5,400	By Gross Profit b/d		2,89,500
To Office expenses		34,600	By Discount		1,900
To Office rent		7,000	By Commission received		4,000
To Advertising		17,000		
To Salaries		31,000		
To Trade expenses		13,000		
To Net Profit		1,87,400		
		2,95,400			2,95,400

Balance Sheet of Mr.Joseph as on 31ˢᵗMarch 2013

Liabilities		Amount ₹	Assets	Amount ₹
Creditors		43,600	Debtors	98,000
Bank overdraft		7,000	Stock of Stationary	5,000
Loan on Mortgage		2,00,000	Loose tools	10,000
Capital	3,65,000		Plant	98,000
(+) Net Profit	1,87,400		Premises	4,00,000
	5,52,400		Closing stock	1,80,000
(-) Drawings	12,000	5,40,400		
		7,91,000		7,91,000

6.13 ADJUSTMENTS

Every business concern should prepare final accounts at the end of the accounting year. The preparation of final accounts includes the determination of net income of an accounting year. All the revenues and incomes are matched with cost of resources consumed called expenses to determine net income. In order to find out true net income, revenues and expenses are matched on accrual basis. Revenue and income earned during an accounting period are compared with expenses incurred during the same period to determine net income on accrual basis.

Sales revenue and other incomes are recorded in the books accounts in a different manner. Sales revenue is recorded immediately soon after completion of sales transaction. It increases either cash or claim to cash in the form of debtors and bills receivable. But, other incomes such as interest, dividend rent etc. are recorded in the books of accounts only on receipt basis. Hence, amount received is adjusted for amount received but not earned and amount earned but not received to determine true profit.

Expenses are recorded in the books of accounts on cash basis. The recordings of expenses require adjustment at the end of the year for amount due but not paid. Moreover, expenditure incurred to acquire fixed assets is charged to Profit and Loss Account for working life of fixed asset. In this case, a portion of fixed asset is charged to Profit and Loss Account as depreciation which requires adjustment at the end of the year. But, there is no outflow of cash in the year in which depreciation charged.

In nutshell, adjustments are made at the end of the accounting period by passing journal entries called adjustment entries or adjusting entries. The very purpose of passing adjustment entry is to find out true profit an accrual basis and portray true and fair financialposition of the business.

The adjustments may be made either before preparing trail balance or after preparingtrial balance. If adjustments are made after preparing trial balance, information about adjustments are given outside the trial balance. In this case, both debit and credit aspects ofadjustments are considered for preparing final accounts. Sometimes, adjustments are made before preparing trail balance. In this case, ledger balances are shown in the trial balance after making adjustments. i.e. Adjusted Trial Balance. So, these balances are recorded only one place while preparing final accounts.

While preparing final accounts, all expenses and incomes corresponding to the period for which the final accounts are prepared must be taken into account, expenses payable and paid in advance, income receivable and received in advance must be taken into account. They are called as adjustments.

Adjustments would appear in two places, namely, either in the Trading account or Profit and Loss account and Assets side or Liabilities side of the Balance sheet. The purpose of adjustment's is to take into consideration all such details necessary to bring the books in perfect order. The several kinds of adjustments and their accounting treatments are as follows:

Closing stock

The unsold goods in stock at the end of the accounting period is called as **closing stock**. This is to be valued at cost or market price whichever is lower.

Adjustment Entry

Closing Stock a/c	Dr	xxx
To Trading a/c		xxx

The value of closing stock will appear on the assets side of balance sheet and on the credit side of trading account.

Outstanding Expenses

Expenses which have been incurred but not yet paid during the accounting period for which the final accounts are being prepared are called as **outstanding expenses**. For example wages outstanding,

Adjustment Entry

Wages a/c	Dr	xxx
To outstanding wages a/c		xxx

Wages outstanding is added with wages account which is shown in the debit side of trading account. Moreover, wages outstanding account is appearing on the liabilities side of balance sheet.

Prepaid Expenses

Prepaid expenses refer to an amount paid in the current accounting year for the services which are going to be received in the subsequent accounting period. Expenses which have been paid in advance are called as **prepaid (unexpired) expenses**. For example insurance prepaid

Adjustment Entry

Insurance prepaid a/c	Dr	xxx
To Insurance a/c		xxx

The prepaid insurance premium amount is deducted from insurance account which is shown in the debit side of profit and loss account. Moreover, insurance prepaid account is appearing in the assets side of balance sheet.

Accrued Incomes or Outstanding Incomes

Income which has been earned but not received during the accounting period is calledas **accrued income**. Otherwise called income earned but not received.

Adjustment Entry

Accrued rent a/c	Dr	xxx
To rent a/c		xxx

Firstly, loss account is shown on the credit of trading account. Secondly, concern account is shown on the asset side of balance sheet as current asset.

Incomes Received in Advance

In otherwise called as unearned income. Income received in advance refers to incomereceived in the current accounting year against which the services are to be rendered in the subsequent accounting year. Income received during a particular accounting period for the work to be done in future period is called as **income received in advance**. For example rent received in advance,

Adjustment Entry

Rent received a/c	Dr	xxx
To Rent received in advance a/c		₹ xxx

Firstly rent received in advance is deducted from the total rent received. These are shown on the credit side of profit and loss account. Secondly rent received in advance is recorded on the liabilities side of balance sheet.

Interest on Capital

Interest on capital means an amount payable to the proprietor or owner of the businessconcern for utilizing the amount which is contributed by him or her as capital. It is treated asbusiness expenses and charged to profit and loss account. In order to see whether the businessis really earning profit or not, it is desirable to charge interest on capital at a certain rate.

Adjustment Entry

Interest on Capital a/c	Dr	xxx	
To Capital a/c			xxx
Profit and Loss a/c	Dr	xxx	
To Int. on Capital a/c			xxx

Interest on capital is recorded on the debit side of profit and loss account. Then interest on capital is added with capital account which is shown on the liabilities side of thebalance sheet.

Interest on Drawings

Cash, goods or any assets of the business concern can be used by the owner for his personal use is called as **drawings**. When interest on capital is allowed, then interest on drawings is charged from the owner. Interest on drawings is an income for the business andwill reduce the capital of the owner.

Adjustment Entry

Drawing a/c	Dr	xxx
To Interest on drawing a/c		xxx
Interest on drawing a/c	Dr	xxx
To Profit and Loss a/c		xxx

Interest on drawings is recorded on the credit of profit and loss account. Interest on drawings is deducted from the capital account which is shown on the liabilities side of balance sheet.

Interest on Loan (Outstanding)

Borrowings from banks, financial institutions and outsiders for business are called loans. Amount payable towards interest on loan is an expense for the business.

Interest on Investment

Interest receivable on investments is an income for the business.

Depreciation

Generally, depreciation is provided only to the fixed assets. In this aspect, depreciation means a portion of depreciable cost of a fixed asset allocated to a particular accounting year and is to be charged to profit and loss account. Depreciation is the reductionin the value of fixed assets due to its use or obsolescence. Generally depreciation is chargedat some percentage on the value of fixed asset.

Adjustment Entry

Depreciation a/c	Dr	xxx
To Asset a/c		xxx

Depreciation amount is recorded on the debit side of profit and loss account. Secondly, the depreciation amount is deducted from the gross value of land and building account and the net amount is recorded on the asset side of balance sheet.

Bad Debts

Debts which cannot be recovered are called **Bad debts.** It is a loss for the business.

Adjustment Entry

Bad debts a/c	Dr xxx	
To Sundry Debtors a/c		xxx
Profit & Loss a/c	Dr xxx	
To Bad debts a/c		xxx

Firstly, a bad debt is recorded on the debit side of profit and loss account. Secondly the bad debts amount is deducted from the sundry debtor who is shown on the assets side ofbalance sheet.

Provision for Bad and Doubtful Debts

Every business suffers a percentage of bad debts over and above the debts definitelyknown as irrecoverable and written off as Bad. This Provision for bad and doubtful debts isgenerally provided at a certain percentage on Debtors, based on past experience. While preparing final accounts, the bad debts written off given in adjustment is first deducted fromthe Sundry debtors then on the balance amount (Sundry debtors – Bad debt written off) provision for bad and doubtful debts calculated.

Adjustment Entry

Provision for bad & doubtful debtors a/c	Dr	xxx
To Sundry debtors a/c		xxx
Profit and Loss a/c	Dr	xxx
To Provision for bad and doubtful debtors		xxx

Firstly, provision for bad and doubtful debts account is recorded on the debit side ofprofit and loss account. Secondly, the amount of provision for bad and doubtful debts is deducted from the sundry debtor which is shown on the asset side of balance sheet.

Bad debts appearing in additional information are deducted from debtors given in trial balance and then, provision required at the end of the year is calculated.

Provision created during the year is debited to profit and loss account and treated as expense of the year.

A bad debt is transferred to provision for bad and doubtful debts account and not to profit and loss account.

A bad debt appearing in trial balance is an adjusted amount. Hence, this amount need not be deducted once again from the sundry debtors amount but only shown on the debit sideof profit and loss account.

If any bad debts amount is recovered, it should be credited to provision for bad and doubtful debts account and to profit and loss account. But, the popular treatment is the bad debts recorded amount credited to profit and loss account as an income.

Treatment of Bad and Doubtful Debts

Profit and Loss Account (Debit Side)

New provision (given in adjustment)	xxx	
(+) New Bad debts (Adjustment)	xxx	
(-) Old bad debts (Trial Balance)	xxx	
(-) Old Provision (Trial Balance)	xxx	xxx

Provision for Discount on Debtors

To motivate the debtors to make prompt payments, cash discount may be allowed tothem. After providing provision for bad and doubtful debts, the remaining debtors are called as **good debtors.** They may pay their dues in time and avail themselves of the cash discountpermissible. So a provision for discount on good debtors at a certain percentage may have tobe created.

Adjustment Entry

Profit and Loss a/c	**Dr**	**xxx**	
To Provision for discount On debtors a/c			**xxx**

Provision for discount on debtors is recorded on the debit side of profit and loss account. Then, bad debts provision for bad and doubtful debts and provision for discount on debtors are deducted from sundry debtors and the net amount is recorded on the asset side ofbalance sheet.

Treatment of Provision for Discount on Debtors

Profit and Loss Account (Debit Side)

Discount allowed	xxx	
(+) New provision (given in adjustment)	xxx	
(-) Old Provision (Trial Balance)	xxx	xxx

Calculation of new provision for discount on debtors

Sundry Debtors	xxx	
(-) New Bad debts	xxx	
(-)Old provision for bad & doubtful debts	xxx	Xxx

Balance Sheet (Asset Side)

Sundry Debtors	xxx	
(-) New Bad debts	xxx	
	xxx	
(-) New provision for bad & doubtful debts	xxx	
	xxx	
(-) New Provision for discount on debtors	xxx	xxx

Provision for Discount on Creditors

Similar to cash discount allowed to debtors, the firm may have a chance to receive thecash discount from the creditors for prompt payment. Provision for discount on Creditors iscalculated at a certain percentage on Sundry Creditors.

Adjustment Entry

Provision for discount on creditors a/c Dr	xxx	
To Profit and Loss a/c		xxx

Firstly, provision for discount on creditors is recorded on the credit of profit and lossaccount. Secondly, the provision for discount on creditors is deducted from sundry creditorswhich are shown on the liabilities side of balance sheet.

Profit and Loss Account (Credit Side)

New provision (given in adjustment)	xxx	
(+) Discount received	xxx	
	xxx	
(-) Old Provision	xxx	xxx

Balance Sheet (Liability Side)

Sundry Creditors	xxx	
(-) New Provision for discount on creditors	xxx	xxx

Common debts

Sometimes, sundry debtors and sundry creditors include amount due from and amount due to a same person. In this case, lower amount of two accounts is known as common debtand is cancelled by passing the following adjustment entry

Adjustment Entry

Sundry creditors a/c	Dr	xxx
To Sundry Debtors a/c		xxx

Firstly, the common debt amount is deducted from sundry creditors account which isshown on the liabilities side of balance sheet. Secondly, the common debt amount is deducted from the sundry debtor which is shown on the assets side of balance sheet.

Abnormal loss of goods

Stock of goods may be destroyed due to fire, theft and accident. If so, this is treatedas abnormal loss of goods. In this situation, a business concern may not take any insurance,may take partly insurance /full insurance.

Adjustment Entry

Loss by fire a/c	Dr	xxx
To Trading a/c		xxx
Insurance company a/c	Dr	xxx
To Loss by fire a/c		xxx

Firstly, loss by fire account is shown on the credit of trading account. Secondly insurance company account is shown on the asset side of balance sheet as current asset.

Deferred revenue expenditure

Deferred revenue expenditure means benefit of expenditure available in more than one year. Therefore, a part of deferred revenue expenditure is written off over a period yearsbenefits received.

Adjustment Entry

Profit and Loss a/c	Dr	xxx
To Advertisement a/c		xxx

Firstly, concern expenses is recorded on the debit side of profit and loss account.

Secondly, the net amount of advertisement is shown on the asset side of balance sheet.

Commission based profit

Sometimes, commission is paid to the manager on the basis of extent of profit earnedby the business concern. There are two methods followed to calculate commission payable to manager. One is before charging such commission another one is after charging such commission.

Before charging such commission

$$\text{Profit} \times \frac{\text{Notinal}}{\text{Rate of commission } 100}$$

After charging such commission

$$\text{Profit} \times \frac{\text{Notinal Rate of commission}}{100 + \text{Rate of commission}}$$

Adjustment Entry (both case)

Commission a/c	Dr	xxx
To Commission Payable a/c		xxx
Profit and Loss a/c	Dr	xxx
To Commission a/c		xxx

Commission account is recorded on the debit side of profit and loss account. Then commission payable account is recorded on the liabilities side of balance sheet.

An over view of Adjustments

S.No	Adjustment	Treatment
1	Outstanding Expenses / Accured expenses	Add with concerned expenses either in the Trading a/c or profit and Loss a/c – DebitSide
		Show it on the liabilities side of BalanceSheet
2	Expenses paid in advance /Prepaid/ Unexpired / Over paid	Deduct from the concerned expenses either in the Trading or profit and loss A/c
		- Debit Side.
		Show it on the Asset side of the BalanceSheet.

S.No	Adjustment	Treatment
3	Income outstanding / Accured Income	Add with concerned income in the creditside of the profit and Loss A/c
		Show it on the asset side of Balance Sheet
4	Income received in advance	Deduct from concerned income in thecredit side of the profit and Loss A/c
		Show it on the liability side of the BalanceSheet
5	Depreciation	Show the amount of depreciation on thedebit side of profit and loss A/c
		Deduct from the value of the concernedasset in the Balance Sheet
6	Bad debts	Show the amount of Bad debts written offthe debit side of the Profit and Loss A/c
		Deduct from the amount of Sundry Debtors on the asset of Balance Sheet
7	Reserve / Provision for bad &doubtful debts	Show on the debit side of Profit & loss a/c
		Deduct from sundry debtors on the assetSide of the Balance sheet.
		Debtors xxx
		(-) Bad debts xxx
		(-) Provision for bad debts <u>xxx</u> xxx
8	Provision for discount on debtors	Show it on debit side of Profit & Loss a/c
		Deduct from Sundry Debtors on the assetside of Balance sheet after making the bad debts and provision for doubtful debtsfrom sundry debtors.

S.No	Adjustment	Treatment
9	Provision for discount oncreditors	Show it on the credit side of the Profit andLoss A/c
		Deduct from the sundry creditors on theliabilities side of the balance sheet.
10	Interest on Capital	Show it on debit side of the Profit and Loss account
		Add with capital on the liability side ofthe Balance Sheet
11	Goods consumed for personal use	Deduct from purchases in the debit side ofthe Trading a/c
		Deduct from Capital in the liabilities sideof the Balance sheet.
12	Interest on Drawings	Show it on the credit side of the Profit &Loss a/c
		Deduct from capital on the liabilities sideof the balance sheet.
13	Interest on Loan	Show it on the debit side of the Profit andLoss a/c
		Add with loan on the liabilities side of theBalance sheet.
14	Closing stock	Credit side of the Trading account
		Assets side of the Balance Sheet.

Problem 20: Pass necessary adjusting entries in the following:

(i)   Wages outstanding ₹ 1,000

(ii)   Depreciation of machinery ₹ 5,000

(iii) Insurance prepaid ₹ 750

(iv)   Bad debts ₹ 500

(v)   Interest on capital ₹ 1,500

Reserve for bad and doubtful debts ₹ 1,000]

Solution:

	Particulars		**Dr ₹**	**Cr ₹**
(i)	Wages a/c	Dr	1,000	
	To wages outstanding a/c(Being wages outstanding)			1,000
(ii)	Depreciation a/c	Dr	5,000	
	To Machinery a/c			5,000
	(Being deprecation provided)			
(iii)	Prepaid insurance	Dr	750	
	To Insurance a/c			750
	(Being insurance prepaid)			
(iv)	Bad Debts a/c	Dr	500	
	To Sundry Debtors			500
	(Being bad debts written off)			
(v)	Interest on Capital a/c	Dr	1,500	
	To Capital a/c			1,500
	(Being interest provided for capital)			
(vi)	Profit and Loss a/c	Dr	1,000	
	To Reserve for Bad & doubtful debts			1,000
	(Being reserve for bad & doubtful debts created)			

Problem 21: The closing stock on December 31, 2015 was ₹ 20,000. There was loss, by fire,of ₹ 5,000 on November 2015. Show how you will deal with this in case.

1. Stock was not at all insured
2. Stock was full covered by insurance policy
3. Stock was partly covered by insurance and the claim of ₹ 300 was accepted bythe insurance company

You are required to show journal entries.

Solution:

	Particulars		Dr ₹	Cr ₹
(1)	Profit and Loss a/c	Dr	5,000	
	To Trading a/c			5,000
	(Being fire loss recorded)			
(2)	Insurance company a/c	Dr	5,000	
	To Trading a/c			5,000
	(Being fire loss will be claimed from company)			
(3)	Insurance company a/c	Dr	300	
	Profit and Loss a/c		4,700	
	To Trading a/c			5,000
	(Being fire claim will be recovered and restwill be loss for the business)			

Problem 22: The following are the balances extracted from the books of Mr.Durai as on 31.3.2014. Prepare Trading and Profit and Loss account for the year ended 31.3.2014 and aBalance sheet as on that date.

Particulars	Dr ₹	Cr ₹
Capital		50,000
Opening stock	10,000	
Machinery	20,000	
Purchases	35,000	
Purchases returns		500
Sales		45,000
Sales returns	500	

Particulars	Dr ₹	Cr ₹
Wages	1,000	
Salaries	2,500	
Office rent	1,000	
Insurance	500	
Sundry debtors	25,000	
Sundry creditors		14,500
Cash	500	
Bank balance	14,000	

Adjustments:

i)   On 31.3.2014 closing stock ₹ 10,000

ii) Outstanding salaries ₹ 500

iii) Prepaid insurance ₹ 250

iv) Bad debts ₹ 500

v)   Provide 10% depreciation on Machinery

Solution:

Trading and Profit and Loss Account of Mr.Durai For the year ending 31.3.2014

Particulars	Amount ₹		Particulars		Amount ₹
To Opening stock		10,000	By Sales	45,000	
			Less: Sales return	500	
			By Closing stock		
To Purchase	35,000				44,500
Less: Purchase returns	500	34,500			10,000
To Wages		1,000			
To Gross Profit c/d		9,000			
		54,500			54,500
To Salaries	2,500		By Gross Profit b/d		9,000
(+) Out standing	500	3,000			
To Office rent		1,000			
To Insurance	500				
(-) Prepaid	250	250			
To Bad debts		500			
To Depreciation :					
Machinery (20,000x10/100)		2,000			
To Net Profit		2,250			
		9,000			9,000

Balance Sheet of Mr.Durai as on 31ˢᵗMarch 2014

Liabilities	Amount ₹		Assets	Amount	Amount ₹
Creditors		14,500	Cash		500
Out standing salary		500	Bank balance		14,000
Capital	50,000		Machinery	20,000	
(+) Net Profit	2,250	52,250	(-) Depre ciation	2,000	18,000
			Prepaid insurance		250
			Sundry debtors	25,000	
			(-) Bad debts	500	24,500
			Closing stock		10,000
		67,250			67,250

Problem 23: From the following prepare Trading, Profit and Loss account and Balance Sheetfor the year 2015.

	₹		₹
Capital	30,000	Sales	1,50,000
Drawings	5,000	Sales returns	2,000
Furniture	2,600	Discount (Dr)	1,100
Bank overdraft	4,200	Discount (Cr)	2,000

	₹		₹
Creditors	13,300	Tax and insurance	2,000
Premises	20,000	General expenses	4,000
Opening stock	22,000	Salaries	9,000
Debtors	18,600	Commission (Dr)	2,200
Rent from tenants	1,000	Purchase Returns	1,800
Purchases	1,13,600	Reserve for bad debts	600
Bad debts	800		

Adjustments: ₹

i)   Closing stock 20,000
ii) Rent to be paid 300
iii) Write off bad debts 600
iv) Prepaid insurance 700
v)   Depreciate premises 5%

Solution:

Dr		**Trading Profit and Loss Account for the year ending 2015**		**Cr**
	₹			₹
To Opening stock	22,000	By Sales	1,50,000	
To Purchases	1,13,600	Less: Returns	2,000	1,48,000

Particulars		Amount	Particulars	Amount
Less: Returns	1,800	1,11,800	By Closing Stock	20,000
To Gross Profit		34,200		
(Transferred to P&L a/c)				
		1,68,000		1,68,000
To Rent outstanding		300	By Gross Profit	34,200
To Bad debts	800		By Rent from Tenants	1,000
(+)New BD	600			
	1400			
(-)Old BD	-600	800		
To Discount		1,100	By Discount	2,000
To Depreciation on premises		1,000		
To Tax and insurance	2,000			
Less: Prepaid	700	1,300		
General expenses		4,000		
To Salaries		9,000		
To Commission		2,200		
To Net Profit		17,500		
(Transferred to Capital a/c)				
		37,200		37,200

Balance Sheet for the year ended 2015

Liabilities		₹	Assets		₹
Capital	30,000		Stock		20,000
(-) Drawings	5,000		Premises	20,000	
	25,000		Less:		19,000
			Depreciation	1,000	
(+) Net Profit	17,500	42,500	Prepaid insurance		700
Rent outstanding		300	Furniture		2,600
Bank overdraft	4,200		Debtors	18,600	
Creditors	13,300	Less: Bad debts	600		
		18,000			18000
		59,700			59,700

Problem 24: The following is the Trial balance as on 31.3.2005. Prepare Trading and Profitand Loss account for the year ended 31st March 2005 and a Balance sheet as on that date.

Particulars	Dr ₹	Cr ₹
Capital		1,00,000
Insurance	1,000	
Drawings	18,000	
Buildings	15,000	
Furniture	7,500	

Particulars	Dr ₹	Cr ₹
Motor van	25,000	
Loan from X @ 12% interest		15,000
Interest paid on the above	900	
Sales and purchases	75,000	1,00,000
Stock (1.4.2004)	25,000	
Salary	15,000	
Octroi	2,000	
Commission received		7,500
Debtors and creditors	28,100	10,000
Bank balance	20,000	
	2,32,500	2,32,500

Adjustments:

1. The value of closing stock on 31.3.2005 is ₹ 32,000
2. Outstanding octroi ₹ 500
3. Prepaid insurance ₹ 300
4. Depreciation: building 2 ½% ; furniture 10% Motor van 10%
5. Provide bad debts ₹ 2,100 and provision for doubtful debts 5%
6. Interest on capital is allowed at 3%
7. Accrued commission ₹ 1,500

Solution:

Trading and Profit and Loss Account for the year ending 31.3.2005

Particulars		Amount ₹	Particulars		Amount ₹
To Opening stock		25,000	By Sales		1,00,000
To Purchase		75,000	By Closing stock		32,000
To Octroi	2,000				
(+) Outstanding	500	2,500			
To Gross Profit c/d		29,500			
		1,32,000			1,32,000
To Insurance	1,000		By Gross Profit b/d		29,500
(-) Prepaid	300	700	By Com. received	7,500	
To Interest	900		(-) Outstanding	1,500	9,000

Particulars	Amount ₹		Particulars	Amount ₹
(+) outstanding	900	1,800		
To Salary		15,000		
To Depreciation:				
Building (15,000x 2.5/100)	375			
Furniture (7,500x 10/100)	750			
Motor van (25,000x 10/100)	2,500	3,625		
To Bad debts		2,100		
To Provision for Doubtful debts (2,8100 – 2,100) x 5%		1,300		
To Int. on capital (1,00,000 x 3%)		3,000		
To Net Profit		10,975		
		38,500		38,500

Balance Sheet as on 31ˢᵗMarch 2005

Liabilities	Amount ₹	Assets			Amount ₹
Creditors	10,000	Bank balance			20,000
Out standing octroi	500	Building	15,000		
Loan from X	15,000	(-) Depreciation		375	14,625
(+) Out standing	900	15,900	Furniture	7,500	
			(-) Depreciation	750	6,750
Capital	1,00,000		Motor van	25,000	
(+) Net Profit	10,975		(-) Depreciation	2,500	22,500
	1,10975		Debtors	28,100	
(+) Interest on capital	3,000		(-) Bad debts	2,100	
	1,13,975			26,000	
(-) Drawings	18,000	95,975	(-) Provision DD	1,300	24,700
			Prepaid insurance		300
			Out standing commission		1,500
			Closing stock		32,000
		1,22,375			1,22,375

Problem 25: From the following Trial balance, prepare the Trading and Profit and Loss a/cfor the year ended 31ˢᵗ December 2009.

Trial balance of Clintan as on December 31, 2009

Particulars	Dr ₹	Particulars	Cr ₹
Purchase	1,50,000	Capital Sales	4,00,000
Salaries	20,000	Creditors	2,50,000
Rent	15,000	Provision For doubt debts	10,000
Insurance	3,000		
Drawings	50,000		1,000
Machinery	2,80,000		
Bank	45,000		
Cash	20,000		
Stock	52,000		
Debtors	25,000		
Freight	1,000		
	6,61,000		6,61,000

Adjustments required:

1. Stock on hand at 31, December 2009 is ₹ 49,000
2. Salaries owing ₹ 3,000
3. Rent and insurance prepaid ₹ 2,000 and ₹ 900 respectively
4. Depreciate machinery by 10%
5. During December Clintan took ₹ 1,000 in goods for his own use
6. Provide 10% for bad and doubtful debts.

Solution:

Trading and Profit and Loss Account of Mr. Clinton for the year ending 31.3.2009

Particulars		Amount₹	Particulars	Amount₹
To Opening stock		52,000	By Sales	2,50,000
To Purchase	1,50,000		By Closing stock	49,000
(-) Drawings	1,000	1,49,000		
To Freight		1,000		
To Gross Profit c/d		97,000		
		2,99,000		2,99,000
To Salaries	20,000		By Gross Profit b/d	97,000
(+) outstanding	3,000	23,000		
To Rent	15,000			
(-) Prepaid	2,000	13,000		
To Insurance	3000			
(-) Prepaid	-900	2,100		
To Depreciation				
Machinery (2,80,000x10/100)		28,000		
Provision for doubtful (25,000x10/100)	2,500			
Old Provision	1,000	1,500		
To Net Profit		29,400		
		97,000		97,000

Balance Sheet as on 31ˢᵗMlarch 2009

Liabilities		Amount ₹	Assets		Amount ₹
Credit ors		10,000	Cash		20,000
Out standing salaries		3,000	Bank		45,000
Capital	4,00,000		Debtors	25,000	
(+) Net Profit	29,400		(-) Provision for DD	2,500	22,500
	4,29,400		Prepaid rent		2,000
(-) Draw ings (50,000 + 1,000)	51,000	3,78,400	Pre paid insurance Mac hinery	2,80,000	900
			(-) Depre ciation Closing stock	28,000	2,52,000 49,000
		3,91,400			3,91,400

Problem 26: From the following Trial balance of Raja as at 31ˢᵗ December 2008, you are required to prepare Trading and Profit and Loss account for the year ended 31ˢᵗ December 2008 and a balance sheet as on that date, after making the necessary adjustments.

Particulars	Dr ₹	Cr ₹
Raja's capital		1,60,000
Raja's drawings	12,000	
Machinery(1.1.2008)	40,000	
Machinery additional (1.7.2008)	10,000	
Stock 1.1.2008	30,000	
Purchase	1,64,000	
Returns inwards	4,000	
Sundry debtors	41,200	
Furniture	10,000	
Freight & duty	4,000	
Carriage outwards	1,000	
Rent & rates	9,200	
Printing & stationery	1,600	
Trade expenses	800	
Sundry creditors		20,000
Sales		2,40,000
Returns outwards		2,000
Postage & telegrams	1,600	
Provision for doubtful debts		800
Discounts		1,600
Rent of premises sub let for year to 30th June 2009		2,400

Particulars	Dr ₹	Cr ₹
Insurance charges	1,400	
Salaries & wages	42,600	
Cash in hand	12,400	
Cash at bank	41,000	
	4,26,800	4,26,800

Adjustments:

1. Stock on 31ˢᵗ December 2008 was valued at ₹ 29,200
2. Write off ₹ 1,200 as bad debts
3. The provision for doubtful debts is to be maintained at 5% on sundry debtors.
4. Create a provision for discounts on debtors and reserve for discounts oncreditors at 2%
5. Provide for depreciation on furniture at 5% p.a and on machinery at 20% p.a
6. Insurance prepaid was ₹ 200
7. A fire occurred on 25ᵗʰ December 2008 in the godown and stock of the valueof ₹ 10,000 was destroyed. It was fully insured and the insurance company admitted the claim in full.

Solution:

Trading and Profit & Loss Account of Mr. Raja for the year ending 31.3.2008

Particulars	Amount ₹	Particulars	Amount ₹
To Opening stock	30,000	By Sales 2,40,000	

Particulars	Amount ₹	Particulars	Amount ₹
To Purchase 1,64,000		(-) Returns inward 4,000	2,36,000
(-) Returns outward 2,000	1,62,000	By Goods destroyed byfire	10,000
To Freight & Duty	4,000	By Closing stock	29,200
To Gross Profit c/d	79,200		
	2,75,200		2,75,200
To Salaries & Wages	42,600	By Gross Profit b/d	79,200
To Rent and Rates	9,200	By Reserve for dis.	
To Printing	1,600		
To Trade expenses	800	On creditors (20,000 x 2%)	400
To Postage & Telegram	1,600	By Rent received 2,400	
To Insurance 1,400		(-) Received in advance 1,200	1,200
(-) Prepaid 200	1,200	By Discount	1,600
To Depreciation:			
Plant & Machinery			

Particulars	Amount ₹	Particulars	Amount ₹
(40,000 x 20 x 100) 8,000			
(10,000 x 20/100 x 6/12) 1,000	9,000		
To Carriage outwards	1,000		
To Furniture (10,000x5%)	500		
To Provision forbad debts (41,200 -1200 x5/100) 2,000			
(+) Bad debts 1,200			
3,200			
(-) Old provision 800	2,400		
To Discount ofdebtors (40,000 – 2,000 x 2/100)	760		
To Net Profits	11,740		
	82,400		82,400

Balance Sheet as on 31ˢᵗ March 2009

Liabilities		Amount ₹	Assets		Amount ₹
Creditors	20,000		Cash in hand		12,400
(-) 2% Discount	400	19,600	Cash at bank Debtors		41,000
Rent received (advance)		1,200	(-) Bad debts	41,200	
			(-) 5% provision (bad debts)	1,200	
Capital	1,60,000			40,000	
(+) Net Profit	11,740		(-) 2% Discount	2,000	
	1,71,740		Insurance prepaid	38,000	
(-) Drawings	12,000	1,59,740	Insurance claim- fire	760	37,240
			Plant & Machinery		200
			(+) Additional		10,000
				40,000	
			(-) Depreciation	10,000	
			Closing stock	50,000	
			Furniture	9,000	41,000
			(-) Depreciation		29,200
				10,000	
				500	9,500
		1,80,540			1,80,540

Problem 27: Mr.Kanna the works Manager and Mr.Kamal, the General Manager are to gettheir remuneration as under.

Mr.Kannan is to get 10% of the profit after charging such 10%

Mr.Kamal is to get 1/5ᵗʰ of the profits after charging all provisions in (i) and (ii)

Additional Information:

Gross profit ₹ 4,000

Various operating expenses ₹ 12,000

Depreciation of fixed assets ₹ 8,000

Profit from the sale of security ₹ 2,000

You are required to prepare Profit and Loss account.

Solution:

Profit & Loss Account

Particulars	₹	Particulars	₹
To Various operating expenses	12,000	By Gross Profit	40,000
To Depreciation – fixed asset	8,000	By Profit from the sale of security	2,000
To Mr. Kannan remuneration	2,000		
To Kamal remuneration	4,000		
To Net Profit	16,000		
	42,000		42,000

Workings:

Profit earned by the company	42,000
Add: Expenses and Depreciation	20,000
	22,000
Less: Kannan remuneration	2,000
(22,000 x 10/110)	20,000
Less: Kamal Remuneration	4,000
(20,000 x 1/5)	16,000

Problem 28: From the following figures, you are required to prepare

i)   Provision for doubtful debts
ii) Bad debts account and
iii) Profit and Loss account

April 1, 2014   Provision for bad debts ₹ 2,500

March 31, 2015   Bad debts ₹ 1,870

Debtors ₹ 20,000

Make provision for bad debts @ 5% on debtors.

Solution:

Dr			Provision for Doubtful Debts a/c		Cr
		₹			₹
2015			2014		
Mar 31	To Bad debts	1870	Apr 1	By Balance b/d	2500
Mar 31	To Balance c/d	1000	2015		
			Mar 31	By P & L a/c	370
		2870			2870

Dr		Bad debts a/c			Cr
		₹			₹
2015			2015	By Provision forBad debts	
Mar 31	To Debtors	1870	Mar 31		1870
		1870			1870

Dr		Profit & Loss A/c	Cr
		₹	
2015			
Mar 31	To Bad debts	1870	
	(+) New provision(2,00,000x5/100)	1000	
	(-) Old Provision	2870	
		2500	
		370	

Problem 29: The following figures appear in the books of Ganesan.

			₹
Jan 1	Bad and Doubtful Debts provision		1,200
	Discount allowed provision		560
Dec 31	Discount allowed during the year		930
	Bad debts written off		470
	Bad debts recovered		25
	Debtors		10,060

Write off further Bad debts Rs. 240 create a discount allowed provision of 2%, createa bad and doubtful debts provision of 10%. Prepare provision for doubtful debts account baddebts account and provision for discount account.

Solution:

Dr	Provision for Doubtful Debts a/c			Cr
	₹			₹
Dec 31 To Bad debts (470+240)	710	Jan 1	By Balance b/d	1200
		Dec 31	By P & L a/c(BF)	492
To Balance c/d (9,820x10/100)	982			
(1,0060 -240 =9820)	1692			1692

Dr	Bad debts a/c			Cr
	₹			₹
Dec 31 To Sundry debtors	470	Dec 31	By Provision for	
	240	Dec 31	Doubtful debts(BF)	710
To Sundry debtors				
	710			710

Dr	Provision for Discount a/c			Cr
	₹			₹
Dec 31 To Discount allowed	930	Jan 1	By Balance b/d	560
To Balance c/d (9,820 – 982=8,838	177	Dec 31	By P & L a/c	547
(8,838 x 2/100)	1107			1107

Problem 30: The following is the Trial Balance of Sivasamy as on 31.3.2016.

Particulars	₹	Particulars	₹
Sundry debtors	1,45,000	Sundry Creditors	63,000
Drawings	52,450	Capital a/c	7,10,000
Insurance	6,000	Return outwards	5,000
General expenses	30,000	Sales	9,87,800
Salaries	1,50,000		
Patents	75,000		
Machinery	2,00,000		
Free hold	1,00,000		
Building	3,00,000		
Stock (on 1.4.2015)	57,600		
Carriage on purchase	20,400		
Carriage on sales	32,000		
Fuel and power	47,300		
Wages	1,04,800		
Return inwards	6,800		
Purchases	4,06,750		
Cash at bank	26,300		
Cash in hand	5,400		
	17,65,800		17,65,800

Adjustments

i)   Stock on 31.3.2016 was valued at ₹ 68,000

ii) Provision for Bad and Doubtful Debts @5% on debtors

iii) Depreciate Machinery by 10%, Patents by 20%

iv) Wages include a sum of ₹ 20,000 spent on the creation of cycle shed foremployees and customers

v)   Salaries for the month of March 2016 amounting to ₹ 15,000 were unpaid

vi) Insurance includes a premium of ₹ 1,700 on a policy expiring on 30[th]September 2016

You are required to prepare Trading, Profit and Loss account and Balance Sheet.

Solution:

Dr					Cr
		Trading and Profit and Loss Account for the year ending 31.3.2016			
	₹				₹
To Opening Stock	57,600	By Sales	9,87,800		
To Purchases	4,06,750	(-) Returns inwards	6,800	9,81,000	
(-) Return outwards	5,000	4,01,750	By Closing Stock		68,000
To Wages	1,04,800				
(-) Cycle shed wages	20,000	84,800			
To Carriage on purchase		20,400			
To Fuel and Power		47,300			

	₹		₹
To Gross Profit	4,37,150		
(Transferred to P&L a/c)	10,49,000		10,49,000
To Provision for bad & Doubtful debts	7,250	By Gross Profit	4,37,150
		(Transferred from Trading a/c)	
To Depreciation: Machinery	20,000		
Patents	15,000	35,000	
To Salaries	1,50,000		
(+) Outstanding	15,000	1,65,000	
To Insurance	6,000		
(-) Prepaid	1,700	4,300	
To General Expenses		30,000	
To Carriage on Sales		32,000	
To Net Profit		1,63,600	
(Transferred to capital a/c)			
		4,37,150	4,37,150

Balance Sheet as on 31.3.2016

Liabilities		₹	Assets		₹
Capital	7,10,000		Stock		68,000
(-) Drawings	52,450		Sundry Debtors	1,45,000	

	6,57,550		(-) Pro vision for bad& doubtful	7,250	1,37,750
(+) Net Profit	1,63,600	8,21,150	(1,45,000 x5/100)		
Outstanding salary		15,000	Machi nery	2,00,000	
Sundry Creditors		63,000	(-) Depre ciation	20,000	1,80,000
			Patents	75,000	
			(-) Depre ciation	15,000	60,000
			Cycle shed		20,000
			Prepaid insurance		1,700
			Free hold		1,00,000
			Building		3,00,000
			Cash in hand		26,300
			Cash at bank		5,400
		8,99,150			8,99,150

Problem 31: The following is the Trial balance of Mr. Kannagi Agencies as on 31ˢᵗ March2009. Prepare Trading and profit and Loss account and Balance sheet for the year ended 31ˢᵗ March 2009.

Particulars	Dr ₹	Cr ₹
Capital		1,00,000
Drawings	18000	

Particulars	Dr ₹	Cr ₹
Building	15,000	
Furniture	7,500	
Motor van	25,000	
Loan from Hari @ 12% interest		15,000
Interest paid on above	900	
Sales		1,00,000
Purchases	75,000	
Opening stock	25,000	
Establishment expenses	15,000	
Wages	2,000	
Insurance	1,000	
Commission received		7,500
Sundry debtors	28,100	
Bank Balance	20,000	
Sundry Creditors		10,000
	2,32,500	2,32,500

Adjustments

1. Closing stock ₹ 32,000
2. Outstanding wages ₹ 500
3. Prepaid insurance ₹ 300
4. Commission received in advance ₹800
5. Allow interest on capital @ 10%
6. Depreciation:

   i.   Furniture 10%

   ii. Motor van 10%

   iii. Building 20%

7.   Charge interest on drawings ₹ 500

Solution:

Dr		Trading Profit and Loss Account for the year ending 2015		Cr	
		₹		₹	
To Opening stock		25,000	By Sales	1,00,000	
To Purchases		75,000	By Closing stock	32,000	
To Wages	2,000				
Add: Outstanding	500	2,500			
To Gross Profit (Transferred to P & L a/c)		29,500			
		1,32,000		1,32,000	
To Insurance	1,000		By Gross Profit	29,500	
Less: Prepaid	300	700	(Transferred from		
To Interest on capital		10,000	Trading a/c)		
To Depreciation:			By Commission	7,500	
Building	375		(-) Received in advance	800	6,700

	₹			₹
Furniture	750		By Interest on drawings	500
Motor Van	2500	3,625		
To Interest	900			
Add: Outstanding	900	1,800		
To Establishment charges		15,000		
To Net Profit		5,575		
(Transferred to Capital a/c)				
		36,700		36,700

Balance Sheet as on 31st March 2009

Liabilities	₹		Assets	₹	₹
Capital	1,00,000		Stock		32,000
(+) Interest on capital	10,000		Prepaid Insurance		300
	1,10,000		Building	15,000	
(-) Drawings	18,000		Less: Depreciation	375	14,625
	92,000		Furniture & Fittings	7,500	
(-) Interest on drawings	500		Less: Depreciation	750	6,750
	91,500		Motor Can	25,000	

(+) Net Profit	5,575	97,075	Less: Depreciation	2,500	22,500
Outstanding wages		500	Sundry debtors		28,100
Commission received in advance		800	Bank balance		20,000
Loan from Hari @12%		15,000			
Outstanding interest		900			
Sundry Creditors		10,000			
		1,24,275			1,24,275

Problem 32: The following is the Trial Balance of Mr. Murugan as on 31st December 2015.

Debit	₹	Credit	₹
Drawings	3,250	Capital	15,000
Stock 1.1.2015	17,445	Return outwards	840
Return inwards	554	Interest on loan to Mani	25
Carriage inwards	1,240	Rent outstanding	130
Deposit with SBI	1,375	Creditors	3,000
Carriage outwards	725	Provision for doubtful debts	1,200

Debit	₹	Credit	₹
Loan to Mani @5% on 1.1.15	1,000	Sales	27,914
Rent	820		
Purchases	12,970		
Debtors	4,000		
Goodwill	1,730		
Advertisement	954		
Bad debts	400		
Patents and rights	500		
Cash	62		
Discount allowed	330		
Wages	754		
	48,109		48,109

Adjustments:

i)   The manager is entitled to a commission of 10% of the net profit. Calculateafter charging such commission

ii) Increase bad debts by ₹ 600 and make provision for doubtful debts 10% andprovision for discount on debtors 5%

iii) The value of closing stock is ₹ 18,792

iv) ₹ 200 of the advertisement charges are to be carried forward to the next year. You are required to prepare Profit and Loss account and Balance sheet.

Solution:

Dr		Trading and Profit and Loss Account for the year ending 31.3.2016		Cr	
		₹			₹
To Opening Stock		17,445	By Sales	27,914	
To Purchases	12,970		(-) Returns inwards	554	27,360
(-) Return outwards	840	12,130	By Closing Stock		18,792
To Wages		754			
To Carriage inwards		1,240			
To Gross Profit		14,583			
(Transferred to P&L a/c)		46,152			46,152
To Bad debts	400		By Gross Profit		14,583
(+) Additional bad debts	600		By interest received	25	
(+) New Provision for			(+) Accured interest	25	50
doubtful debts (4000-600=3400)	340		(1000 x 5/100)		

(3400x10/100)	1,340	
(-) Old provision		
For doubtful debts	1,200	140
To Carriage outwards		725
To Advertisement	954	
(-) Carried forward – prepaid	200	754
To Rent	820	
To Discount allowed	330	
To Provision for discountOn debts (3,060 x5/100)	153	
To Managers commission (11,711 x 10/110)	1,065	
To Net Profit (Transferred to capital a/c)	10,646	
	14,633	14,633

Balance Sheet as on 31.12.2015

Liabilities	₹		Assets	₹	₹
Capital	15,000		Sundry Debtors	4,000	
(-) Drawings	3,250		(-) Bad debts	600	
	11,750			3,400	
(+) Net Profit	10,646	22,396	(-) Provision for doubtful debts	340	
Rent outstanding		130	(3,400x10/100)	3,060	
Sundry Creditors		3,000	(-) Provision for discount on debtors	153	2,907
Managers Commission		1,065	(3,060x5/100)		
			Stock		18,792
			Advertisement prepaid		200
			Deposit with SBI		1,375
			Loan to Mani		1,000
			Accrued interest		25
			Goodwill		1,730
			Patents and rights		500
			Cash		62
		26,591			26,591

Problem 33: From the following trial balance prepare trading and profit and loss account forthe year ended 31.12.2009 and a Balance Sheet as on that date.

Debit	₹	Credit	₹
Purchases	11,870	Capital	8,000
Debtors	7,580	Bad debts recovered	250
Returns inwards	450	Creditors	1,250
Bank deposit	2,750	Return outwards	350
Rent	360	Bank overdraft	1,570
Salaries	850	Sales	14,690
Travelling expenses	300	Bills payable	1,350
Cash	210		
Stock	2,450		
Discount allowed	40		
Drawings	600		
	27,460		27,460

Adjustments

a. The closing stock as on 31.12.2009 was ₹ 4,200
b. Write off ₹ 80 as bad debts and create a reserve for bad debts at 5% on sundrydebtors
c. Three months rent is outstanding
d. Interest on bank deposit ₹ 135 credited by the bankers and interest onoverdraft ₹ 157 debited by them in the pass book have not been entered in thebook

Solution:

Dr	Trading and Profit and Loss Account for the year ending 31.3.2009		Cr	
	₹			₹
To Opening stock	2,450	By Sales	14,690	
To Purchases	11,870	(-) Returns inwards	450	14,240
(-) Return outwards	350	11,520	By Closing stock	4,200
To Gross Profit (Transferred to P&L a/c)		4,470		
		18,440		18,440
To Reserve for bad debts	375		By Gross Profit	4,470
(+)New Bad debts	80	455	By Bad debts recovered	250
To Interest on overdraft		157	By Interest on bank deposit	135
To Rent	360			
(+) outstanding rent	120	480		
To Discount allowed		40		
To Salaries		850		
To Travelling expenses		300		
To Net profit (Transferred to capital a/c)		**2,573**		
		4,855		4,855

Balance Sheet as on 31.12.2015

Liabilities	₹		Assets	₹		
Capital	8,000		Stock Debtors			4,200
(-) Drawings	600		(-) Bad debts	7,580		
	7,400			80		
(+) Net Profit Rent outstanding Sundry CreditorsBank overdraft Bills Payable	2,573	9,973	(-) Reserve for bad debts(7500 x5/100)	7,500	375	7,125
		120	Cash			
		1,250	Bank deposit			
		1,570				210
		1,350				2,728
		14,263				14,263

Workings

Bank balance	2,750
(+)Interest on bank deposit	135
	2,885
(-) Interest on over draft	157
Closing bank balance	2,728

Problem 34: The following is the Trial Balance was extracted from the books ofMr.Krishnanan as on 31ˢᵗ December 2014.

Debit	₹	Credit	₹
Plant and Machinery	20,000	Capital	80,000
Manufacturing wages	34,500	Sundry creditors	44,560
Salaries	15,850	Bank loan	15,000
Furniture	10,000	Purchase returns	1,740

Debit	₹	Credit	₹
Freight on purchases	1,860	Sales	2,50,850
Buildings	24,000	Reserve for bad debts	2,000
Manufacturing expenses	9,500		
Insurance	4,250		
Goodwill	2,500		
General expenses	8,200		
Factory fuel and power	1,280		
Sundry debtors	78,200		
Factory lighting	950		
Opening stock	34,200		
Motor car	12,000		
Purchases	1,02,000		
Sales returns	3,100		
Bad debts	1,400		
Bank charges	400		
Cash in hand	4,200		
Cash in bank	1,120		

Prepare the Trading and Profit and loss account for the year ended 31st December 2014 and the Balance sheet as on that date taking into consideration the following information.

1. Stock in hand on 31st December 2014 was valued at ₹ 30,500
2. Depreciation plant and machinery by 10%, furniture by 5% and motor car by ₹1,000

3. Bring provision for bad debts to 5% on sundry debtors
4. A commission of 1% on the gross profit is to be provided for work manager
5. A commission of 2% on net profit after charging the works managers' commission is to be credited to the General Manager.

Solution:

Dr	Trading and Profit and Loss Account for the year ending 31st December 2014		Cr	
		₹		₹
To Opening Stock		34,200	By Sales 2,50,850	
To Purchases	1,02,000		(-) Returns inwards 3,100	2,47,750
(-) Return outwards	1,740	1,00,260	By Closing Stock	30,500
To Manufacturing Wages		34,500		
To Freight on purchase		1,860		
To Manufacturing expenses		9,500		
To Factory fuel and Power		1,280		
To Factory lighting		950		
To Gross Profit		95,700		
(Transferred to P&L a/c)		2,78,250		2,78,250
To Depreciation:			By Gross Profit	95,700
Plant & Machinery	2,000		(Transferred from	
Furniture	500		Trading a/c)	
Motor Car	1,000	3,500		
To Salaries		15,850		

To Provision for bad debts	3,910			
(+) Bad debts	1,400			
	5,310			
(-) Reserve for bad debts	2,000	3,310		
To Freight on sales		2,140		
To Insurance and tax		4,250		
To General expenses		8,200		
To Bank charges		400		
To Work Managers' commission (95,700x1/100)		957		
To General Managers' commission		1,142		
To Net Profit (Transferred to capital a/c)		55,951		
		95,700		95,700

Balance Sheet as on 31st December 2014

Liabilities	₹		Assets		₹
Capital	80,000		Stock		30,500
(+) Net Profit	55,951	1,35,951	Plant & Machinery	20,000	
Sundry Creditors		44,560	(-) Depreciation	2,000	18,000
Bank Loan		15,000	Furniture	10,000	

Liabilities	₹	Assets		₹
Work Managers' commission	957	(-) Depreciation Motor	500	9,500
General Managers' commission		Car	12000	
		(-)	1000	11,000
		Depreciation Sundry	78200	
		debtors	3910	74,290
		(-) Provision for bad debts (78,200 x 5/100)	24,000	
		Buildings Goodwill		25,000
				1,120
		Cash at bank		4,200
	1,97,610	Cash at hand		1,97,61

General Manager's commission should be calculated on net profit. Net profit before calculation of commission of general manager is 57,093. General Manager Commission is 2% on netprofit

$$57,093 \times 2/100 = 1,142$$

Problem 35: From the following particulars extracted from the books of Mr.Suman, you arerequired to prepare a trading, profit and loss account for the year ended 31st December 2008and a balance sheet as on that date, after making the necessary adjustments.

Debit	₹	Credit	₹
Suman's capital	2,08,000	Investments	40,000
Suman's drawings	12,000	Cash at bank	26,600
Purchases	90,000	Bills payable	5,000
Returns inwards	2,000	Stock 1.1.2007	35,000
Land and buildings	60,000	Wages	32,000
Plant and machinery	1,00,000	Sundry creditors	40,000
Sales	2,10,000	Postage and telegrams	1,400
Returns outwards	1,000	Insurance charges	1,600
Salaries	12,000	Gas and fuel	2,700
Office expenses	2,500	Bad debts	600
Office furniture	5,000	Office rent	2,600
Discount(Dr)	1,200	Freight and duty	9,000
Sundry debtors	26,600	Loose tools	2,000
Interest on investments	4,000	Factory lighting	1,600
Cash on hand	2,400	Provision for doubtful debts	800

Adjustments:

1. Stock on December 31, 2008 was valued at ₹ 66,000
2. Wages ₹ 1,600 and salaries ₹ 600 were outstanding
3. Insurance prepaid ₹ 400
4. A new machine was installed on September 30, 2008, costing ₹ 14,000 but itwas not recorded in the books and no payment was made for it, wages ₹ 1,000paid for its erection have been debited to wages account

5. Loose tools were valued at ₹ 1,600 on 31ˢᵗ December 2008
6. Depreciate Plant and Machinery by 10% p.a, Furniture by 5%, p.a and Land and Building by 2% p.a
7. Of the sundry debtors ₹ 600 are bad and should be written off
8. Maintain a provision of 5% on sundry debtors for doubtful debtors
9. Stock valued at ₹ 1,500 was destroyed by fire on 25.12.2008 but the insurance company admitted a claim for ` 1,000 only.

Solution:

Dr		Trading and Profit and Loss Account for the year ending 31ˢᵗ December 2008		Cr
	₹			₹
To Opening stock		35,000	By Sales	2,10,000	
To Purchases	90,000		(-) Returns	2,000	2,0,8000
(-) Returns	1,000	89,000	By Closing stock		66,000
To Fright & Duty		9,000	By Stock destroyed by fire		1,500
To Wages	32,000				
(-) wages for erection	1,000				
	31,000				
(+) Outstanding	1,600	32,600			
To Gas and Fuel		2,700			
To Factory lighting		1,600			
To Gross Profit (b/f)		1,05,600			
		2,75,500			2,75,500

To Salaries	12,000		By Gross Profit		1,05,600
(+) Outstanding	600	12,600	By Interest on investments		4,000
To Office expenses		2,500			
To Discount		1,200			
To Postage & Telegram		1,400			
To Insurance	1,600				
(-) prepaid	400	1,200			
To Office rent		2,600			
To Bad debts (600 + 600)		1,200			
To Reserve for bad debts	1300-	500			
	800				
To Loss by fire		500			
To Depreciation:					
Plant & Machinery	10,375				
Furniture & Fittings	250				
Land & Building	1,200				
Loose Tools	400	12,225			
To Net Profit		73,675			
		1,09,600			1,09,600

Balance Sheet as on 31st December 2008

Liabilities	₹	₹	Assets	₹	₹
Capital	2,08,000		Cash in hand		2,400
(-) Drawings	12,000		Cash at bank		26,600
	1,96,000		Investment		40,000
(+) Net Profit	73,675	2,69,675	Debtors	26,600	
Sundry creditors	40,000		(-) Bad debts	600	
(+) for machine purchased	14,000	54,000		26,000	
Bills payable		5,000	(-) Reserve fordoubt ful debts	1,300	24,700
Out standing expenses:			Stock in trade		66,000
Wages	1,600		Prepaid insurance		400
Salaries	600	2,200	Loose tools		1,600
			Insurance claim due		1,000
			Furniture & Fittings	5,000	
			(-) Depreciation	250	4,750
			Plant & Machinery	1,00,000	

Liabilities	₹	Assets		₹
		(+) Addition	15,000	
			1,15,000	
		(-) Depreciation	10,375	1,04,625
		Land & Building	60,000	
		(-) Depreciation	1,200	58,800
	3,30,875			3,30,875

Problem 36: From the following balances taken from Sriraman on 31st December 2010,Prepare the final statement.

Particulars	₹	Particulars	₹
Capital	3,00,000	Purchase returns	8,460
Purchases	2,40,000	Bad debts	4,200
Sales	4,21,110	Bad debts provision	9,720
Drawings	52,800	Insurance	3,900
Opening stock	34,380	Discount received	570
Rent (Cr)	6,300	Sales returns	12,720
Wages	18,840	Buildings	75,000
Carriage outwards	50,820	Sundry debtors	1,86,210
Carriage inwards	6,930	Furniture & fittings	10,500
Postage	4,440	Salary	29,610
Cash in hand	47,550	Administrative expenses	4,020
Additions to building	21,000	Sundry creditors	56,760

Adjustments:

i) Stock on 31st December 2010 is valued at ₹ 42,870

ii) Depreciate the existing building @2.5% and additions building @2% andfurniture @10%

iii) Write off bad debts from the books at ₹ 1,710

iv) Provision for bad debts on debtors @ 5%

v) Salary outstanding was ₹ 1,710

vi) Rent to be received during the year 2010 is ₹ 400

vii) Unexpired insurance ₹ 720

viii)Interest on capital @5%

Solution:

Trading and Profit & Loss Account of Mr. Sriraman for the year ending 31.12.2010

Particulars	Amount ₹		Particulars		Amount ₹
To Opening stock		34,380	By Sales	4,21,110	
To Purchases	2,40,000		(-) Returns inwards	12,720	4,08,390
(-) Returns	8,460	2,31,540	By Closing Stock		42,870
To wages		18,840			
To Carriageinwards		6,930			
To Gross Profit		1,59,570			
		4,51,260			4,51,260
To Salary	29,610		By Gross Profit		1,59,570
(+) Out standing	1,710	31,320	By Rent	6,300	

Particulars	Amount ₹		Particulars	Amount ₹	
To administrativeexp		4,020	(+) Out standing	400	6,700
To Postage		4,440	By Discountreceived		570
To Insurance	3,900				
(-) Prepaid	720	3,180			
To Carriageoutwards		50,820			
To Depreciation:					
Building	1,875				
Building (new)	420				
Furniture	1,050	3,345			
To Int. on capital		15,000			
To Bad debts	4,200	1,710			
(+)Bad debt written off	1,710				
(+)New Provision	9,225				
(186210-1710 x 5/100)					
(-)Old Provision	9,720	5,415			
To Net Profit		49,300			
		1,66,840			1,66,840

Balance Sheet as on 31.12.2010

Liabilities	Amount ₹		Assets		Amount ₹
Capital	3,00,000		Building	75,000	
(+) Net Profit(-) Drawings	49,300		(+) Additions	21,000	
	3,49,300			96,000	
(+) Int. on capital	52,800		(-) Depreciation	2,295	93,705
Sundry Creditors	2,96,500		Cash in hand Sundry Debtors	1,86,210	47,550
Salary outstanding	15,000	3,11,500		1,710	
		56,760	(-) Bad debts write off	1,84,500	
		1,710		9,225	
					1,75,275
			(-) New Provision 5%Closing	10,500	42,870
			Stock Furniture	1,050	
					9,450
			(-) Depreciation 10%		400
					720
		3,69,970			3,69,970
			Rent receivable Prepaid insurance		

QUESTIONS

FILL IN THE BLANKS:

1. Closing stock is_____in the trading account.
2. Direct expenses appear in the debit side of the_account.
3. Indirect expenses appear in the_______side of the profit and loss account.
4. Bad debt is a.expense.
5. By preparing profit and loss account__can be find out.
6. All incomes are_____in the profit and loss account.
7. 'Salaries and wages' appear on the____account.
8. Balance sheet shows the_____of a business
9. ____ account enables the trader to find out gross profit or loss.
10. Net Profit is transferred from Profit and loss account to_account.
11. Outstanding expenses are shown on the_______side of the balance sheet.
12. Closing stock is valued at Cost Price or_____price   whichever is lower.
13. Interest on drawings is credited in____account.
14. Depreciation is deducted from the concerned__in the Balance sheet.
15. Debts which are not recoverable from Sundry debtors are termed as ____.
16. Outstanding income is an____.
17. Provision is_against profit.
18. Reserve is__against profit
19. Depreciation is_____against profit

[**Answers:** 1. Credited, 2. Trading, 3. Debit, 4. Selling,
        5. Net profit or loss, 6. Credited, 7. Profit   and
        loss account, 8. Financial position, 9. Trading,

10 Capital, 11.Liabilities, 12.Market, 13.Profit & Loss Account, 14.Fixed Assets, 15. Bad debts, 16. Asset, 17. Charge, 18. Appropriation, 19. Charge]

CHOOSE THE CORRECT ANSWER

1. Trading account is prepared to find out
   a)   Gross profit or loss   b)   Net profit or loss
   c)   Financial position

2. Opening stock is
   a) Debited in trading account
   b) Credited in trading account
   c) Credit in profit and loss account

3. Fixed assets have
   a) Short life   b)   Long life   c)   No life

4. Wages is an example of
   a) Capital expenses   b)   Indirect expenses
   c) Direct expenses

5. Capital is a
   a) Income   b)   Assets   c)   Liability

6. Cash in hand is an example of
   a)   Current assets   b)   Fixed assets
   c)   Current liability

7. Drawing must be deducted from
   a) Net profit   b)   Capital   c)   Gross profit

8. Net profit is added to
   a) Gross profit   b)   Drawings   c) Capital

9. Returns inwards are deducted from
   a) Purchases   b)   Sales   c)   Returns outward

10. The Profit and Loss account shows
    a) Financial position of the concern   b) Net profit or Net loss
    c) Gross profit or Gross Loss

11. Rent outstanding is
    a) a liability   b) an asset   c) an income

12. Interest on capital is added to
    a) Expense A/c   b) Income A/c   c) Capital A/c

13. Interest on drawings is deducted from
    a) Income A/c   b) Capital A/c   c) Expense A/c

14. If sales revenue is ₹ 8,00,000, cost of goods sold is ₹ 7,10,000 and operating expenses are ₹ 80,000 the gross profit is
    a) ₹ 60,000   b) ₹ 70,000   c) ₹ 90,000

15. The sale of by- products would be credited to
    a) Trading a/c   b) Manufacturing a/c
    c) Profit & Loss a/c

16. Sales are equal to
    a) Cost of goods sold - Gross Profit
    b) Cost of goods sold + Gross Profit
    c) Cost of goods sold

17. Opening stock ₹ 7,400, Purchases ₹ 41,600, Closing stock ₹ 5,000 cost of goods sold is
    a) ₹ 50,000   b) ₹ 44,000   c) ₹ 36,000

18. Gross profit is the difference between
    a) Sales & expenses
    b) Sales and indirect expenses
    c) Sales and cost of sales

19. Work in progress is a component of
    a) Fixed assets   b) Tangible assets   c) Intangible assets

20. Accounting process comes to an end after preparing
    a) Trial balance   b) Final account   c) BRS

21. Preliminary expenses is an example of

    a) Current assets   b) Fixed assets   c) Fictitious asset

22. Which one of the following is example of personal a/c?

    a) Capital a/c   b) Cash a/c   c) Building a/c

23. The excess of current assets over current liabilities is called

    a) Net worth   b) Net Working capital

    c) Gross working capital

24. Balance Sheet is prepared primarily for the benefit of

    a) Owners   b) Creditors   c) Management

25. If outstanding salary appears in trial balance, it is taken only to the

    a)   Trading account   b)   Balance Sheet

    c)   Profit and Loss account

26. Prepaid expenses can be described as

    a) Paid in advance   b) Received in advance

    c) Not to be paid

27. Octroi is debited to

    a) Trading account   b) Profit and Loss account

    c) Balance Sheet

28. Free sample paid by manufacturer is debited to

    a) Trading account   b) Profit and Loss account

    c) Balance Sheet

29. Goodwill is an example of

    a) Current asset   b) Fixed assets   c) Fictitious asset

30. Which one of the following arrangements represents the order of liquidity?

    a) Cash, B/R, Stock and Debtors

    b) Debtors, Cash, B/R and Stock

    c) Cash, B/R, Debtors and Stock

[**Answers:** 1.(a), 2. (a), 3. (b), 4. (c), 5. (c), 6. (a), 7. (b), 8. (c), 9. (b), 10 (b), 11 (a), 12 (c), 13 (b), 14 (c), 15 (b), 16 (b), 17 (b), 18 (c), 19 (b), 20 (b), 21 (c), 22 (a),

23 ((b), 24 (a), 25 (b), 26 (a),27 (a),28 (b), 29 (c), 30 (c)]

OTHER QUESTIONS

---

1. What is a Trading account?
2. "Profit and Loss account" – Explain
3. What do you mean by a "Balance Sheet"?
4. Explain the objectives of preparing final accounts.
5. What are the items appearing in the debit and credit side of trading account?
6. What are direct and indirect expenses?
7. Write the difference between trial balance and balance sheet.
8. What do you mean by current assets?
9. What do you mean by Assets? Classify the assets with suitable examples.
10. What is an outstanding expense?
11. What is prepaid expense?
12. What is income received in advance?
13. What is bad debt?
14. Write notes on provision for discount on Creditors.
15. What is adjusting entries?

EXERCISE

1. From the following balances prepare Trading, P & L account for the year ended31.12.2001 and Balance sheet as on that date.

Particulars	₹	Particulars	₹
Capital	30000	Debtors	17078
Cash	3418	Sales	29360
Purchases	35640	Return outwards	1756
Creditors	3920	Drawings	2600
Rent	700	Rent owning (Cr)	160
Bill Payable	2690	Discount (Dr)	270
Trade charges	460	Return inwards	2460

Additional information

i)   Closing stock ₹ 12800

ii) Depreciation on furniture 10% p.a

iii) Provide for doubtful debts 5% on debtors

iv) Goods costing ₹ 500 were used by the owner.

(Ans: Gross Profit ₹ 5,856; Net Profit ₹` 2,782; Balance Sheet ₹ 36,452)

2. From the following balances prepare Trading, P&L account for the year ended31.12.2009 and Balance sheet as on that date.

₹		₹	
Capital	30000	Furniture	2600
Bank o/d	4200	Premises	20000
Creditors	13800	Discount (Dr)	1600

Stock	22000	Tax and insurance	2000
Rent (Cr)	1000	Carriage	1800
Sales	150000	Debtors	18000
Commission paid	2200	Purchases	110000
Salaries	9000	Sales returns	2000
Bad debts	800	Discount (Cr)	2000
Drawings	5000	General expenses	4000

Additional information

a. Stock on 31.12.2009 ₹ 20000
b. Interest on capital at 5%
c. Depreciation on premises ₹ 300 and on furniture ₹ 260
d. Reserve 5% on debtors for doubtful debts
e. Unexpired insurance ₹ 200

(Ans: Gross Profit ₹ 34200; Net Profit ₹ 14840;   Balance Sheet ₹ 59340)

3. The following are the balances extracted from the books of Mr.Ramakrishnan as on31.12.2011.

₹		₹	
Buildings	15000	Capital	20000
Machinery	10000	Purchase returns	1000
Furniture	1000	Sales	140000
Opening stock	16000	Sundry creditors	4800
Purchases	94000	Discount earned	500
Sales returns	500	Reserve for bad debts	300
Sundry debtors	15000	Suspense account (Cr)	20000
General expenses	800	Cash at bank	4700

Cash in hand	300	Salaries	14000
Rent	4000	Commission	1400
Rates and taxes	600	Bad debts	200
Insurance	400	Discounts allowed	700

Additional information

i) Outstanding expenses:
   a. Salaries ₹ 1400
   b. Commission ₹ 150
   c. Rent ₹ 1000

ii) Insurance prepaid ₹ 100

iii) Stock on 31.12.2011 ₹ 20000

iv) Maintain the reserve for bad debts at 5%

v) Depreciate:
   a. Machinery by 5%
   b. Motor car by 10%
   c. Furniture by 6% and
   d. Building by 7%

Prepare Trading and Profit and loss account for the year ended 31.12.2011 and abalance sheet as on that date.

(Ans: Gross Profit ₹ 50500; Net Profit ₹ 23590; Balance Sheet ₹ 70940)

4. From the flowing Trial balance has been extracted from the books of Mr.Rajarajan on 31.12.2005. From these particulars prepare Trading and Profit and Loss account for theyear ending 31.12.2005 and also balance sheet as on that date.

Debit	₹	**Credit**	₹
Machinery	4000	Capital	9000
Cash in hand	500	Sales	12000

Debit	₹	Credit	₹
Cash at bank	1000	Bank loan	4000
Wages	1000	Sundry creditors	4500
Purchases	8000	Dividend received	300
Stock 1.1.2005	6000		
Sundry debtors	4400		
Bills receivable	2900		
Rent	400		
Interest on bank loan	50		
Commission	250		
General expenses	800		
Salaries	500		
	29800		29800

Adjustments
a)   Closing stock 31.12.2005 ₹ 8000
b)   Wages outstanding ₹ 100
c)   Salaries unpaid ₹ 100
d)   Rent prepaid ₹ 150
e)   Commission ₹ 50
f)   Interest on bank loans not yet paid ₹ 400

(Ans: Gross Profit ₹ 4900; Net Profit ₹ 2800; Balance Sheet ₹ 20950)

5. From the following Trial Balance and other particulars, prepare Trading and profit and Loss account for the year ended 31.12.2007 and balance sheet as on that date.

Debit	₹	Credit	₹
Interest	1500	Capital	22000
Rent	500	Bills payable	4000
Insurance	200	Sundry creditors	20000
Plant and machinery	20000	Bank overdraft	20000
Sundry debtors	20000	Loan on mortgage	30000
Wages	30000	Sales	96400
Stock (Opening)	5000	Bills receivable	3000
Salaries	7000		
Loose tools	21000		
Cash in hand	1000		
Business premises	40000		
Stationary	500		
Office expenses	700		
Purchases	42000		

Adjustments:

Closing stock was ₹ 8000;

Wages outstanding ₹ 600;

Salaries unpaid ₹ 200;

Rent due ₹ 150;

Insurance prepaid ₹ 50;

Bad debts written off ₹ 200.

(Ans: Gross Profit ₹ 26800; Net Profit ₹ 16400; Balance Sheet ₹ 113350)

6. From the under mentioned trial balance of Z ltd, prepare trading, profit and loss accountand balance sheet for the year ended 31st December 2010.

Debit	₹	Credit	₹
Opening stock	30000	Equity shares	
Rent and rates	6000	(1000 shares of ₹ 100 each)	100000
Purchases	60900	5% debentures	25000
Wages	55200	Sales	175000
Discount	1500	Creditors	8000
Fuel	2570	Bank overdraft	12000
Buildings	70000	Discount	2200
Carriage inward	1175	Transfer fee	100
Sundry debtors	20000	Return outwards	100
Goodwill	28000		
Plant and machinery	25000		
Loose tools	6000		
Advertisement	3000		
General expenses	4400		
Bad debts	1030		
Debenture interest	625		
Miscellaneous expenses	3000		
Insurance	1000		
Cash in hand	3000		

a. Authorize capital of the company is ₹ 200000

b. Stock on 31.12.2010 ₹ 35000

c. Depreciation plant and machinery at 9% and revalue loose tools at ₹ 41000

d. Allow 2 ½ % discount on debtors and 2% as bad debts reserve.

(Ans: Gross Profit ₹ 60255; Net Profit ₹ 136335; Balance Sheet ₹ 181960)

7. The following balances are extracted from the books of Mr.Ravichandran on 31.12.2014. Prepare Trading and Profit and Loss account for the year ending 31.12.2014 and a balance sheet as on that.

Trial Balance as on 31.12.2014

Debit	₹	Credit	₹
Furniture and fittings	640	Capital	12500
Motor vehicles	6250	Provision for bad debts	200
Buildings	7500	Sundry creditors	2500
Bad debts	125	Sales	15450
Sundry debtors	3800	Bank overdraft	2850
Stock 1.1.2014	3460	Purchase returns	125
Purchases	5475	Commission	375
Sales returns	200		
Advertising	450		
Interest	118		
Cash	650		
Taxes and Insurance	1250		
General expenses	782		
Salaries	3300		
	34000		34000

The following adjustments are to be made:

a) Depreciate buildings @ 5% furniture and fittings @10% and motor vehicles@ 20%

b) Stock on 31.12.2014 was ₹ 3250

c) ₹ 85 are due for interest on overdraft

d) Salaries 300 and Taxes ₹ 120 are outstanding

e) Insurance amounting to ₹ 100 is prepaid

f) One third of the commission received is in respect of work to be done nextyear.

g) Write off further 100 as bad debts and provision for bad debts is to be madeequal to 5% on sundry debtors

h) Purchases included purchase of furniture ₹ 200 on 1.1.2014

(Ans: Gross Profit ₹ 9890; Net Profit ₹ 1916; Balance Sheet ₹ 20396)

8. From the following Trial balance of Kandasamy as on 31.3.2013, prepare Trading account and Profit and Loss account for the year ended 31.3.2013 and a balance sheet as on that date after making necessary adjustments.

Trial balance

Debit	₹	Credit	₹
Kandasamy drawings	12000	Kandasamy Capital	60000
Furniture and fittings	4000	Returns outward	2000
Plant and machinery	30000	Sales	130000
Opening stock	20000	Creditors	12000
Purchases	80000	Loan at 6% .p.a taken from	
Salaries and wages	22400	M.Meena on 1.10.2012	10000
Debtors	20400	Discount	600

Debit	₹	Credit	₹
Return inwards	5000		
Postage and telegrams	1500		
Rent, rates and taxes	3600		
Bad debts written off	400		
Trade expenses	200		
Interest on loan from MeenaInsurance	150 800		
Travelling expenseSundry expenses Cash in hand	500 300		
Cash at bank	3050		
	10300		
	214600		214600

Adjustments:

a. Closing stock
    a. Cost price ₹ 21000
    b. Market price ₹ 25000

b. Of the debtors 400 are bad and should be written off. Create a reserve for baddebts at 5% on sundry debtors and a reserve for discount on debtors 2 ½ %

c. Salaries ₹ 800 for March 2013 were not paid

d. Interest on capital is to be calculated at 6% p.a and on drawings ₹ 330

e. Prepaid insurance amounted to ₹ 100

f. Depreciation furniture and fixture by 5% and plant and machinery by 10%

g. Make a reserve for discount on creditors @ 2%

(Ans: Gross Profit ₹ 48000; Net Profit ₹ 9795; Balance Sheet ₹ 83775)

9. Pass necessary journal entries

   a. Depreciation at 10% is to be charged on machinery ₹ 1,00,000

   b. Insurance unexpired ₹ 200

   c. Closing stock ₹ 55,000

   d. ₹ 2,000 to be transferred to reserve fund

   f. Goods worth ₹ 2,000 distributed as free samples to customer

10. Give journal entries for the following

    a. Machinery of the book value 3500 sold for 3000

    b. Goods worth ₹ 1000 taken by the proprietor for his domestic use

    c. Loss of stock by fire ₹ 6200 insurers admit the claim for only ₹3000

    d. Sales tax paid on goods purchased ₹ 1250

11. Give journal entries for the following transaction

    a. An amount of ₹ 2000 is due from Jaya. He has become insolvent and only 40% wasrealized from his estates

    b. A piece of old machinery whose book value is ₹ 2800 has been sold for ₹ 3300

    c. Goods worth ₹ 1250 and cash ₹ 750 were used by the proprietor

    d. Loss by fire of stock of goods ₹ 3500, insurance company admitted the claim for ₹ 3000 only.

www.ingramcontent.com/pod-product-compliance
Lightning Source LLC
LaVergne TN
LVHW041448170726
843492LV00005B/1144